DUNPHY
A Football Life

DUNPHY

A Football Life

Jared Browne

NEW ISLAND

DUNPHY: A FOOTBALL LIFE
First published 2012
by New Island
2 Brookside
Dundrum Road
Dublin 14

www.newisland.ie

PRINT ISBN: 978-1-84840-162-4
EPUB ISBN: 978-1-84840-163-1
MOBI ISBN: 978-1-84840-164-8

British Library Cataloguing Data. A CIP catalogue record for this
book is available from the British Library

Typeset by JM InfoTech India
Cover design by Mariel Deegan
Printed by xxxxx xxxxxx

New Island received financial assistance from
The Arts Council (An Comhairle Ealaíon), Dublin, Ireland

10 9 8 7 6 5 4 3 2 1

Contents

About The Author

J ared Browne was born in Tralee, County Kerry in 1979. A talented young footballer, Browne received trials with Manchester United in 1995 at the age of fifteen and at Liverpool a year later. He has also repre-sented the Republic of Ireland at schoolboy level, earning a cap against Northern Ireland for the Under-15 team in 1995. Browne left football at the age of twenty to pursue a university education which has led to him obtaining a Bachelors Degree and a Masters Degree in Philosophy. A qualified solicitor, he now lives and works in County Kerry.

www.jaredbrowne.net

Acknowledgements

Special thanks to my agent Jonathan Williams for helping to make this book happen. Thanks to everyone who assisted in the publishing process. Thanks to *When Saturday Comes, The Blizzard and The Guardian* sports section for keeping me in touch with exemplary football writing. Thanks to the National Library of Ireland.

In researching this book I found the excellent, *Inverting the Pyramid: The History of Football Tactics* by Jonathan Wilson and *Red Mist: Roy Keane & the Football Civil War* by Conor O'Callaghan, to be essential reading.

Introduction

Eamon Dunphy was an ordinary footballer who became an extraordinary football journalist and television analyst. Of the many former players who have made the switch from football to a career in the media, few, if any, have done it with as much as ease and success as Dunphy. In fact his post-football career is where he has made his name; it easily overshadows his forgettable playing days at a succession of English lower division clubs.

As a footballer, Dunphy was little more than a journeyman, eking out a modest living throughout a tough and inglorious career. As a media personality, however, he is a household name and one of the most recognisable faces in Ireland. He has fashioned a diverse mini-empire of his own within Irish journalism, tirelessly innovating and promoting himself across all sectors of the media. In 1978, when he left behind professional football, along with the financial security it had provided him with since he was a teenager, he took a calculated risk to try and make an independent living through football analysis. It was a courageous move, given the unstable nature of such work, but Dunphy backed himself, knowing, perhaps, that he was his own greatest asset. Driven by the pressing need to develop and sustain a lasting source of income, Dunphy's strategy was to excel in numerous fields of the media so that he would not have to rely on any one source of income. Speaking of his early career plans to *The Irish Times* in May 2010, Dunphy said, 'Survival was always the name of the game for me'. When you've been poor, when you've been a footballer, when you've had to finish your career at 33 and do something else, the objective was always survival. I'd still be in that mode.' This fear of poverty, together with the knowledge that, on leaving football, he had no formal qualifications, has ensured that Dunphy has never taken his opportunities for granted.

He has been indefatigable in his ambition and in the range of work he has taken upon himself. Dunphy has written for several newspapers, including the *Sunday Tribune, Sunday Independent, The Irish Times, Ireland on Sunday, Irish Daily Star* and in Britain for *The Independent On Sunday, The Observer* and *The Times.* Furthermore, he penned a best-selling football memoir, *Only a Game?*, covering his last season at Millwall FC – the book that first established his writing credentials. In 1992, together with writer, Roger Titford, he reprised the confessional style of *Only a Game?* by penning *More than a Job?: The Players' and Fans' Perspectives* (a study of his 1975/76 promotion-winning season with Reading FC), and in 1994, he released *Eamon Dunphy's World Cup Diary: More than a Game* (a critical account of the Republic of Ireland's performances in the 1994 World Cup). He has also written a highly regarded football biography, *A Strange Kind of Glory: Sir Matt Busby & Manchester United.* In addition to these works, he has ghosted Roy Keane's extremely successful autobiography, *Keane: The Autobiography.*

Aside from print, Dunphy has also worked extensively in radio, producing and presenting the exceptional current affairs show *The Last Word* on Today FM from 1997 to 2002. He has had two separate talk radio shows with Newstalk: the first ran from 2004 to 2006, while the second lasted from 2010 to 2011. In the intervening period he hosted a Sunday morning show, *Conversations with Eamon Dunphy*, for RTÉ Radio 1. In television, Dunphy has worked as a football analyst for RTÉ since the 1978 World Cup and it is in this capacity that he is best known, having becoming a veritable fixture of Irish television. He became the first male presenter of the internationally acclaimed quiz show *The Weakest Link* in 2001, lasting for one season, and he hosted a single season of his own late night talk show, *The Dunphy Show*, which aired on TV3 in 2003.

Although he had been working as a part-time television analyst with RTÉ for two years previously, his first full-time position came in 1980 with the start of a new Irish newspaper, the *Sunday Tribune*. Dunphy managed to land the role of soccer correspondent with the help of a referral from Irish political correspondent Vincent Browne. From the beginning, he marked himself out as different. The young writer was straight-talking, combustible and frequently offensive to the subjects of his writing; in other words, he was impossible to ignore, a quality that has served him well as an analyst. He arrived with a bang, determined to call it as he saw it, regardless of the opprobrium that often ensued from his acid put-downs and sensational irreverence. He has remained, throughout his career, a divisive figure, loved by some, reviled by just as many. Dunphy has accumulated enemies with a collector's zeal, and has never strayed far from the headlines. He has no greater pleasure than pushing upstream, all the while blaspheming against received wisdom about the game that is his passion.

Dunphy stands out as an extremist with purist views about how football should be played. He has, on many occasions, incurred the wrath of his own country, not least when he objected vociferously to the management style of Republic of Ireland boss Jack Charlton at the 1990 World Cup. He was vilified for his unpatriotic stance, becoming deeply unpopular with the public at large, but in time such an outsider position would become common ground for Dunphy. He occupied it again in 2002 when he sensationally announced on RTÉ that he would be supporting Ireland's opponents in that summer's World Cup, as a protest against Irish manager Mick McCarthy's decision to send home Roy Keane. In more recent years, his trenchant opposition to the current Irish manager, Giovanni Trapattoni, has merely confirmed this trend. Yet, although Dunphy has certainly invited hostility, his star has never waned and this is because, above all, he is compelling. However one might describe him, 'boring' would hardly be fitting. In the otherwise often grey world of football punditry Dunphy could never be charged with being dull. He rarely fails to stoke the flames, providing, in equal parts, scandal and illumination to his audience with original and challenging ideas. He is unpredictable and this makes him unfailingly interesting. He has had an iron grip on the Irish public's attention for over thirty years and his staying power shows no signs of flagging.

This book charts the course of Dunphy's changing opinions on Irish and British football since the writing of *Only a Game?* in 1976. In that time he has voiced shocking, but unerringly provocative and impossible to ignore, broadsides against numerous respected figures within the game: from the international managers of the Republic of Ireland (Mick McCarthy: 'The boil on the arse of humanity'; Jack Charlton: 'A bully' and 'a bloody belligerent toerag') and of England (Terry Venables: 'A hollow man' whose cv is 'riddled with failure') to Premier League stars of past and present, such as Ronaldo ('a cheat', 'a clown', 'a puffball' and 'a disgrace'), Steven Gerrard ('a nothing player'), David Beckham ('a hero designed ... for the pages of *Hello!* magazine'), Niall Quinn ('a creep')and Roy Keane ('the perfect human being', when he liked him and 'a bullshitter', 'an asshole' and 'a media-tart' when he stopped liking him).

The book also looks specifically at Dunphy's role on RTÉ's football coverage and his on-screen dynamic with long-term colleagues John Giles, Liam Brady and Bill O'Herlihy. In this capacity, he has been unflinching in his assessment of the low standard of British television football analysis, accusing the *Match of the Day* crew of Gary Lineker, Alan Hansen, Mark Lawrenson and Alan Shearer of talking 'like they're on sleeping pills' and Sky Sports of treating its viewers as unintelligent, beer-swilling 'couch potatoes'. I provide, in chapter 8, an extended analysis of these views, comparing the RTÉ panellists to their British counterparts, Sky Sports and the BBC.

Although this book argues that Dunphy has been one of the best and most fascinating football analysts at work in Ireland or Britain in the last three decades, it also deals with his frustrating side – his occasional factual inaccuracies, his overreliance on shock value, his frequent habit of contradicting himself – and attempts to answer some of the intense criticism that he has been the target of throughout his tumultuous career. Dunphy has not been one to shrink in the face of adversity, never shirking from facing his critics head-on, in a good, honest tussle. This book is written in the same spirit of open debate and does not hold back in order to save Dunphy's blushes. It portrays the captivating football analyst that he is, with all his complications.

Chapter 1

'Nobody ever makes it after leaving Old Trafford'

Eamon Dunphy was born on 3 August 1945 and grew up in the north Dublin suburb of Drumcondra. His childhood, while never destitute, was a difficult one. His parents, Margaret and Paddy, and younger brother, Kevin, shared a single room in the Richmond Road area. Owing to lack of space, he and his brother slept on the floor. His father was a builder's labourer and later a hospital orderly, but was frequently out of work because of the straitened economic times of Ireland in the 1950s, a situation that added to the family's hardship. Nonetheless, his youth was made easier by having devoted parents whom he has frequently described in highly affectionate terms. Of their influence on his life Dunphy has said:

> They were poor, honest, devout good citizens. They raised their children to believe in those same values, and they suffered greatly to do that. They weren't the me-generation that I was. They

were really good people, and not just them but all of their generation.

Dunphy, speaking to the *Irish Examiner* in April 2010, has described growing up in Dublin during this period as 'a grey, bleak time', with football the only thing to temporarily lift the gloom. In his own words, he was a 'street kid' who spent as much of his time as possible outdoors playing the game he loved. Commenting on this time, in a television interview with TV3 journalist Ursula Halligan in January 2010, he noted: 'Football was a liberation from the frailties that I felt were besetting me: we were poorer than other people; my clothes weren't great; I wasn't a big fella.'

He may have been slight in stature – a fact he attributes to having begun smoking at age eight – and burdened by harsh economic restraints, but his ability gave him a way out, bringing him the opportunity of first representing Dublin, and then the Republic of Ireland at under-15 schoolboy level, the traditional way of being noticed by English First Division scouts. Dunphy had dreamed of being a professional footballer at the highest level and for aspiring young players in 1950s' Dublin that unequivocally meant Manchester United.

Soon, the dream began to become reality when Billy Behan, former Manchester United goalkeeper and then Irish scout, began calling to Dunphy's home. Behan, the same scout who had already introduced Irish players such as John Giles, Liam Whelan, Jackie Carey and Joe Carolan to Sir Matt Busby, now wanted Dunphy to follow suit. He met stiff resistance from the young player's mother, however, who, according to Dunphy, was strongly anti-English and did not support what was an uncertain move for her teenage son. It began what Dunphy has referred to as an extended wooing process, with the determined Behan

– noted for his ability to win over the trust of nervous parents – even turning up one Christmas with a turkey, in an attempt to seal the deal. The situation caused considerable tension at home as Dunphy's father attempted to convert his sceptical wife to the idea. Eventually, after he had spent a year working as a messenger boy for an upmarket tweed shop, Kevin & Howlin Ltd on Dublin's Nassau Street, his mother relented. She would not stand in the way of his football career.

On 3 August 1960, his 15th birthday, Dunphy went to Manchester for a two-week trial. 'It was 35 minutes and Busby watched. That was it, in Chorlton, a cricket facility. Just amazing.' He passed the test and was taken on as an apprentice the same year, beginning his involvement with professional football. For the teenage Dunphy, this was the realisation of a long-held boyhood dream. As a wide-eyed thirteen-year-old he had watched the famed Busby Babes demolish Shamrock Rovers in Dublin and was smitten. 'They beat Shamrock Rovers 6-0 at Dalymount Park and I was there. It was in the early rounds of the European Cup, September '57. The whole city was "waow". It was like Elvis or the Beatles coming. Magical.'

In his biography of Sir Matt Busby, Dunphy describes arriving at a club that was still living in the shadow of the Munich air disaster: a tragedy that had claimed the lives of eight Manchester United players on 6 February 1958 when the team's plane failed to take off on the third attempt from Munich's Riem Airport:

> Nobody mentioned it. The clock on the wall over the forecourt bore the words 'February 6th 1958'. That was all. This was a modest, and it seemed, entirely appropriate memorial. There was no need for an ostentatious memorial, the grief was

profound. But it was not our grief, rather Bobby's [Charlton], 'The Boss's [Sir Matt Busby], Jimmy's [Murphy], the grief of those who'd belonged to another club.

Dunphy signed a professional contract with Manchester United in 1962 and joined illustrious names like Bobby Charlton and Denis Law on the club's books. Dunphy, however, with such quality to contend with, was unable to break into the first team during his three years at Old Trafford and remained no more than a promising squad player. In the 1965 close season, Dunphy had a choice: languish on the fringes of this admittedly great club or move elsewhere to play regular first-team football. He opted for the latter and agitated successfully for a move. He writes in his account of Busby's life:

> I left Old Trafford that summer. This mattered little to anyone but me ... I had been a promising youth team player but was neither strong enough nor good enough to make progress in this born again football club. I asked for a transfer. The Boss saw me in the office. There was a saying that nobody ever makes it after leaving Old Trafford. This was an article of United faith. Busby reminded me of this. Players are desperate to come to Manchester. They don't choose to leave ... As I was hardly going to make it in Manchester terms I wondered why he bothered in my case. But he did. He wanted me to stay another year. I, concealing my awe, remained firm.

Dunphy's hand was strengthened and encouraged by the knowledge that Birmingham City, another First Division club, had expressed an interest in signing him for £8,000, an option he favoured. Dunphy did get his move, but on Busby's terms: a week later, in August 1965, he was sold to York City for £4,000, a club newly promoted to the Third Division. According to Dunphy, Busby had little fondness for former players coming back to haunt him, as John Giles had done after Manchester United sold him to Leeds United in 1963. Dunphy, from the club's point of view, was placed safely out of harm's way: a whole two division's distance from being able to embarrass the great man. Dunphy's time at York City was brief, with the player making only 22 appearances and scoring three goals, before securing a transfer to Millwall in the Second Division in January 1966. He made his debut for the south London team against Workington on 28 January 1966, thus beginning his longest stint at any one club. Spanning eight years, Dunphy would make 303 appearances for the Lions, scoring 25 times, as a regular first-team player. These years would come to represent the peak of Dunphy's playing career, taking him up to his twenty-eighth birthday and being the highest level of club football he would enjoy.

His time at Millwall would end in acrimony at the start of the 1973/74 season when he found himself out of the team and in search of a new club. This season was not in vain, however. Dunphy kept a careful diary of his last troubled months at the Den which was subsequently published to high acclaim. *Only a Game?* has come to be regarded as a seminal account of the footballer's life and remains in print today, thirty-six years after its first publication in 1976. It is the book that helped Dunphy to find a career in writing beyond his existence as a footballer.

Dunphy departed Millwall in December 1973 to join Third Division Charlton Athletic for a fee of £20,000. He played 44 times for the club, scoring three goals. His final move in English football came in 1975 when he switched to Reading, a club he would make 77 appearances for, scoring three goals, until his retirement from the English game in 1977. He finished his playing career in his native Dublin, playing until 1978 with Shamrock Rovers under the management of his life-long friend and international colleague John Giles.

Although Dunphy's club career was distinctly average, he did manage to represent his country 23 times during his time at Millwall. He made his debut in Paris on 10 November 1965 in a World Cup qualification play-off match against Spain, a game that Ireland lost 1-0. His last cap came in 1972 in a 4-1 defeat to Austria in a European Nations Cup qualifier.

First, however, we join Dunphy in 1973, age 28, at the beginning of a pivotal season in his football and journalistic future. It is when the player starts to become the writer with the creation of *Only a Game?*, Dunphy's ground-breaking account of a football career in terminal decline.

Chapter 2

Eight years in The Den:
becoming a writer

Eamon Dunphy's *Only a Game?* stands in a small and select tradition of compelling football autobiographies. It is a forthright account of the travails of a journeyman footballer who has plied his trade in the lower divisions of the English game, away from the spotlight of the top division. This is a footballing world unadorned by television coverage and the associated advantages of wealth and stardom. Football at this level really does seem like a job. Although this occupation was of a radically different nature to the ordinary nine to five existence, it still, unmistakably, had something of the strain of daily work. By today's stellar standards, the pay was extremely low, the conditions difficult, and the players were all too intimate with the stock-in-trade of everyday life; they were versed in mortgages, bills, car loans and the repetitive toil of simply making ends meet. These players may have been living their dreams, by lining up every week for a professional football club, yet in the ambiguous context of the Second Division, this was no guarantee of an escape from the ordinary.

In its frank appraisal of this unglamorous world, *Only a Game?* can be read as the antidote to the typical showbiz autobiographies of today's overpaid football stars. Dunphy's autobiography plumbs the depths of the footballer's life and has been called by *Financial Times* columnist Simon Kuper 'the best footballer's account of British football' and by Richard Williams of *The Guardian* 'the first footballer's diary to deal with the game's disappointments and humiliations'. This is history written by the losing side, and it is all the more fascinating for it.

The old Second Division could be a grim place and the life of the professional footballer just as unpleasant. In an age before the cult of celebrity was upon us, Dunphy shows us the life of an ordinary footballer at a very ordinary football club, Millwall FC. In the early 1970s, professional footballers earned modest wages and their employment rights were poorly developed. The 1973/74 season featured in *Only a Game?* is only some thirteen years after the £20 maximum wage for footballers was abolished, owing to the lobbying of the Professional Footballers' Association, led by Jimmy Hill. Add to this the lack of freedom of contract, and the fact that all players faced an uncertain future after football, without adequate qualifications for any other form of work, and you will begin to understand that this life had its considerable challenges.

In this footballing environment, the playing pitches were terrible and the training pitches even worse. In winter, players had to navigate a muddy sludge as the playing surfaces felt the strain of the wet British weather. Summer could be little better with some pitches becoming a solid mass of divots and bumps. Before you could even enjoy your football, you had to cope with the playing surface, a challenge that most modern professionals in the top two divisions will never have to face. The stadiums were another aspect of the game that did not exactly encourage flowing football. Speaking candidly of The Den, Millwall's down-at-heel ground, Dunphy gives us the following account:

> The place was distinctly lacking in ambiance. Having wound their way through a maze of narrow streets off the Old Kent Road, visiting teams would draw up outside what looked like a derelict factory. Here, grey was the primary colour. What wasn't grey needed a coat of paint. The pitch was tight – and bumpy. The visitors' dressing room was dark and narrow, as welcoming as a British Rail loo. Only good teams and brave players survived their introduction to the Lions' Den.

The Den, and its like, were the venues in which Dunphy pursued his craft. Theatres of dreams they were not. They were classic, intimidating cauldrons, where, as Dunphy puts it, 'the fans were as hostile as the decor' and the image that comes to his mind is that of a 'raucous dockland music hall.' Simon Inglis, in his authoritative work *The Football Grounds of Great Britain*, substantiates Dunphy's description of Millwall's downtrodden ground before it received its modern-day revamp. He notes that finding The Den was an achievement in itself, with a patchwork maze of streets leading up to its unspectacular narrow gateway. Once there, he highlights the depressing spectacle awaiting the intrepid stranger: 'The Den is a tight enclosure, dominated by the drab, weathered tones of its uniform roofs and terracing'; the combined effect of the 'walls, the police hut, the dark stand and the low roofs make it resemble a huge trap.'

To play and thrive in these environments, you had to have steel in your backbone and a real love of the game. These were the days of the hard man, when tackling from behind was commonplace, and when the skilful ball-player was something of an endangered species. Such players were under threat because there is nothing more anti-football than the tackle from behind. Aside from the obvious perils of permitting such play, the tackle from behind was ruinous, because it neither encouraged players to present for the ball nor to retain it when they had received it. A player will not dwell on the ball and wait for the opportune moment to release it, if he knows, that at any moment, he might be suddenly upended from behind. For an intelligent ball-player like Dunphy, who was not physically strong enough for professional football, this was not comfortable territory.

Speaking of this period, Dunphy informs us that 'This was the Second Division whose traditional hardness had been reinforced by the inclusion in every side of Peter Storey/Norman Hunter clones, complete in every detail except talent.' Peter Storey (Arsenal) and Norman Hunter (Leeds United) were prime examples of the infamous hard men of British football.

Yet, despite the odds, in these distinctly unromantic surroundings Dunphy builds a vision of and an argument for the beautiful game, an unremitting belief in how the game should be played, as opposed to how it is routinely played. In the drab surroundings of Second Division football, Dunphy holds fast to an ideal, a determination to believe that there is something great about the game of football, something more than the kick-and-rush football of the division in which he plays. He expounds and elaborates on this vision time and again in *Only a Game?* It quickly becomes evident to the reader that Dunphy was a thinking man's footballer and *Only a Game?* contains the seeds of his mature football analysis off the field. In it we see the emergence of Dunphy's now highly recognisable views on the game.

There is abundant evidence to show that Dunphy the analyst and football critic is very much a part of *Only a Game?* Readers will recognise his thoughtful and strident views, his tendency to polarise opinion, and a distinct predilection for not being too far away when controversy is abroad.

The beauty of *Only a Game?*, however, is that we get insightful and intelligent football analysis from the perspective of someone who was then still playing the game, from an insider still immersed in the world of the professional footballer. This is what separates it from many autobiographies of its kind. The book gives a player's view of the game with searing honesty. He shows the game as it is and exposes the psychology of the professional footballer in all its discomforting inconsistencies. As Nick Hornby has put it, 'What sets it apart is its honesty and lack of sentimentality.'

The quality of *Only a Game?* is partially explained by the fact that by the time Peter Ball, editor of the book and Dunphy's literary confidant, persuaded him to write the memoir Dunphy had matured as a person and a footballer. He had not floated aimlessly through the seasons of his playing career uncritically imbibing received wisdom along the way. Dunphy reflected on the nature of football, forming his own philosophy of the game. What makes a good player? Is there a correct way to play football? What is good and bad coaching? What role does psychology play in a footballer's performance? These are all issues tackled seriously and with some insight in the pages of Dunphy's autobiography, and, in doing so, he develops a standpoint on the game that goes beyond the straightforward motivations of the ordinary footballer. He reflects on the very condition of the game of football and on what it means to be a professional in this most popular of sports.

Dunphy has an almost instinctive feel for the soul of the game. He speaks of himself and other players as being artists, not mere sportsmen who simply enjoy the game as athletes would. For Dunphy, the footballer is much more than an athlete. He is a creator of possibilities, an artist whose tool is the football and whose canvas is the football pitch.

Moreover, in Dunphy's exalted vision, spirituality and football meet. This is revealed very early in the memoir, where we find Dunphy describing the bliss that comes from relaxing after a demanding training session. Any athlete will be able to identify with Dunphy's words. Describing his daily pre-season training routine, he says: 'You spend the morning working, from half past ten until twelve, then have some lunch, then work again in the afternoon. You finish about four and you are really knackered. Yet it is a marvellous spiritual feeling. You have worked hard and are cleansed.' Dunphy then continues, in almost religious tones, to elaborate on how pre-season training expunges the guilt of the footballer who has succumbed to temptation throughout the languorous summer break.

We are indeed a long way from the relentless dullness of many footballers' autobiographies. *Only a Game?* is not part of that tradition, the tradition that respected football writer Brian Glanville, writing in the preface to Dunphy's book, refers to as the 'ghosted pap which, with its endless banalities and disingenuousness, has so long been inflicted on us'. Agree or disagree with him, Dunphy is a player who has something to say about the game.

By the time he wrote his diary on the 1973/74 season, Dunphy had already developed the free-thinking, controversial style for which he has become known as a writer and broadcaster. His relationship with the then Millwall manager Benny Fenton illustrates the point well. Throughout the season covered in his diary, Dunphy's association with Fenton became heavily strained. Fenton was essentially a traditional Football League manager whose patience with Dunphy's outspoken persona had begun to wear thin. Their disagreement culminated in Fenton characterising Dunphy as a dangerous political type, who talked a good game but could not do it on the pitch where it mattered. The ostensible reason for their fall-out had been Dunphy's advice to a colleague who was agitating for a move from Millwall. Dunphy counselled his playing colleague to coerce the club into making a public statement in order to force their hand in relation to his proposed move.

This, to any football manager, and certainly to the old school kind of which Fenton was an example, was little short of treason. Dunphy was promoting player power. For Dunphy, players were used and abused far too often in the game, and Fenton could see this combustible element surfacing in Dunphy. He had Dunphy categorised as a troublemaker. Clearly, for a footballer, Dunphy was thinking far too much, and, worse still, he was encouraging his fellow players to do likewise. Someone had to go and it was not going to be Fenton. The result was a series of events being put into motion which would see Dunphy hand in a transfer request and move to Charlton Athletic only a few months into the 1973/74 season.

Inevitably, players of Dunphy's kind clash sooner or later with football managers. A football club is run as a dictatorship, with the unquestioned authority of the manager holding sway. Players are expected to take orders and be obedient, just as soldiers are expected to follow their superior's commands. Independent thought is not encouraged, because player power is the dread of any manager. There is little place for democracy in a football club and Dunphy simply had too much of the democrat in him. He was possessed of a healthy awareness of his rights, a trait in a player that would make it very difficult for him to get along with a traditional Football League manager like Benny Fenton.

In *Only a Game?* we even get a detailed analysis of how democracy solved a serious dispute between Millwall's captain, Dennis Burnett, and Benny Fenton. After Burnett failed to appear for a pre-season practice match in the summer of 1973, Fenton handed him a one-week suspension and proceeded to call a squad meeting to convey the news to his players. The novelty of this gathering was that Fenton genuinely consulted with and sought the opinion of his players. Fenton wondered if his decision to send Burnett home had been extreme? Perhaps it was a proportionate response? After much debate, Fenton is persuaded to telephone Burnett, and what began as a serious stand-off between two entrenched egos is settled with a remarkably laconic invitation to Burnett: 'Come back for lunch, and we'll forget about it.' Burnett returns and the matter is forgotten.

One has to marvel at how few words were needed to resolve this conflict between captain and manager. It, more than anything else, points to the special bond that joined these men. Histrionics and dramatic gestures of contrition became redundant when it was this easy to access a shared understanding.

Although Dunphy rightly points to the unusual act of democracy between manager and players, he is perhaps setting himself up for a painful fall. This is an isolated incident, where rank was forgotten and roles were temporarily equalised, and could not be seen as any significant revolution in the interaction between manager and players. The true reason for it surely lies in the unusual crisis of having your captain and most important player alienated. Fenton would not have made exceptions for any other player, a lesson that Dunphy was soon forced to learn.

In later years, when writing an introduction to the 1986 second edition of *Only a Game?*, Dunphy had softened his stance on Fenton, realising that he had given the manager a raw deal. Dunphy moves his ire upstairs to the boardroom, targeting the real 'bastards', whom he now sees as being responsible for the plight of Millwall FC during those years. Fenton was caught between selfish professional footballers and a demanding board of directors, who did not understand the game, yet put no less pressure on Fenton for that. Dunphy touchingly describes Fenton readying himself for an encounter with his paymasters. He says, 'I can still see him now, after a particularly satisfying performance by 'his boys', standing in front of the dressing room mirror, comb in hand, readying himself for a triumphant boardroom entrance.' Although this is ostensibly a happy moment, Dunphy acutely conveys the subtle degradation at play here: a football man forced to justify himself before non-football men.

Dunphy even admits to guilt for his part in Fenton's downfall, saying that he, like all footballers, was selfish, and he goes so far as to say that if there was a hero in *Only a Game?* it was Benny Fenton. This is a significant shift, because the first edition of *Only a Game?* pointedly had a different hero, namely the 'good pro'. The careful reader will notice that Dunphy's chronicle is not dedicated to family and friends but, in fact, to this most elusive of figures, the 'good pro'.

Who, exactly, is this 'good pro' figure by whom he sets so much store? According to Dunphy, his greatness is both in sporting and personal terms. 'His goodness has to do not just with his talent but with his spiritual state' and, although he may not always be the greatest player, he compensates for it with the enduring qualities of 'integrity, nobility of spirit, dedication to duty and commitment to cause'. For Dunphy, in the heat of battle, the 'good pro' is always on hand to offer support. When your team is defending, he is tracking his man and, conversely, when the team is attacking, he is always making himself available for a pass, whether it be in the first or the last minute of play. He is, in other words, more than a footballer, his 'moral courage' showing that he always accepts responsibility in 'attack or defence, at home or away, in January mud, April wind or August sunshine'. This man for all seasons is arguably the origin of Dunphy's oft-repeated phrase, 'real football people', whom he frequently acclaims, in stark contrast to the collection of men in blazers who typically control the game from their ivory towers.

Is this vaunted figure, the 'good pro', just a fiction, a creation of Dunphy's nostalgia, or can we put faces to this ghost-like spectre? One salient example can be found in Dunphy's biography of Sir Matt Busby, where Dunphy describes Busby's playing days. Busby, he notes, never shirked responsibility: 'He wanted the ball, was never afraid, always coaxing by example' and Dunphy elaborates, saying that Busby had 'moral courage, the willingness to make mistakes for others, to carry their burden on the days when they weakened'. He was not one of the sunshine boys, but one of the 'quiet men, dependable and diligent'. He was precisely the kind of honest hero whom Dunphy seeks to commemorate in his diary. This man of decency is for Dunphy a moral counterweight to the gilded decadence of modern football stars, whom Dunphy has described as being mired in 'the bloated, celebrity-haunted circus that is the contemporary Premiership'.

In order to dispel a myth, and, lest we think that Dunphy's honest hero is all selfless work rate and no talent, one could point to Dunphy's constant admiration for Paul Scholes, a player who possesses just as much ability as honesty. If any modern player fits Dunphy's 'good pro' tag, it is surely the Manchester United midfielder and, in *Only a Game?*, a serious respect of such talent lies alongside Dunphy's aforementioned appreciation of the less aesthetic qualities of heart and endeavour.

This is clear from the overwhelming sense in Dunphy's memoir that there is a correct way for football to be played and an incorrect way. He presents an expressive, open style of football, where the ball is caressed and nurtured in a fluent and unrushed passing game. In this world, the opposition is overcome not by hard graft, but by guile and stealth, and the sheer joy of being creative. This is the fabled beautiful game, and the game with which Dunphy wishes to identify.

Footballers, when playing this way, develop an intuitive and unspoken form of communication, a mutual enjoyment of the rhythm and flow of something greater than themselves which can be revealed through playing the game the right way. Early in the book, we see a startling instance of this when Dunphy likens the relationship between two midfielders to that of the intimacy of lovers. He says: 'It's a form of expression – you are communicating as much as if you were making love to one another.'

This is an image of footballers that flies in the face of the machismo that so regularly dominates football and footballers' relationships. It is joyous expression. 'It's an unspoken relationship, but your movements speak, your game speaks.' Dunphy's point is that when two midfielders work together, when they play one-twos, when they play through balls to each other, they are sharing and creating something special. Such communication does not need words. The art and flow of football says it all. As inspiring as this may sound, it remained largely an ideal, the exception to the rule.

The reality of football at the lower levels of the game is something very different, and it is a reality that even Dunphy the idealist succumbs to from time to time.

The harsh reality of the old Second Division was kick-and-rush. It was a world where honesty, graft and effort brought results and where creativity was seen as a dangerous luxury. In Dunphy's words, 'bite and fight are the order of the day' and the imperative is studs first, think later. This is a world where ideals die hard and where the beautiful game is regularly at risk of being reduced to a mere battle of might and wills. The lower divisions of the Football League, it should be remembered, are more about surviving than thriving. Exciting, crowd-pleasing football comes a distant second in the weekly struggle to edge a few places up the table. One rule dominates proceedings: the survival of the fittest.

As a player, Dunphy found it hard to fit into this playing environment. He was a wispy but talented midfield playmaker whose game was based more on craft than on physicality. Commenting on this period in *The Independent on Sunday*, Dunphy has said: 'I thought football was very hard. I wasn't strong or athletic enough. The *Rothman's Yearbook* showed me as 9st 4lb. The next lightest anywhere was a stone heavier. It was partly because I'd been smoking since I was eight, partly my metabolism.'

In 1964, during his spell at Manchester United, the club's annual programme compared Dunphy favourably to Denis Law for 'his natural ability, fair hair, lean build and willingness to tackle hard.' With such a frame, Dunphy had to base his game on nous and artistry, qualities that found scant sympathy in the old Second Division. Speaking in an interview with *The Guardian* in November 2004, Dunphy assessed his ability in the following terms: 'I was a midfield general. I just wasn't very strong. But I was skilful. I didn't have the strength and athletic prowess you need to go to the top, but I was decent enough.'

Dunphy wanted his football to be graceful and for Millwall to play with skill, but undoubtedly, to some extent, Dunphy's loftier thoughts on the game are brought down to earth by the grim reality of lower level football and by his physique. At times, perhaps, it affects his judgment. At these points we see a tension emerging in the book between Dunphy's dearly held vision of the game and the murky reality that surrounded him daily in the Second Division. On the one hand, Dunphy presents a visionary and almost poetic image of football. In his conception, football, when played correctly, is an art form, with fine, flowing passing movements an imperative.

However, Dunphy seems all too aware that frequently, if not most of the time, the game is in fact more about perspiration than inspiration, the player more artisan than artist. This does not diminish the ideal, however. To say that football is played a certain way week in, week out does not mean that it is the correct way. The ideal, then, is something that Dunphy seeks to kindle and revive, even though the evidence before his eyes forms a brutal riposte to his aesthetic pretensions.

Consequently, it is not altogether surprising that at times Dunphy seems to relent in the face of the reality around him. This is evidenced by his attitude to a young Gordon Hill, a player who would go on to sign for Manchester United in 1975 and be capped for England six times between 1976 and 1977. Hill had obvious natural skill and dribbling ability, qualities that should have drawn Dunphy's admiration. Yet Dunphy is dismissive of Hill's undoubted talents. He sees Hill as a luxury that Millwall cannot afford, a player who may have ability, but whom Dunphy ultimately writes off as a showman and individualist, someone who is not a team player and will consequently not go very far in the game.

Perhaps it is unfair to accuse Dunphy of getting it wrong here. Predicting the future of young promising players is far from a science; many young players with obvious ability regularly fail to live up to their vaunted potential. However, it is interesting to wonder if, in this isolated instance, it is the Second Division talking, and not the idealistic Dunphy whom we see elsewhere and still see today.

This same ambiguity can be recognised in Dunphy's mature football analysis. He is a passionate exponent of the beautiful game, yet he despises and rails against the kind of skilful player who does not put in an honest shift for the team. We shall come to see that the 'good pro' remains very much a live figure in Dunphy's analysis of the modern game.

Dunphy's passion for football is another quality that is very evident throughout his autobiography. Although, it is almost a cliché to speak of football people having a passion for the game, unmistakably we see this quality in Dunphy during these early years.

There is one particularly revealing moment in *Only a Game?* that illustrates this point. Dunphy discovers a young apprentice footballer in tears at the Millwall training ground; he has just been informed that he will not receive a professional contract. This is the moment that every trainee footballer dreads. These young players are the human detritus of football, casually cast aside at a young age, without adequate preparation for what lies ahead, and with no immediate prospects. Dunphy comforts the player, assuring him there is a future outside of football, but to no effect. It is the end of this teenager's world as he knows it, and in order to stop the youth becoming what Dunphy terms 'factory fodder', he makes sure that the boy is set up in a catering course. Dunphy, then, goes on to condemn the football establishment for not caring for its younger players, and that more should be done to give them a proper chance to prove their worth before they are unceremoniously shoved away from the professional scene.

If more evidence of this passion were needed, we could point to Dunphy's vivid description of the footballer's arch fear, that of being dropped. Dunphy describes how easily it happens and how, when it first comes, the dreaded event is over in a moment. Your name is simply not on a piece of paper. Where before you were a first-team player, you are now a substitute. It happens without notice, leaving you unprepared for the resulting shock. It is up to you, the player, to try to make sense of the situation. Why was I dropped? Will I play first team football again? Does the manager still believe in me? Am I still wanted? Is there a point any more if I am just a reserve?

The first time Dunphy is dropped at Millwall was particularly brutal for him. At a training practice match, he is simply given a reserve team bib without as much as a word of explanation. The cold truth hits Dunphy hard and the attendant sense of injustice follows rapidly. He cannot reconcile himself to the way he has been informed of his sudden demotion, describing it as a dagger in the back: 'A snap of the fingers, and you are gone. Out. All the commitment, all the emotion, all the hard work, all the belief. Everything gone.' Yes, Millwall had lost to a very poor Carlisle United team on the previous weekend, but Dunphy is sure it was not entirely his fault. He had tackled, he had grafted, he had sweated for the team, as well as playing his own more creative midfield game. Dunphy is left on the verge of tears, but he bites his lip, and heads to the other end of the pitch to join the reserves. To a senior player, utterly unaccustomed to reserve football, it is banishment pure and simple.

For anyone who might think this is an overreaction and that Dunphy simply needed to grow up and deal with being dropped, I ask them to compare the professional footballer's job to that of an ordinary worker. Do people suddenly and routinely get demoted in their workplace without any notice from their superiors? Is it a regular occurrence for an office worker to come to work on a Monday morning and find his desk gone and that his job simply has been removed over the weekend? Obviously not. If this were to occur in an ordinary workplace, trade unions would be consulted and legal action would almost certainly follow. Workers' rights and employment legislation would be invoked, and a general sense of scandal would prevail.

If a footballer is demoted, however, it is different. He is expected to shut up and get on with it. He is often not even informed of the reason why he has been dropped, another basic right that an ordinary worker would enjoy. The footballer is left to his own thoughts and devices. He joins the reserves, adjusts as best he can, and tries to find the motivation from within himself to get back in the first team.

Dunphy gives us an insight into the feelings a footballer goes through in these situations. After driving home to his wife and bursting into tears, he describes himself going shopping with her to get his mind off matters, but to no avail. He says: 'It's eating into you the whole time. You can't think about anything else for one minute. You go home and you are restless, edgy. The whole time you are thinking "What am I going to do?" '.

Later in the book, when Dunphy has been dropped again from Millwall's first team and is on the verge of a transfer, he describes the void in the footballer's life when regular Saturday football is replaced by the dreaded Mid-Week League for reserve teams. This league, which exists by necessity and in which nobody seems to have any interest, Dunphy describes as 'death on every level'. In place of the adoring crowds at The Den, substitute the fabled one man and his dog, and an impression of the dearth of atmosphere at these games becomes clear. It also means playing on a Wednesday evening instead of in the traditional Saturday game, and Dunphy tells of the sense of consequent aimlessness that comes over the footballer when his Saturday is devoid of football.

When he was part of the first team, Dunphy's whole week was leading to Saturday. Discussing preparation, he says:

On Fridays you have steak for dinner because it is good for you. And you go to bed early because it is good for you. You stay chaste because it is good for you. Your whole life has a point. And that point is three o'clock on a Saturday afternoon. Your life is very purposeful. And when you aren't playing there is a big void.

Dunphy's portrayal of the lost footballer, struggling for a sense of meaning after being marginalised from the first team, is an affecting meeting between existential angst and the ordinary footballer.

If we were in any doubt about the intense feelings that are generated when a player is dropped, we can look to a revealing interview that Dunphy gave to *The Independent on Sunday* in May 2004. During the interview, when asked what keeps him awake at night, surprisingly Dunphy does not talk of the usual fears that might haunt an ageing man. Instead, he informs us, his nightmare is being dropped by Millwall. In this nocturnal horror scene, Dunphy finds himself back at The Den being summoned by Benny Fenton for some ominous purpose. He explains: 'If I have a bad dream, it's always about being left out of the side and standing outside the manager's office at the Old Den.' This is proof indeed of the lingering power of the footballer's insecurity. Dunphy then goes on to explain how his wife Jane inquired about the causes of his disturbed sleep. He explained, and she replied, 'Who the hell is Benny Fenton?'

I have already alluded to the larger than life presence of the manager in a football club and the way in which his will overshadows all decision-making in the club, a will that brooks no disagreement or disaffection. The manager controls the club and players in a quasi-tyrannical manner, and the presence of Fenton in Dunphy's dreams does nothing to dispel this notion. The spectre of the football manager, 'the Boss', lives on in Dunphy's psyche.

Indeed, Dunphy's perspicacity for laying bare the mind of the footballer is what originally marked out *Only a Game?* as a ground-breaking work of football writing. In a 'warts and all' analysis, Dunphy outlines the often selfish and ignoble motivations that drive the professional footballer. This is the unedifying, egoistical reality that lies disturbingly close to the surface.

An apt illustration of this occurs in the aftermath of Dunphy being dropped, an occasion when he makes some of his most honest and revealing admissions about the footballer's mindset. After Millwall lost 3-2 to Sheffield Wednesday in October 1973, a game that Dunphy watched from the stands, he admits to being inwardly delighted at the result because it means his chances of a recall are obviously improved. In the dressing room, after the game, he describes imitating the outward pretence of gloom while inwardly being very pleased with himself. He says:

> And when they get beaten, as we did last night, what do you do? You act. Because you can't come in with a big smile all over your face. Everybody else is sick. But you aren't. You are pleased. So you come in and make faces; pretend that you are sick like the rest of them. But everyone knows that you are acting.

This is refreshingly truthful, and what many of us will have secretly believed about footballers for a long time. How often do we hear professional footballers uttering tired phrases: it's the team that matters; the three points are the main thing, it's not about my performance, it's about the team. These are myths, and Dunphy has the honesty to expose them. Footballers, like all sportspersons, are solitary creatures, concerned primarily for their own survival before all else. Beneath the unvarying cluster of platitudes that eulogise the value of the team ethic lies an inherently selfish beast. Hence a player's own career and performance level come first, while the fate of the team lags behind in second place. Even the success of the team is for Dunphy not something you share: 'It is your glory. You [the team] only achieve it together. But you don't share it. Everyone sets out to achieve it, and the team is your means to that end.'

This is a lot more like the truth. In reality footballers are driven by the search for personal success and the pursuit of footballing greatness on the pitch. And why not? Is this not why young players passionately want to make the grade? Concern for the team is a by-product of the individual player's pursuit for greatness and it cannot be any other way. The public face of football is a communal event; the private face lurks in a far more egocentric place, and Dunphy does not shirk from diagnosing it when he tells us 'sport is basically a lonely thing for every individual in it.' Looked at from this perspective, a football team is really a team of eleven individuals mandated to perform together.

The piquancy of *Only a Game?* in its unsparing dissection of professional football can be partly explained by the fact that Dunphy is slowly becoming aware of the impending end of his career. He will not lead this privileged life forever, and, being dropped, and made surplus to requirements, brings this fact into stark relief. There is a heavy note of the endgame about this book, and the closing chapter, 'Saturday Nights in Hell', chronicling

Dunphy's creeping disillusionment and departure from Millwall, marks the beginning of the downward slide.

It should be remembered that Dunphy began his football career as a trainee at Manchester United. He had daily contact with George Best, Bobby Charlton and Denis Law. Anyone who played at the same club as these men had to be changed by that experience. Dropping to the lower divisions can only seem like failure after the exalted company one kept in the environment of Busby's Manchester United.

The truth is that Dunphy began near the summit and kept falling thereafter. This gives *Only a Game?* an unmistakable tinge of regret, a sense of unrealised potential, a suggestion that the great opportunity has already passed for Dunphy and that he is approaching the denouement of his career. He is in the winding-down stage.

It must be a difficult moment for a professional footballer to realise that his powers are waning and that the most has not been made of the chance given to him, a chance that presents itself to very few and that can come only once. The moment for Dunphy surfaces in the preseason of 1973, on his twenty-eighth birthday, when he is contemplating the season ahead. It was going to be a make-or-break season for him: the season when he hoped he would finally attain promotion and play in the First Division, the place where all footballers long to test their abilities. The moment creeps up on Dunphy, filling him with fear for his future. He says:

> Twenty-eight, the age when insecurity like a slowly descending fog appears on the horizon. You begin to wonder what is coming from the Provident Fund, about a testimonial, sometimes at night about retirement – the end. How much

longer will you spend your summers in this idyllic
way dreaming of glory? ... It's a shock to realize
how rapid the descent is from pinnacle to valley.

Little did Dunphy know just how rapid his own descent
would be in the end. Only three months into the 1973/74
season and after being substituted in a 0-1 defeat to
Middlesbrough, Dunphy sees the writing on the wall. His
time at Millwall is coming to an abrupt and unceremoni-
ous end. The Millwall team that has played together for
so many seasons is being broken up and Dunphy paints
a bleak picture of his football future: 'With each passing week, I'm deteriorating back into that dreadful limbo
where your confidence goes, your belief in yourself is
eroded, your appetite for the game diminishes. Deep
down inside I believe that I can play. I know I could succeed, achieve something in my career.' This is the sadness
of *Only a Game?*: unrealised hopes and cheated desires –
the lot of the journeyman footballer.

Dunphy may have hoped for one last attempt at promotion to the First Division, but this hope is eclipsed by
the feeling that he has reached his peak and his career
is fading away. For what awaited Dunphy were not the
heights of the First Division but the lows of the Third
Division with Charlton Athletic. After falling out with
Benny Fenton, and becoming marginalised at Millwall,
Dunphy decided that he needed regular football and so he
joined Charlton Athletic in December 1973. Even though
the Third Division was a serious step down, Dunphy
chose Charlton because they wanted him. One cannot
underestimate the desire for a footballer to be wanted, to
feel he is an integral part of something. This must have
seemed like deliverance, compared to the crippling disenchantment that Dunphy had begun to feel at Millwall.

After much negativity, he simply wanted something positive, Third Division or not.

His parting analysis of Millwall, after eight years, is pithy and to the point: 'A failed football club in October. A depressing place.'

As he muses on his new challenge, Dunphy likens footballers to roses, saying, 'In good soil they bloom; on stony ground they don't.' If Dunphy hoped to bloom, it was not to be at Charlton. After beginning well, Charlton looked like promotion candidates to the Second Division, with Dunphy a major influence from central-midfield, but, in the end, the challenge faded and Dunphy was dropped for a number of games near the end of the season. At the end of the 1973/74 season Theo Foley, the manager who had signed Dunphy, was sacked, and after a difficult next season under Andy Nelson, Dunphy was given a free transfer to Reading in the Fourth Division.

He played an important role in the Reading team that won promotion to the Third Division in the 1975/76 season. However, the following season was a constant battle for survival, and Reading and Dunphy found themselves once more in the Fourth Division. In a way, it is the inevitable destination for a lower league footballer, moving from club to club, dropping a division each time.

In a painful paradox for Dunphy, the greatness of his diary lies in the fact that it is essentially an account of failure, an unfolding of disillusionment with the game of football, and not a success story.

Failure, arriving unexpectedly in the middle of the 1973/74 season, is the catalyst for Dunphy to look back on his career in order to draw out its significance and to ask where he goes from here. Where there might have been tales of glory, there are only frustrating 'what might have beens', unexplored possibilities and missed opportunities, hopes turned sour, the raw material of recrimination, not celebration. As Dunphy has put it, *Only a Game?* records 'the bitter end of a journey that was not always bitter'.

Dunphy did not feel appreciated by Millwall for his years of service, and in an interview with *The Irish Times* in 2010 he has cited a sense of being exploited as one of his abiding memories of leaving English football.

An account of bitterness it may have been, but the importance and originality of *Only a Game?* should not be underestimated. Its relevance can be understood with more exactness when we consider the tradition of British sports writing out of which it came. As Simon Kuper pointed out in his article 'Sporting Fictions', Dunphy's book was one of the first noteworthy accounts of football written from a working-class perspective. Frequently, when it came to a choice of material, British writers overlooked football, and instead favoured the games of cricket and rugby. Football was condescended to and considered not worthy of literary expression, while nothing unusual was thought of whole chapters being devoted to cricket matches in some novels.

An instructive example, highlighted by Kuper, of the proliferation of cricket references in English literature can be found in L.P. Hartley's novel *The Go-Between*, where a central chapter in the book is devoted to a detailed description of a cricket match between the upper- and lower-class citizens of the community. The match is not just a literary diversion. In fact, it plays an important role in advancing the plot and the characters' various relationships. Such a serious role for a football match, however, was not conceivable in this uneven literary environment where many writers seemed to lack a basic appreciation of the game.

This literary imbalance meant that the few exceptional works that were devoted to football tended to be written by those who either did not understand or appreciate the game fully. This led to a skewed vision of the footballer, for as the critic D.J. Taylor has put it, such works 'tend to be written by educated gentlefolk who have observed the game from afar' and who, consequently, cannot do justice to the sport.

Dunphy, by writing with an insider's understanding, is the opposite of this literary tradition. He writes about football from personal experience, as an active, self-aware participant, and not as a detached and disinterested observer. For this reason, Dunphy's work can be most accurately compared to David Storey's great rugby league novel, *This Sporting Life*. Although *This Sporting Life* is a novel and *Only a Game?* a work of non-fiction, Kuper argues there is a major crossover of subject matter and treatment. In both books, we find raw and authentic accounts of the life and toils of the sportsman; descriptions of the sporting life with which ordinary footballers and rugby players could genuinely identify. In these works, the voice of the working-class sportsman finds eloquent expression, something not always audible in British sporting literature.

Ostensibly a football book, *Only a Game?* is, in truth, more than just that. It is a book full of the energy of human endeavour, attempting to exhibit the very normal struggle to achieve something lasting, despite everything.

On the publication of *Only a Game?*, it became clear that Dunphy was more than a footballer and that a promising career in writing was a genuine possibility. Although *Only a Game?* established his credentials, Dunphy's beginnings in writing pre-date this period. In fact, Dunphy had already begun writing a column for the *South London Press* newspaper before the end of his Millwall career.

It was here that his controversial views first found voice, in a weekly column entitled 'Dunphy's Diary'. His rebellious spirit and anti-establishment views, aired weekly, had the expected effect. They caused outrage in certain football circles. Dunphy was seen as a traitor to the game and to the people who work so hard to make clubs function. He had taken the easy money and become one of the resented journalist fraternity. It is to Dunphy's credit that *Only a Game?* includes the full text of a blunt critique of his column, which originally appeared in the match programme for a game between Millwall and Leyton Orient on 24 November 1973, only days before he would sign for Charlton Athletic.

In this short, acerbic piece, penned by an unknown writer, Dunphy is censured for becoming another armchair critic, getting his thirty pieces of silver for betraying honest, hard-working football people. Ostensibly the piece is a response to Dunphy's support of those arch rebels of the game at the time, Brian Clough and Malcolm Allison, and his related criticism of football's 'little people': those who had opposed Clough and Allison.

Dunphy is accused of veiling his column in a cloak of idealism in order to hide the fact that he is just another hired hack from Grub Street. The anonymous writer says:

> Is it ideals which inspire this blowing of one's top? If history is any guide, most idealists existed in poverty. Today's so-called idealists, by virtue of the communications media, get paid for their outbursts. They also get paid for remaining loyal to those who provide them with a living, a very good living at that.

This is an interesting point about the independence of media football commentators. To what extent can their views be trusted when they have a paymaster to keep contented? Are Eamon Dunphy's many celebrated outbursts motivated by concerns of ego and financial gain, or is his unwavering perspective on the game simply natural and integral to him as a pundit? According to the match programme writer, Dunphy's strident views are damaging to the game: 'You change the game by ordered thought, not by outbursts which boost your own ego, which give you a headline in a local or national newspaper.'

Dunphy, the anti-establishment rebel, the carefree stoker of controversy, was already under attack even before he had become a full-time journalist, nearly twenty years before he would be reviled so publicly for his outspoken views on Jack Charlton's management of the Republic of Ireland national team.

After writing *Only a Game?*, Dunphy contributed a highly regarded column to a Reading newspaper, before making his true journalistic breakthrough in 1978, when he contributed a series of well-received articles to *The Irish Times*, covering the World Cup of that year. It was this World Cup that saw the beginnings of Dunphy's long-standing television role as a football analyst for RTÉ, teaming up with Bill O'Herlihy to cover the tournament.

On returning to Dublin, Dunphy continued to work in football, playing for and taking the post of youth team coach at Shamrock Rovers in 1977, where John Giles was now manager. Giles had enjoyed a long playing career in England from 1959 to 1977 with Manchester United, Leeds United and West Bromwich Albion, while also holding the role of international player-manager with the Republic of Ireland national team from 1973 to 1980. Giles and Dunphy planned to return Shamrock

Rovers to more successful times, hoping that the professionalisation of the club would bring about the required transformation. However, after three years of effort, the yield was a single FAI Cup victory in 1978 (Dunphy's only winner's medal in senior football), and Dunphy departed in a hail of recriminations. Speaking in an interview given for Daire Whelan's *Who Stole Our Game? The Fall and Fall of Irish Soccer*, Dunphy blamed the smallmindedness of the League of Ireland for the failure of the project. He said: 'They [the League] didn't want us to rise because they knew that they couldn't rise and they didn't want a professional club dominating the League as they put it.'

Although the experience may have left him bitter, it did give Dunphy his only taste of European club football. Following their success in the 1978 FAI Cup, Shamrock Rovers entered the European Cup Winners' Cup where Dunphy and his team mates competed in two ties. In the first round they were drawn against the Cypriot club Apoel Nicosia. Rovers won 3-0 on aggregate, winning the first leg 2-0 in Dublin and then completing the victory with a 1-0 away win in the second leg. Consequently, in the second round they met the Czech Republic club Banik Ostrava but were comprehensively defeated 6-1 on aggregate. In Dublin, the first-leg result was a 3-0 win for the Czech team and in the return fixture it was a 3-1 scoreline in their favour.

After leaving Shamrock Rovers, Dunphy turned to journalism, tellingly, in a symbolic exchange, handing over his FAI Cup winner's medal to the person who gave him his NUJ card, and he tells us: 'I have never been back to a League of Ireland ground since.'

His one last dalliance with football occurred in 1982 when Dunphy put himself forward as a candidate for the vacant managerial post at Millwall. Although Dunphy was now settled in Ireland, the thought of realising his dream of managing Millwall was enough to turn his head. It was a short-lived dream, however, because the then-chairman, Alan Thorne, favoured George Graham for the post. How Dunphy would have fared as a manager of a football club is a question consigned to the interesting 'what-ifs' of history. After this setback, Dunphy became committed exclusively to a life of writing and broadcasting work.

Although it would be easy to draw a line between Dunphy the footballer and Dunphy the writer, his writing grew organically out of his experience as a professional footballer. It was the fact that Dunphy, as a player, was already reflecting on the game, forming and expressing thoughtful insights, which shows us that he was always a writer-in-waiting.

In fact, Dunphy has said that football was the perfect preparation for journalism, making the point that if he could survive football, then he could survive any of the challenges that journalism might present.

When we look at Dunphy now, we see a seasoned journalist and a football analyst on television and radio. It looks as if it could have been no other way. Not so apparently. If we return to the pages of *Only a Game?*, we find a young Dunphy highly critical of the journalist profession. He describes an uneasy stand-off between footballers and journalists. He talks of the deep mistrust that footballers have towards journalists, the concern that a journalist will bring preconceived ideas to a story and make the player say what the story needs him to say, not what the player actually wants to say. The journalist is the proverbial wolf in sheep's clothing, winning the player's trust in person in order to sell them out all the better in print. Dunphy must surely have dwelled on this conflict before committing himself to a writing career. He must have been aware that players would likely see him in a different light. There would now be an air of suspicion surrounding him which he would have to work to dispel if he wished to gain the trust of players.

In fact, Mick McCarthy, in his diary of Italia '90, *Captain Fantastic: My Football Career and World Cup Experience*, has pointed to the shock felt by many of the Irish squad when they discovered Dunphy's true colours. According to McCarthy, they were conned into believing that Dunphy, as a former footballer and Irish international, would be more understanding of their situation and, he claims, they did not foresee the highly critical tone of Dunphy's writings.

Indeed, going back even further, as we have seen, Dunphy was accused by others of betraying the game when he published his thoughts in his first weekly column in the early 1970s. He was branded a traitor, and interestingly, in the introduction to the second edition of *Only a Game?* Dunphy professes almost guiltily that he is now one of them, a journalist. He seems to carry the accusation of traitor with him into his writing: 'Now I am among them, the type of people who watch sport and presume they know what is going on out there, the type of people who run the world, who regard sport as, well, a simple thing, only a game, the type of people the sportsman secretly despises.'

This, once more, is the presence of the 'good pro' in Dunphy's writings. As if in deference to this honest 'bastion of decency' and noble 'embodiment of sporting virtue', Dunphy seeks to retain the 'good pro' almost as an artistic companion. It is as if this consciousness tempers his views by keeping awake within him a grounding sense of guilt, for having crossed over and having become one of those who do not play the game but yet presume to know the game. It is as if the memorialising of the 'good pro' makes good Dunphy's act of betrayal.

Indeed, more than one writer has pointed to the continued presence of the 'good pro' in Dunphy's writings, and nowhere more so than in his controversial ghostwriting of Roy Keane's 2002 autobiography, *Keane*. Can his strange attraction and admiration for Keane be explained by the fact that in him Dunphy saw the highest example of the 'good pro', the perfect embodiment of all those previously nebulous qualities to which Dunphy had alluded, but could not sufficiently pin down into any one player? Joyce Woolridge has argued this very point in an article called 'Good pro, bad PR' which appeared in the English football magazine *When Saturday Comes*, claiming that Dunphy, the ghostwriter, haunts the pages of Keane's autobiography a little more than is appropriate for one whose role is supposed to be simply that of a mouthpiece and not a rewriter of fact. According to Woolridge, Dunphy inevitably ends up presenting an idealised image of Keane that fits the parameters of his own subjective notions of the 'good pro'. Keane, the flawed man, is reshaped as Dunphy's virtuous pro, in an act, that for Woolridge, amounts to an unauthorised usurpation of Keane's authorial voice.

More detailed questions about Dunphy and Keane's relationship, and the precise nature of the true voice of Keane's autobiography, will have to wait for the later chapter on Dunphy's relationship with Keane. For the moment, it is enough for us to see that the 'good pro' will not go away. He has not remained in 1973, as a casualty of the aborted season that spawned *Only a Game?* He has life in him yet, as an active presence in Dunphy's football analysis. Whether he is the product of Dunphy's sentimental imagination, or a real flesh and blood character, he remains the fulcrum around which Dunphy's values and views on the game orbit, the cornerstone of his football analysis.

Chapter 3

Are we *all* part of Jackie's Army?: Dunphy and Jack Charlton

J ack Charlton became the manager of the Republic of Ireland football team in unusual circumstances. It was the kind of badly organised event for which the Football Association of Ireland (FAI) would become notorious, and more than lent itself to the natural suspicions of conspiracy theorists.

When the FAI sought a new manager for the national team, to replace Eoin Hand, in 1986, four candidates were presented to the public: John Giles, Liam Tuohy, Jack Charlton and Billy McNeill. However, privately, it was understood that Bob Paisley, the most successful manager in Liverpool's history, was the man the FAI actually intended for the job. At the FAI meeting to choose the new manager, the Paisley plan seemed to be following the script when, unexpectedly, an unknown member changed his preference, thus depriving Paisley of the required number of votes. A second ballot was held and Charlton emerged as the surprise victor. Paisley, who had allegedly received private assurances from the FAI that the job was as good as his, was waiting at home for a call that never came.

A week later, Charlton held his first press conference to meet the Irish press, and the long-running conflict between Dunphy and Charlton had its first very public manifestation.

Dunphy, asking his first question, wasted little time in raising doubts about the cloak-and-dagger fashion by which Charlton had been appointed, and quizzed one FAI official as to why Paisley had not been given the job, as had been anticipated. Dunphy had campaigned for Paisley's candidacy and was less than happy with the choice of Charlton. Charlton interrupted Dunphy and refused to allow the question to be answered and, instead, invited Dunphy outside to settle the matter, before barging out of the press conference himself.

From the very beginning, Dunphy and Charlton were at loggerheads, and it seems that this mutual dislike has survived the years unscathed. During a RTÉ radio interview in October 2008 with the late Gerry Ryan, Charlton dismissed Dunphy as a know-nothing critic, and disparagingly referred to him as 'that guy off the telly who tells everyone he used to be a footballer'. Dunphy, for his part, as late as 2002, writing in *Ireland on Sunday*, labelled Charlton a 'large, belligerent, bloody-minded English toerag' for his criticism of Roy Keane during the Saipan affair. The feud persists to this day and was a constant source of interest and debate during Charlton's long managerial reign.

Charlton managed Ireland from 1986 to 1996. Before his stewardship, Ireland had not participated in a World Cup or a European Championship. In stark contrast, under Charlton's guidance Ireland qualified for two World Cups and one European Championship, managing to get past the first round in each tournament. In Charlton's period Ireland played 93 games, won 46, drew 30 and lost

17, keeping 32 clean sheets while conceding only 41 goals. Add to this list the odd highly impressive competitive victory against major footballing nations such as England and Italy, and it becomes clear that Charlton's legendary status in Ireland was indeed earned.

This is real success at the highest level and, as such, it must be taken seriously, however one views the tactics Charlton used. Jack Charlton brought the Republic of Ireland football team to where they had never been – major tournaments – and turned them into a team ranked seventh in the world on the eve of the 1994 World Cup. Furthermore, when he resigned in 1996, football had never been more popular in the country, with unprecedented numbers joining the game at all levels and age-groups.

One cannot deny how serious an achievement this is, and clearly it would be ridiculous to ignore the fact that Charlton transformed the game of football in Ireland, but, yet, it is reasonable to ask, could Ireland have done better? Could a different man with a different football philosophy have achieved more than Charlton did with his no-nonsense percentage game?

Charlton's statistics are very impressive but, as common sense teaches us, statistics can conceal as much as they reveal. There was another side to Charlton's Ireland. This enviable résumé was achieved at a serious cost to the footballing culture of Ireland. In other words, it was achieved through the frequent use of unreservedly utilitarian football of, at times, the most numbingly direct kind. It was 'route one' football, plain and simple, without any accoutrements to garnish it. However, it undoubtedly was working, and so in general terms, commentators remained content.

After performing well at Euro '88, Charlton was firmly established in his role, and by the time Ireland had qualified for Italia '90 there was a general and impassioned support for the Charlton way. By this stage, the adopted Englishman was effectively a national hero. However, this comfortable tranquillity was about to be upset by an upstart, former footballer turned journalist, at a press conference in Sicily in 1990. It emerged that not quite everybody was 'part of Jackie's Army', despite what the Irish team's official World Cup song had suggested. There was one very vocal dissenter who had deserted from the camp and Charlton did not like it.

At this infamous press conference, held in Palermo, Ireland's base during the first round, pandemonium was unleashed when Charlton noticed Dunphy amongst the press corps. After Dunphy ventured a question about Ireland's highly disappointing first round draw with Egypt, Charlton became enraged. He pointedly refused to answer Dunphy's question before storming out of the room. One journalist who was present that night, Ian Ridley, has described the scene: 'The atmosphere was tense. Everybody knew something was about to kick off. It looked innocuous enough as Eamon Dunphy took his seat at the press conference, but when Jack Charlton spotted him, sparks flew.'

The bee in Charlton's bonnet was Dunphy's tirade, only days earlier, against Ireland's derisory 0-0 result with Egypt. After watching a truly shocking ninety minutes of what can only tenuously be called football, Dunphy – working as an analyst for Irish state broadcaster RTÉ – launched his pen across the studio, proclaiming the performance to be a disgrace and that he was ashamed of Irish football. Writing, subsequently, in *The Independent*, he reasoned that Charlton had, 'One of the best teams in Europe and he turned them into a pub side.'

These words may seem harsh, but for those of us who have not yet been able to forget that terrible encounter with Egypt, they may not be harsh enough. In this particular match it seemed that Charlton was not only determined to restrain his players but was also intent on turning them into bad footballers. Ireland huffed and puffed for ninety minutes with uninspiring dead-end tactics and could not break down a poor, but organised Egyptian team. It has generally come to be understood as the worst performance, and game, of the Charlton era. Those who have sympathies for Dunphy's view see the Palermo incident as a decisive victory for him. Perhaps Charlton had no answer to Dunphy's confrontational style of questioning in that press conference and consequently had no choice but to get out of the heat.

But Charlton has a very different interpretation of the encounter. In his book *Jack Charlton: The Autobiography*, Charlton says that his only regret about the incident was that, by walking out, he gave Dunphy publicity that he did not deserve. Given the opportunity to relive the moment, he claims he would have simply ignored Dunphy's question and turned to another journalist. Charlton is speaking with the benefit of hindsight here, and history tells us that such a calm and reasoned response to opposition is not really in his DNA. As we shall see, he cultivated a convenient habit, during his tenure of the job, of walking away from journalists whenever unpalatable topics were raised.

Of course, the rumble in Palermo was not the origin of Charlton's enmity towards Dunphy. Charlton tells us in his autobiography that he first dismissed Dunphy as a journalist on the flight home from Germany after Euro '88. At first, Charlton said he was willing to tolerate Dunphy, but 'All that changed on the flight back to

Dublin when I read a scurrilous piece he had done on [Mick] McCarthy. There and then I said, "you can stick it up your arse, you little prat. There is no way I want anything more to do with you".' Charlton concludes by saying: 'I'm a professional who has been appointed to do a job and the last thing I need is a journalist trying to tell me how to do it. I promptly dismissed him to the point where I never read his stuff.'

Returning to the Palermo incident, whatever view one takes of the matter, it is fairly evident that it did little for Dunphy's popularity at home, while Charlton was more celebrated than ever. These were the heady days of Jackie's Army, what Declan Lynch has referred to in his book *Days of Heaven* as Ireland's 'summer of love'. Ireland's miracle year came in 1990. The country was on a thrilling wave of optimism at this time, with Charlton at the centre of it all. Writing in 1994, after Ireland's exit from the World Cup, Dunphy described the excitement surrounding Charlton in the following incendiary terms:

> Public opinion, in the context of the Charlton myth, is nothing more than the congealed igno-rance of a nation dazzled to the point of mass hysteria. The minority who know their football well enough to distinguish between fact and fan-tasy have long since decided that even though the show is great, the football of the Charlton era has been, too often, lousy.

Dunphy's job as a journalist was to prise the facts from the mesh of fantasy and myth in which a nation is typi-cally gripped when it comes to the national team. The 'Charlton myth' is a recurring phrase in Dunphy's writ-ings and he reserves special scrutiny for it. This is the sacred cow that he wants to debunk and in the process open the eyes of the Irish people. In Dunphy's mind, this emperor had no clothes and this would have to be exposed whether the Irish people wanted to see it or not. He dared to raise doubts about the Charlton regime and was immediately branded a traitor. Dunphy found himself in the midst of a strange and powerful backlash and was in danger of being run out of town.

Amazingly, his safety was actually at risk on his return to Ireland after the 1990 World Cup. It is difficult to believe that this occurred only twenty years ago in a civilised society. Speaking of the negative public reaction, Dunphy has said: 'It was serious. I was physically attacked. When I came back from Italia '90, I was caught up in the mob and could have been killed. I had hate mail and my son was roughed up. We'd [The Republic of Ireland] never done anything and now we'd been to the World Cup quarter-finals. Everyone became a football expert.'

Looking back, it seems fair to say that the euphoria of Italia '90, with its attendant resentment towards Dunphy, had a distinctly patriotic air about it. It had little to do with football and a lot to do with so-called 'Irishness' and the particular national crusade on which Charlton was taking the country. Principally what the Irish wanted was the adventure, to feel unreservedly good about something, and, if the football was less than exemplary, that could be ignored. Undoubtedly, though, the ferocity of the reaction betrayed the fact that Dunphy was merely making explicit an implicit understanding on the part of the Irish people: the football was retrograde and terrible to behold, yet the prevailing mood did not allow for such beliefs to be openly expressed, and so it found a derivative and negative expression in the scapegoat form of Dunphy.

At the time, many writers sought to capture and celebrate this mood of triumph, but in the process they only helped to bury, rather than expose, the uncomfortable truths lurking within the Charlton era. A particularly culpable example of this vein of writing came from Roddy Doyle in a piece entitled 'Italia '90 Jacko's Army', published in *The Observer* in November 1993. Doyle takes the well-trodden path down that most clichéd of writing avenues: capturing the *zeitgeist*, and, in the process, doing his level best to portray the Irish fan as a hybrid of jolly drunkard and lovable buffoon. Doyle smothers rational thought by shouting loudly enough, dismissing Dunphy's criticisms by branding him a member of 'the gang of miserable little fuckers waiting for things to go wrong' and concludes: 'None of them are really Irish, that's the problem.' No comment need be added to this. It buries itself in its own stupidity. It does exhibit, however, the pernicious and visceral patriotism that dominated football analysis at this time, emasculating rational thinking, and which, precisely, Dunphy was protesting against.

Clearly, though, whatever its merits, the Irish found confidence and unprecedented unity in this journey, and Dunphy seemed determined to puncture that, hence the vitriol.

The real sting in the tail of this national hysteria, for Dunphy, however, was an unquestioned acceptance of the Charlton way. If Charlton was a hero, then he had to be beyond reproach, and all we could do as proud Irish men and women was to row in behind him. Ian Ridley summed up this mood in an article published in *The Guardian* in August 2002: 'This was a small nation reaching World Cups and hang the methods. The joy and self-esteem they brought were worth it. If the price of the craic was uncritical cheerleading, so be it.' In fact,

Dunphy has highlighted how even the media, and football journalists of the time, were taken in by the halo effect surrounding everything Jack Charlton did. He put it in the following way: 'The media's job should have been to say: "This king has no clothes". Instead, they fell in line and perpetuated the myth of Big Jack.' Although Dunphy was in the minority, he was not alone, as John Giles has revealed in his autobiography. He too shared Dunphy's anti-Charlton sentiments, arguing that the former Irish manager was patently unable to make the best of the talent at his disposal.

What exasperated Dunphy so much, however, was the denigration of Irish football implicit in the euphoria of the Irish fans, with Charlton as the spearhead and focal point of this fervid movement. For Dunphy, the Irish supporters were just along for the ride and doing their best to live up to the 'lovable Irish' caricature wherever international football took them. Where Dunphy wanted the emphasis to be on football, the nation was locked into the limited belief that they 'were a small country with no great footballing tradition, splendid supporters, providers of the fairy tale dimension to the tournament'. In Dunphy's eyes, the Republic of Ireland was letting itself down as a footballing nation by inviting the world to see it in outmoded, stereotypical terms. It was an expression of a basic lack of confidence. Ireland might not be the best team in a World Cup, but the Irish could at least make sure they were the best fans.

It is to his continuing credit that Dunphy took an unwavering stance to such stereotyping and, whether or not one agreed with his views, you had to admire him for holding fast to his principles, despite being reviled for this in Ireland. After hearing so much of the same line, it was refreshing to hear someone question the Charlton regime. As Conor O'Callaghan has put it, speaking of Dunphy's bullish stance, in *Red Mist: Roy Keane & the Football Civil War*: 'Amid all the flag-waving, each of his hectoring invectives came as a blessing, like a cloudburst after months of sun.'

Detractors of Dunphy, however, argue that he chose the contrary position in order to garner plaudits and so advance his own career. Charlton himself has described Dunphy as the 'original contrary journalist. If you said black, he'd call white. He seemed to agree with nothing or nobody'. The implication, here, is that Dunphy courted controversy on the basis that all publicity is good publicity and that his real motivation was self-serving.

Further than this, Charlton's supporters argued that the manager's style was eminently realistic. Ireland had limited players therefore a limited style of play was a necessity. To open up and attempt to play flowing, attacking football would have been tactical suicide since the Irish team was simply not good enough to play in such an expansive way.

If only this were true, the debate would be very short indeed. However, when we examine many of the players at Charlton's disposal, this argument begins to look questionable. Advancing the point, Dunphy has put it in the following terms: 'Think of Mark Lawrenson, Paul McGrath, Packie Bonner, Liam Brady, Ronnie Whelan, David O'Leary and Denis Irwin. One of the best teams in Europe and he turned them into a pub side. He actually preferred [Mick] McCarthy to O'Leary.'

Clearly, Ireland did have the players to play a more adventurous game and to compete realistically with the best. However, Charlton's flair for the pragmatic put an end to this possibility. Brady, comfortably Ireland's best midfielder and ball-player, was progressively marginalised until he quit international football, and the era of Mick McCarthy at centre-back was ushered in because David O'Leary, a cultured centre-half, was used as a reserve only, when selected.

The popular belief is that Ireland overachieved under Charlton, but we have to ask the question: in the light of the foregoing, is it possible that Ireland in fact under-achieved under his stewardship?

We must take these concerns seriously and put Dunphy's views to the test. Was Charlton's coaching fundamentally flawed and was there a better way for Irish football at this juncture? In order to make this evaluation, we should examine the tactics Charlton championed as manager of Ireland.

The mantra used to describe the Charlton years was 'put them under pressure'. This was the principal tactical idea behind Ireland's play. However, putting teams under pressure is not really a tactic at all. Every good team should put the opposing team under pressure, but they also have a plan for when they retrieve possession of the ball. An instructive example comes from Josep Guardiola, the manager of Barcelona FC at the time of writing this book. Although Barcelona are correctly fêted as the best current example of the passing game, at a coaching conference in the summer of 2009 Guardiola gave a paper, not on the merits of the passing game, but on pressurising opponents in order to win back possession. This illustrates that putting pressure on the ball is important even to a cultured team like Barcelona, but it is only half their strategy. The other half involves keeping the ball once they get it back, something Ireland was specifically instructed not to do under Charlton.

In a balanced team, then, both putting pressure on the ball and retention of it will receive due attention. But to simply announce 'put them under pressure' as one's entire plan, as Charlton did, is to attempt to elevate the ordinary to the level of strategy. Try as one might, vigorous running and harrying of opposition players alone will never be a virtue, no matter how much a team applies itself to it. There is no magical alchemy here. This is one base metal that will not become gold through sheer effort. A pressure game alone, with no constructive plan for what a team will do once it recovers the ball, is a serious limitation and not something to be celebrated.

In a revealing piece in *The Irish Times* in February 2000, Charlton explained the idea behind what he termed 'the pressurise game': 'You played the ball in behind people and, when you had them turning to face their own goal, you pressurised them. It meant that when they got the ball and wanted to come out a bit you were in there on top of them.' Charlton elaborates further in his autobiography, explaining that one of the key roles of his midfielders was to give the ball to the full-backs who would then launch it into the opposite corner of the pitch, with the Irish players immediately moving forward to restrict the area.

So this was the key to the Charlton game. The idea was to force the opposition team to face in the wrong direction, towards their goal, and then apply as much pressure as possible. The hoped-for result would be panic, and this might lead to an error, or an interception, upon which Ireland could then capitalise. Of his tactical instructions to his players, Charlton described it in the following words: 'That's going to be our game, lads, get the buggers turning, get the ball behind them, and stir them up till they're crazy with the annoyance of it all.'

Midfielders were merely functional in Charlton's tactics. Such players dwelling on the ball, displaying enterprise and creative initiative, was out of the question for Charlton. The ball had to go forward at the earliest opportunity and he says in his autobiography that 'Only when the ball was in the last third of the field were our players allowed to decide for themselves how to play.'

In other words, in Charlton's approach, midfielders were forbidden from expressing themselves on the ball. Their job was not to play a passing game but to simply get the ball forward at the earliest available moment, either by giving it to their full-backs or by launching it forward themselves. Indeed, in many instances the midfielders would not even see the ball because it would be sent over their heads by defenders aiming for the centre-forward. They would be involved only if they were lucky enough to meet one of the knock-downs from Niall Quinn or Tony Cascarino, for example.

Charlton, it seems, viewed the midfield with fear and suspicion, seeing it as the place where you usually lose possession, rather than as a part of the pitch where productive possession originates. It seems that Charlton was not interested in creative football. In typically strong language, Dunphy has claimed that Charlton's 'narrow mind, mistrust of originality and fearful spirit' precluded the possibility of the team being in any way creative.

This phobia towards midfield play is, of course, exactly why Charlton could never properly accommodate the playmaking abilities of Liam Brady, possibly the most talented ball-player Ireland ever possessed. The Brady issue, for Dunphy, was the epitome of everything that was wrong with the Charlton system. In Dunphy's eyes, if a manager could not incorporate such a talent into the side, then the problem lay not with any deficiency of the player, but with the manager's system.

Charlton's style strangled the creative impulses of midfielders in that their role was limited to carrying out simple functions, and any deviation from this was strictly forbidden. Obviously, this was not a system that would call on Brady's unique creative talents, and Charlton almost speaks of Brady's range of skills as a collection of bad habits acquired throughout his long career. Describing Brady's role in the team, Charlton says: 'All his life, he'd been accustomed to taking balls off the back four and then playing through midfield. Now, our defenders were banned from giving it to him in those situations.' In Charlton's world, receiving possession, and building constructively from that platform, is akin to a dangerous disease from which top midfielders from major European clubs seem to suffer. Because, essentially, that is what Brady was: a gifted midfielder who had graced Serie A for seven seasons, playing with no less a club than Juventus along the way, and yet Charlton felt his style of football needed correcting.

The predictable unhappy end to this mismatch between pragmatic authoritarianism and creative midfield play was Brady's premature retirement from international football in September 1989. Charlton substituted Brady with eight minutes remaining in the first half of a friendly match against Germany. For Brady, this was a humiliation too far, and he promptly announced his retirement after the game.

According to Dunphy, Brady was effectively pushed into retirement, worn down by Charlton's attritional style of play. His natural ability was fettered because he was forced to operate in a straitjacket tactical system that allowed for no variation. The upshot was that one of Ireland's greatest players would not play at a World Cup, and Ireland went on to play at Italia '90, the following summer, without Brady. What made it all the more outrageous for Dunphy was that a player like Mick McCarthy, of limited ability, would actually captain Ireland at that tournament and be viewed by Charlton as the lynchpin of the team.

In *Jack Charlton's World Cup Diary*, Charlton expresses the view that Brady was very much past his best by the time Italia '90 came around, and that the friendly match against Germany proved that he did not have the running power needed for international football. For, as Charlton reveals in his autobiography, running was the key to Ireland's game. Perspiration and not inspiration would be the Charlton litmus test. If you could not run for ninety minutes, then you were not going to figure in his plans, regardless of your ability. It was that stark. Writing in his autobiography about the first time he scouted Jason McAteer, Charlton says: 'I was impressed by his ability to run and run when I went to watch him at Bolton [Wanderers]. That was the essence of our match plan and I reckoned he could fit into it.'

True, Brady did not have the legs of his youth, at the age of 32, in 1989. However, when Charlton claims that he was not able for international football, what he really means is that Brady was not suited to Charlton's vision of international football – a high-tempo running game. Brady most certainly would have been a huge asset to a footballing team with a style of play that could have maximised his abilities.

Think of Arnold Mühren, who at 37 had played a starring role for Holland a year earlier at Euro '88. The Dutch played in such a way that Mühren's age and lack of stamina were simply not a factor, and his playmaking abilities flourished at the highest level. Or if one prefers a modern-day example, take Paul Scholes, who, regularly dominates games for Manchester United, even though he is thirty-seven years old and also lacks the stamina of old. For Sir Alex Ferguson, it is not a question of accommodating Scholes. Because of Manchester United's passing game, Scholes is in fact a vital component of the team.

This was Dunphy's point when he so vehemently opposed Liam Brady's marginalisation. The problem, in his view, was with the system and the manager, not with the player. In his mind, with a more cultured football style, Brady could have played a pivotal role for Ireland. However, according to Dunphy, writing in *The Independent*, Charlton's mind-set blinded him to this vision. Charlton's take on football, Dunphy says, is: 'The folly of a limited coach who has never really known how best to deploy the wonderful players available to him, the fear of a bully confused by talent, determined to mask his confusion by projecting the image of sturdy conviction.'

It is abundantly clear that, Jack Charlton was a 'my way or no way' kind of manager and this is why Dunphy has frequently referred to him as a bully. Evidence from other players about Charlton's treatment of Brady supports Dunphy's claims. Andy Townsend, Charlton's loyal captain after Mick McCarthy's retirement in June 1992, has commented in the *Daily Mail* that when Charlton took over, he made it very clear that there would be serious recriminations for players who deviated from his tactics. Townsend concludes: 'Ask David O'Leary and Liam Brady who, despite their talent, were soon ex-internationals.' Ronnie Whelan provides further evidence of Charlton's attitude. Whelan has frequently been outspoken in his criticism of Charlton's tactics and has said that players were left with a stark choice: 'If you didn't do it, you were not in the team.'

Speaking on RTÉ's World Cup 2010 coverage, Whelan told of how hard it was to swallow his principles and conform to Charlton's long-ball edict. He explained how he found it extremely difficult to continually direct balls in behind the opposing full-backs, when his better instincts were to play it on the ground in the midfield. He said that as soon as he reverted to type and began to express himself on the ball, as he would have done at Liverpool, he was out of the team. On the same programme, Dunphy made the supporting point that, at the time of Charlton's tenure, Whelan was one of the best midfielders in the world, yet was ordered to play a primitive, retrogressive style of football.

In fairness to Charlton, these elementary tactics, which tended to alienate players of Brady's and Whelan's calibre, did actually function very effectively against many teams, and Whelan concedes this point. Most teams did not like the thought of trying to play passing football when they were put under intense pressure or were simply not good enough to do so. However, the pressure game, as outlined by Charlton, had one serious flaw: it was based squarely upon a commitment to repeatedly concede possession. In a strange feat of logic, Irish players were under orders to give away the ball in order to get it back. What, though, if the ball did not come back? What if the opposing team actually retained the ball under pressure? In these situations, Ireland had no answer.

The question then is: would it not be easier to just keep the ball when you have it and start building attacks, instead of handing it over to the opposing team as soon as you have it? Unfortunately, this would not be the way the Irish team would go about its business. Instead, they would be committed to a hugely inefficient style of play where possession would be relinquished and the players would be asked to keep running and closing down the opposition. Eventually, the ball could present itself in a dangerous position where a goal chance might occur.

By using these tactics, Ireland was not doing enough to win games. They stopped other teams from playing but did not contribute enough to games to guarantee durable success at the highest level. Roy Keane has highlighted this in *Keane: The Autobiography*, when he makes the point that Charlton and his assistant, Maurice Setters, had one-track minds when it came to basic tactics. Speaking of their insistence on a running game, despite the brutal heat and humidity of midsummer in the United States, Keane says: 'The opposing theory, that we might conserve our energy in heat that we'd never encountered before, the idea that we might pass the ball and make the opposition do the running, never seemed to have occurred to Jack and Maurice.'

The group game against Egypt at Italia '90 cruelly exposed the limits of this one-dimensional running game. The Egyptians relentlessly closed down the Irish and the team had no answer. Egypt did an Ireland on Ireland. They put Ireland under pressure, to return to that unfortunate mantra. There was not a lot of nuance to Charlton's tactics, and if one lesson could be taken from this encounter, it was the absence of subtlety in Ireland's play. It was all or nothing. Plan A had better work, because there was no Plan B in the tactical cupboard waiting to be dusted down and pressed into action if it was needed.

A team playing football, retaining possession patiently, and waiting for the moment to strike, could have played their way through and around Egypt. Not Ireland, though. Yes, the team had top-level international players who were more than capable on the ball, but, with Charlton at the helm, passing the ball was simply not an option.

Frank Stapleton, in his autobiography, *Frankly Speaking*, even pointed to the fact that the one player who could have unlocked Egypt that day, Liam Brady, was sitting in the stands as merely an interested observer.

This was Dunphy's point when he threw his pen across the RTÉ studio during the post-match coverage. Ireland's talented players were being asked to play beneath their normal level and were forbidden from expressing themselves on the ball. And so a very poor Egyptian team negated Ireland effectively.

As Charlton's last tournament as manager of Ireland, the performances at USA '94 are a good way to evaluate his tactics. It is an opportunity to examine what progress the team had made in the eight years since Charlton had taken charge. After narrowly failing to qualify for Euro '92 in Sweden, Charlton's Ireland successfully qualified for the World Cup in 1994. The tactics he employed are once more instructive and show the merit in Dunphy's arguments against Charlton's brand of football.

Although no one can deny Charlton his success, with the impressive first round victory over Italy to attest to this, it is obvious that there was something seriously wrong with the general tactics he adopted in the tournament. If one were to pinpoint the problem, it would have to be that Charlton's preferred style of play again had a fundamental bias against ball retention.

Put simply, Ireland did not retain enough possession throughout the 1994 World Cup and this all comes back to Charlton's philosophy. His approach to football was based on neutralising opponents with a high-tempo pressure game. This meant that Ireland had to do a huge amount of running in any particular game because Charlton's focus was not on ball retention. The Irish players would not try to play their own game, but would try to stop opponents from playing their game. This is negative football, in that the focus is on stopping the opposition team playing rather than on trying to play your own passing game.

However, accepting this, any analysis must be fair and cannot ignore the facts. This technique was successful and Ireland achieved some very impressive results by using these tactics. They also qualified for successive World Cups out of difficult qualifying groups. However, the crucial point about Charlton's tactics is that they were limited, inefficient, and seriously underused the talents of the players at his disposal. Yes, the team achieved substantial success, but it could have been significantly better considering the prowess of the Irish players.

In *Jack Charlton's American World Cup Diary*, Charlton talks openly about his tactics. We can begin to see the gaps in his arguments when we look at his analysis of the group game against Mexico, where Ireland lost 2-1 to an ordinary Mexican team that eventually failed to progress beyond the group stage. Essentially, Charlton blames the weather conditions for the defeat. He reasons that the Mexicans were used to the high temperatures and humidity of Orlando while the Irish players were not. Speaking of his pre-match thoughts, he admits that he even dreaded the encounter: 'We must walk out on Friday for a noonday kick-off with a team thoroughly familiar with these kinds of conditions.' This was true, but hardly a comprehensive explanation of events.

What Charlton does not mention is that the true reason the weather is such a concern is because Ireland did not retain possession of the ball and so were forced to expend huge amounts of energy trying to get it back. Possession, it should be noted, is eminently practical.

Keep the ball and you both conserve energy and increase your chances of winning. The obvious corollary is that you decrease your chances of losing. This, however, is not an admission Charlton is prepared to make. Instead, the heat is made to fully explain why the Irish players were outplayed by an average side.

The Mexico match was a painful example of the problems with Charlton's pressure game. According to Roy Keane's account, Charlton's plan was to bombard the little Mexicans with high balls launched from the back by Packie Bonner, and then to pressurise them when they were turning to face their own goal. The Irish players duly attempted this, but the problem they faced was that the ball did not come back. The Mexicans dealt with the high balls and kept possession, so Ireland was left chasing shadows in 110°F. Charlton's solution to the problem of the heat was to concede possession and run. Is it any wonder that the Irish forward Tommy Coyne suffered serious dehydration during the group stage?

In the aftermath of this game, Dunphy asked Charlton at a press conference about the tactic of playing the ball back to Bonner. Charlton's explanation was that energy conservation was behind it and not just the object of sending long balls forward from Bonner's kicks. Dunphy, however, subsequently pointed out the flaw in this reasoning, stating that: 'The alternative to his [Charlton's] point of view, in relation to energy conservation in this exacting climate, is that infinitely more effort is required winning back the possession that Bonner wastes, by decree, than is necessary.' Dunphy concludes, with reference to the Mexico game: 'Some of Friday's weariness was caused by the heat. Some by Jack Charlton's tactics.' This reasoned argument shows that Dunphy cannot be dismissed as merely an out-of-touch idealist demanding aesthetically pleasing football for its own sake. He demanded passing football, too, for the very obvious reason that it is essentially more efficient than the long-ball game, because the ball does the work and not the players.

Even Ireland's training was dominated by running. Roy Keane gives us a revealing insight into the nature of the Irish training regime before the opening game against Italy. Of the management team, Keane says: 'The one idea Big Jack and Setters had was to run the bollocks off us every day. The theory was that we'd get used to being knackered and therefore wouldn't wilt during games.' This was not a wise training technique and was likely to prematurely tire the Irish players before the tournament even began. Even Graham Taylor, the England manager from 1990 to 1994, admitted that the high tempo pressure game which he, like Charlton, favoured was insufficient when the climatic conditions made it impossible to continue running for long periods. The point is further proven, and can be elaborated upon, when we look at Ireland's games against Norway and Holland.

The Norway game is of particular interest from a tactical point of view because it was a clash between two almost identical systems and football philosophies. Separately, but equally, Egil Olsen, the Norway manager, and Charlton had arrived at the very same tactics. This game was going to be like against like, pressure against pressure, with little or no possession of the ball in between.

Early in his career, Olsen had completed a master's degree dissertation on what could be called the percentage game. This involved maximising the amount of times the ball went forward in any game. This, he reasoned, arguing on the basis of statistical analysis, was the surest way to guarantee victory and long-term success for a team. If the ball is going forward at every available opportunity, the argument goes, common sense dictates that you will score enough goals over a game or season to ensure the greatest possible success.

Lest we become carried away by the positive sound to this theory of football, we should emphasise the important qualification that, for Olsen, the ball must go forward *via the quickest route*. Logically, this can mean only long-ball football, since this is the fastest way of getting the ball into the opposition team's box.

Olsen did not disappoint. Long-ball football is certainly what he had in mind. Perhaps the phrase 'air raid' would be more apt, when we consider the amount of long passes that Norway launched into opposition penalty areas at the 1994 World Cup. Incredibly, a favourite tactic of Olsen's – used repeatedly at USA '94 – was to place a tall, bruising centre-forward on the left flank (stand up, Jostein Flo) where he would typically be marked by a shorter right-back. Cue Norway's own right-back, and a barrage of right to left long-balls designed to take advantage of the players' height discrepancy. Olsen even invented a name for these right to left missiles: 'reachers' he dubbed them, without any discernible sense of humour.

The obvious parallel here is with Charlton's preference for employing a tall target man up front to flick on long-balls launched by his full-backs. In *Jack Charlton's World Cup Diary*, covering Italia '90, Charlton informs us: 'In our match plan, we employ a target man up front and a runner to get the knock-ons. Tony Cascarino, Frank Stapleton and Niall Quinn are all capable of doing the first job.' If more evidence were needed, we can go back to Charlton's early managerial days at Middlesbrough when he employed Alan Foggon, a strong, no-nonsense centre-forward, as a target man for his long-ball game during the years 1973 to 1976. Again, as manager of Newcastle during the 1984/85 season, Charlton deployed what writer Ken Sproat has called the 'twin battering rams' of Tony Cunningham and George Reilly, whose job it was to be on the end of long balls dispatched from the rear. And, finally, during his stint as manager of Sheffield Wednesday from 1977 to 1983, one of Charlton's first signings was the big target man Andy McCulloch.

This is more compelling evidence to show that Charlton has always had only one way of playing, and the ability of the Irish players was simply not a relevant consideration for him. He would impose the same type of game regardless of the personnel at his disposal.

When we consider the similarities between Olsen's Norway and Charlton's Ireland, is it any wonder that the game ended in a scoreless draw, a stalemate born out of an intense phobia towards possession football and the natural ability of footballers. It was the perfect draw; absolute nullity on a football pitch with twin tactical systems seamlessly dissolving into and neutralising each other in the afternoon Florida heat.

At the heart of this game were two managers with a profound mistrust of their players' abilities and an insistence that they conform to a rigid and limited tactical schema. Let's hear Charlton's own words after the Norway game. Discussing his half-time team talk he said: 'By half-time neither side had created a chance of note but that suits me fine. I get down to the dressing room at the break and I preach again the gospel of vigilance and avoiding unnecessary risks.'

This is the voice of a manager who has almost no regard for the way football is played. He freely admits that he could not care less that his own team had not 'created a chance of note' in forty-five minutes of football. If the result is the right one, then what of the manner by which it is achieved? This is all very fine if your objective is to hang on for ninety minutes against a very ordinary Norway team, but how are you going to defeat the Dutch, the Germans and the Brazilians, in the later stages of the tournament. How are you going to win the World Cup? By not creating a chance of note?

This brings us to the point Dunphy made after the 1994 World Cup concerning Charlton's ambitions for the team. In Dunphy's opinion, Charlton was clearly just happy to be at the World Cup and had no actual belief in Ireland's ability to make serious progress in the tournament. Writing in *The Independent* Dunphy said: 'Watching from close range, it was clear that he, more than anyone else, was content just to be at the finals.'

The point behind what Dunphy is saying here is that Charlton did not play winning football. He played holding football. Even in the Italy game, where the Irish players were individually brilliant, Ireland managed only one goal and that was a fortuitous half-volley by Ray Houghton from a miscued clearance by Franco Baresi. In other words, Ireland was out to hold Italy primarily, and if a chance to score arose, then well and good, and this is just how the game played out.

By any analysis, it would have been very difficult for Ireland to win the World Cup, but with Charlton's negative tactics it became an impossibility. How was Ireland going to get to the final? By grinding down every team they met with incessant running and a rigid defensive line-up? This was not a recipe for winning games. It was a recipe for respectability and a dignified exit when the real football began in the second round. Yes, the Irish team was difficult to beat, but this often just added up to heroic draws and not all-important victories.

As harsh as it may sound, Dunphy was right about Charlton's limited approach, and it was not just Jack Charlton who was happy to simply participate. Ireland, as a nation, may have settled for too little when they could have expected such a great deal more, judging by the standard of player at their disposal.

The players who went to that tournament were not content to just show up for the preliminaries before heading home to a blaze of applause when the serious games began in the knock-out stages. For professional players, the World Cup is the greatest stage of all, and each Irish player would have wanted the greatest possible success for himself and the team. Charlton, however, was not on the same wavelength. In his view, the Irish players were just not talented enough to have grand ambitions and to play the kind of expansive passing game that could have brought success. In a piece published in *The Irish Times* in February 2000, Charlton said as much, when explaining his choice of long-ball football over possession football. Speaking of the leading football nations as being past masters of the possession game, he states:

> I decided it was no good coming to Ireland and trying to build a successful team playing exactly the same as the game's leading nations. They had been good at this type of game for ten or fifteen years before us and for me to think we could match them with our resources was nonsense.

Charlton, in a dubious and rather bizarre distinction, drew a sharp line between so-called continental players and Irish players and seemed to suggest that the divide was akin to an immovable law of nature.

Conor O'Callaghan, in his excellent book *Red Mist: Roy Keane & the Football Civil War*, describes Charlton's view of continental players with great wit and precision. He relates how, 'In footage of matches from the seventies, defenders in possession stroll out with all the unhurried freedom of nudists on a beach. Jack was the first to recognise that and, famously, instructed the Irish team to "put them under pressure".' O'Callaghan concludes: 'According to the Book of Jack, tanned handsome men from hotter climes were naturally more skilful than us with the ball, but found wanting when it came to argy-bargy.'

Objectively, this is a flawed argument because Charlton will find it very hard to persuade anyone that Roy Keane, Paul McGrath, Ray Houghton, Andy Townsend and Steve Staunton could not pass the ball as well as continental players. What exactly did he think they were doing week in, week out with their clubs in the Premier League and Champions League? At the time of the 1994 World Cup, Roy Keane was playing at central-midfield for Manchester United, while Paul McGrath, one of the greatest players to have represented Ireland, was featuring for an Aston Villa side, along with his colleagues Townsend, Staunton and Houghton, which had finished second in the Premier League only a year earlier.

This is a point that Dunphy has made on numerous occasions. Ireland had some of the best players in Europe, but this fact was obscured behind the fog of Charlton's system. If we go back to earlier squads, we can point to other accomplished passers of the ball: Ronnie Whelan, Liam Brady and Mark Lawrenson come to mind.

As the abundant empirical evidence suggests, all the players who made up Ireland's midfield at the 1994 World Cup were cultivated ball-players. It was not a question of the player's ability; it was a question of Charlton's attitude.

Clearly, Charlton is not being honest about his choice of tactics. The truth is that he knew only one way of playing and that was always a long-ball game. It was the very same when he managed English clubs, and nothing had changed when he took charge of Ireland. He did not appraise the Irish players and decide that, unfortunately, they were just not good enough to play a possession game. He understood very well that they were talented players, but he simply knew of no other tactical system. As Tom Humphries put it in *The Legend of Jack Charlton*: 'The new Charlton technique didn't appear to be tailored so much to the team's talents as [to] the manager's beliefs.' There would be no football played, regardless of the quality of player at Charlton's disposal. This was set in stone from day one of his tenure and it never changed during his ten years in charge.

Roy Keane points out that during some international games the players would begin to pass the ball around as they did at club level, contrary to Charlton's express wishes. Keane highlights the first-round victory over Italy as an example of this, when Ireland started moving the ball about comfortably in the second-half after Italy had faded from the contest. In his autobiography Keane writes: 'This sometimes happened on good days with Big Jack's Ireland. We'd throw out the game plan and do what came naturally to most of us. Just play the game the way we would for our clubs.'

With tactics as ill-conceived and short-sighted as Charlton's, the Irish were always in danger of being seriously found out in the second round of the tournament, and this is essentially what happened when they met Holland in Orlando. The Dutch, being one of those leading nations that had been quite good for fifteen or twenty years at spraying the ball about, were going to be a serious proposition.

Charlton's success with Ireland was remarkable in many ways, but his old-fashioned up-and-at-'em tactics were cruelly exposed against the Dutch. It was going to take so much more than long balls and pressure to defeat Holland. And as Dunphy has emphasised, the Irish players did have that something more, but it was successfully shackled by Charlton's negative tactics. Ireland were comprehensively beaten 2-1 by the Dutch, with Paul McGrath's late goal coming as a consolation.

What went wrong in this game to bring their tournament to such an abrupt halt? Basically, Ireland's non-possession game came back to haunt them yet again. The Dutch, much like the Mexicans, only with better technique, did not give back the ball once the Irish had conceded it to them. They were good enough to keep the ball, even under pressure, and to that Charlton's system had no effective answer.

This, then, was the great flaw in this tactical system and it was not only Charlton and Ireland who had been taught a painful lesson. England, under Graham Taylor, was nursing the same wound after finding that their brand of pressure game was just not good enough at this level. They had failed to even qualify for the 1994 World Cup, finishing third in their qualifying group behind Norway and Holland.

Surprisingly, Taylor, a long-time advocate of the long-ball game, admitted as much during his tenure as Watford manager, from 1977-87, where he developed and honed his pressure game. As football writer Jonathan

Wilson has noted, although Watford's high-tempo blend of long passes and intense harrying overwhelmed domestic opponents in the English League, it was found wanting when they stepped on to the European stage. Why? Taylor explains: 'We were playing sides who were prepared to sit deep, play short passes, hold the ball and pick us off, who had fans who weren't demanding they thump the ball forward.' And when Watford was thrashed 7-2 on aggregate by Sparta Prague in November 1983 in the third round of the UEFA Cup, Taylor was even more emphatic: 'It was men against boys. When you gave the ball away, they didn't give it back to you.'

Interestingly, Dunphy often compared Charlton's Ireland to Taylor's England in that they used the same simple-minded system, and in the end, it proved inadequate for both teams.

The comparison, however, gains substantially more weight when we see the common source of Charlton's and Taylor's tactics. Both were graduates of the FA training school at Lilleshall in England where they fell under the influence of Charles Hughes, the FA's coaching director. Hughes espoused an incredibly basic long-ball game, rooted in pragmatic arguments, and supported by a detailed statistical analysis. Hughes, in turn, had assimilated these ideas from the influential Charles Reep, a former wing commander turned football analyst and statistician, who first formalised and articulated the theory of the long-ball, pressure game. His and Hughes's big idea was that 80-90% of goals are scored from five passes or fewer, thus justifying a long ball game which traded on percentages. If the ball was being sent into the opposition penalty area with sufficient frequency, the theory went, eventually the goals would come. Obviously, the logic here was seriously flawed. It said nothing about how long sequences of passing often lead to free-kicks, which can then produce goals with one or two passes, or how chains of passes tire the opposing team, allowing your players even more opportunities to score.

In this vision of the game, players were chess pieces and were given simple functions to be carried out as part of the match-plan. The system was everything and the player had a value only insofar as he could perform his allotted function within that framework. Allied to the impression that Hughes and Reep made on Charlton was the influence of Alf Ramsey, whom Charlton cites in his 1990 World Cup diary as one of his major inspirations. Ramsey won the 1966 World Cup with England, using a robustly utilitarian approach to the game and was one of the first advocates of what Jonathan Wilson has termed 'the English Pragmatism'. Hughes and Reep continued confidently in this tradition of pragmatism, with England's 1966 triumph as proof of its validity.

As Dunphy has pointed out, Charlton and Taylor were trying to impose the same tactics on their respective national teams, and this equivalence had its roots in the fact that they had both diligently studied and applied the Reep/Hughes system. In concrete terms, the long-ball game they favoured meant that neither could easily accommodate talented ball-players, and both managers, consequently, showed a marked disinclination to select creative play-makers. Witness Charlton's marginalisation of Liam Brady and Taylor's corresponding disinterest in the remarkable ability of Matthew Le Tissier. If further examples were needed, we could even highlight Charlton's ill-fated tenure as Newcastle United's manager in the 1984/85 season, when Charlton's long-ball game largely bypassed and dispensed with the undoubted talents of Peter Beardsley.

The fates of Charlton and Taylor part ways, however, when we see the radical disparity between the reactions each received from their football nations. Both espoused the same long-ball game, yet Taylor was roundly castigated by the English media, becoming a veritable figure of fun, while Charlton became a national hero in Ireland. This can partly be explained by the obvious fact that Charlton had greater success on the pitch than Taylor, but it is not the complete account. The other cause is, as Dunphy has said repeatedly, the fact that Ireland had little or no expectations, and were happy to take any success, however it was procured. Taylor, on the other hand, had to answer to the English media and public, where football expectations are immoderately high. Charlton's taskmaster was a lot easier to please, and so he remained in command long after Taylor had left the post of England manager.

Another, perhaps less perceptible but no less powerful reason for the differing fortunes of Charlton and Taylor lies in their respective personalities. Where Charlton was confident, charismatic and brimful of ebullience, Taylor appeared fussy, pedantic and schoolteacher-like. Both managers presided over limited tactical systems, yet Charlton had the force of personality to paper over the cracks and sweep everyone along. Taylor, unfortunately, played into the willing hands of Fleet Street, with a personality short on charm and likeability. In the end he fell victim to a shameful tabloid smear campaign.

Dunphy has also pointed to the mesmerising effect that Charlton's persona had on the Irish people, becoming, in the end, a bona fide public relations masterstroke. According to Dunphy, Charlton was 'determined to mask his confusion by projecting the image of sturdy conviction. In public relations terms that act has worked, worked beyond his wildest dreams, elevating him to the status of a national hero.'

If we look at examples, we can see that Charlton did indeed have a natural talent for the art of public relations, always being very careful about how to project his personality and how to portray himself in just the right manner. With Charlton, there was undoubtedly an excess of personality, a surfeit of behaviour if you like, acting both as distraction and compensatory force for serious deficiencies in substance.

A case in point occurs in his autobiography, where Charlton is forever reminding us of his passion for hunting and fishing, always depicting himself as a simple man with honest, wholesome pursuits. He even tells us that he has bought a house in the West of Ireland, so good is the fishing to be had there. After being subjected to this barrage of field sport information – he devotes a whole chapter to the topic – was I the only reader who suspected Jack of trying to sell us the reluctant saviour story? The idea here being that he would gladly have spent the second half of the 1980s and the first half of the nineties fishing for salmon, knee-high in a West of Ireland river, had not the FAI portentously summoned him to the helm, in order to drag the Irish team into the twentieth century.

The success of this image, however, was that Charlton managed to blend it so seamlessly with his managerial role. He was just lovable Big Jack rolled into one irresistible package. Barney Ronay, in *The Manager: The Absurd Ascent of the Most Important Man in Football*, has highlighted this public face of Charlton with great wit. He says of him: 'In his hands football, and indeed life itself, seemed no more than an extension of rambling, fishing and field sports, a matter of colour in your cheeks, a good long walk and maybe a fresh trout down the front of your trousers.'

The field sports phenomenon does not stop here though. When interviewed by Pat Kenny on *The Late Late Show* in May 2002, at the height of the Saipan saga, Charlton was asked to comment on Roy Keane's famous outburst towards Mick McCarthy which led to Keane being sent home. Charlton paused, for dramatic effect, and said that he needed filling in because he happened to have spent the last week on the bank of some unspecified river, consumed no doubt by the innocent and invigorating pursuit of decent country living. Kenny obliged, and gave Charlton a transcript of Keane's expletive-laden tirade in order to spare viewers' ears.

It does stretch all credibility to be asked to believe this kind of disingenuous account. The most important event in Irish football history, the biggest story of the 2002 World Cup, which was headline news all over the world, and Charlton needs updating because he has spent the last week fishing? This is just another instance of the kind of public relations exercise at which Charlton became so adept during his spell as Ireland's manager.

Another aspect of the Charlton regime that irritated Dunphy was the lack of professionalism behind the scenes, and more interestingly, Dunphy has claimed that the players were of the same opinion. Speaking of the abuse Dunphy received for opposing Charlton, he states: 'People said I was being controversial for the sake of it by not supporting the regime. But I knew the players shared my opinion. They thought it was a joke, a shambles.'

This is quite a contentious claim for Dunphy to make, given that he is purporting to speak for the many individuals who played under Charlton. However, at least one major incident can be highlighted which displays this lack of professionalism and the considerable unrest there was among the Irish players.

It occurred at the 1994 World Cup when Maurice Setters had been left in charge of training for the day. Under the intense heat of a midsummer sun, Setters ran the players into the ground before asking them to finish off with a full eleven-a-side match. The players regarded this training regime as punishing and counterproductive. Led by their captain, Andy Townsend, the players walked off the training ground in open mutiny, ignoring Setters' frantic injunction to get back on the pitch. Unfortunately for Charlton, the press was present in numbers and seized upon it as an instance of conflict and high treason in the Irish camp. The matter, however, was successfully covered up when Charlton convinced the media that it was just a minor disagreement between Roy Keane and Maurice Setters and not a full-scale revolt led by the captain and endorsed by the full squad.

An incident such as this cannot be underestimated, and that it should occur at the World Cup finals, when players would be loath to jeopardize their place in the team, is compelling proof that they were not completely happy with Charlton's management.

We know from Keane's autobiography that he was not impressed by Charlton's methods. In his opinion, Charlton was no tactical mastermind, and he records how his team talks often fell short of the required detail, tending to be emotive when they should have been technical. Keane cites half-time against Holland at the 1994 World Cup as a salient example of Charlton's style. Ireland was 2-0 down and in need of a tactical change of direction. However, by Keane's account, all Charlton delivered was bombast: 'At half-time, when a real manager can earn his corn by adjusting his tactics to meet the demands of any given situation, the great man offered nothing, except bluster.'

The defeat against Holland proved Keane's point. Charlton had no back-up plan. Ireland went back out for the second-half and never looked like winning the game.

Another farcical incident that tends to support Dunphy's claims about Charlton's lack of professionalism is the infamous 'Harry's Challenge' fiasco. The day before Ireland was to play Austria at Lansdowne Road in a qualifier for Euro '96, Charlton decided to take the squad to Harry Ramsdens. Harry Ramsdens, for those not familiar with the venerable institution, was a fish and chips restaurant on the Naas Road, on the outskirts of Dublin. Harry's eponymous challenge consisted of giant size portions of haddock and chips with baked beans or peas, followed by dessert. Charlton urged the players to eat, and they duly obliged. The next day, several players apparently reported their legs failing them late in the game, as Ireland were defeated 1-3 at home to Austria, thus severely denting any hopes of qualifying automatically for Euro '96.

Clearly, this is unacceptable preparation for any game of football, at club or international level, and that Charlton could not see this raises doubts about his understanding of fitness levels and would certainly tend to substantiate Dunphy's claims that the regime was a shambles. It got worse, however, when it became evident that Charlton had a stake in Harry Ramsdens, and stopped off with the Irish players presumably to give the establishment an injection of publicity.

Other former players have given similar accounts of Charlton's rough and ready attitude to training and match preparation. In a documentary on Roy Keane, entitled *Roy Keane: A Life of Controversy*, aired on TV3 in April

2009, John Aldridge spoke of looking forward to joining the Irish camp for international matches, because it came as a welcome reprieve from the disciplined lifestyle enforced at club level. He recounts how the team once went on a four-day drinking spree before the crucial European Championship qualifier against Austria in 1995. According to Aldridge, all the players enjoyed the international trips immensely, since it gave them the freedom to drink, and indulge in the kind of carnivalesque atmosphere that was unthinkable at their clubs.

In a piece written for *Ireland on Sunday* in May 2002, Dunphy roundly criticised Charlton for pinning the blame for this inept organisation on the FAI, when the real culprit was he himself. For Dunphy, it was Charlton's responsibility to confront the FAI on all relevant matters relating to pre-match preparation, but he repeatedly failed to do so and, in the process, presided over ten years of amateur preparation.

In the wake of Ireland's exit from the 1994 World Cup, Dunphy, writing in *The Independent*, berated Charlton, claiming that his one-dimensional, narrow-minded philosophy was holding back the Irish team. Dunphy described Ireland as being reduced by Charlton's negative football, to the lowly status of 'beggars at a banquet' in what was an otherwise exciting and open World Cup.

Clearly Dunphy wanted Charlton out, but what was needed instead? According to Dunphy, the solution was a man of vision: someone who could articulate a grander scheme, who would encourage the Irish players to grow and express themselves; a manager who could lead the Irish players 'towards some realisation of their dreams'.

But, although Charlton's players may have nurtured dreams, he himself was resolutely no dreamer and, yet, all the great managers were just that: consummate dreamers.

They articulated a grand plan, a strategy that would lead to enduring success with football of the highest quality. Busby, Shankly, Paisley, Ferguson, Wenger: each one a dreamer. Charlton, on the other hand, was pragmatism itself, with his zealous commitment to results-driven, functional football.

Dunphy's point is that Charlton had no vision and, consequently, had nothing noble to bring to football. In other words, he could not offer a way of playing the game that would both excite and edify football fans. For Charlton, football was only about results – often draws in Charlton's case – and the players under him were manipulated accordingly. Any individualism was crushed by his dogmatic insistence on the monotonous long-ball game.

By Dunphy's reckoning, Charlton could never be a great manager because he was the type to control and ultimately stifle players, when he should have inspired and encouraged them to play. Even as far back as *Only a Game?*, Dunphy made the point that a good coach will seek to liberate his players while a lesser coach will seek to dominate and control his players with rigid tactics and strictly defined roles for each of them. He tells us that coaching 'should be about showing people how to express themselves. How to express their own abilities within the framework of the team. Not subjection, but liberation.' And subjection is exactly how Dunphy viewed Charlton's relationship with the Irish players.

Interestingly, Dunphy's views here tie in with other theories current in the 1970s. As Barney Ronay points out in *The Manager: The Absurd Ascent of the Most Important Man in Football*, the Dutch team at Ajax in the 1970s had developed a theory of coaching focused on the concept of the en-skillment of players. This entailed the manager's presence being restrained in favour of achieving this objective. The manager's role was to inspire and free his charges and, consequently, players were encouraged to think on their feet by developing the ability to play football in any position on the pitch. It is from these ideas that the famous Dutch 'total football' philosophy originated. At its core was a fundamental trust in players' abilities.

This can be contrasted with the British coaching tradition out of which Charlton emerged, where the manager's presence dominates proceedings and the player is ordered to conform to a strict managerial blueprint for how the game will be played. Player freedom, and the development of footballing skills, is sacrificed for the sake of organisational unity. Although other famous and highly successful British managers, such as Brian Clough, were similarly authoritarian in manner, Clough did not extend this control to imposing a simple football style upon his players. On the contrary, his teams were noted for their freedom from the limitations of excessive coaching and could not be compared to any team of Charlton's.

In *Football: A Sociology of the Global Game*, Richard Giulianotti elaborates on these theories, linking them to work practices and the general relationship between manager and worker. Speaking of the early 1970s, the period in which Charlton received his coaching instructions at Lilleshall, Giulianotti writes as follows:

> At this time, 'scientific' approaches dominated modern football. The FA coaching supremo, Charles Hughes, was promulgating the functional purity of 'direct football'. Through the simplified method of management by objectives (MBO), teams were instructed to play the 'long ball' as data analysis 'proved' that up to 90% of goals came from less than five passes.

Giulianotti, concludes that this scientific approach effectively 'amounted to industrial de-skilling'. Comparing this British theory of management with the more enlightened approach on the Continent he further writes:

> During the late 1960s and 1970s the Dutch side Ajax fashioned 'total football', a more fluid and attacking style of play. All team players needed to be highly adaptable and capable of playing in most outfield positions. Total football's industrial philosophy was nearer to an 'en-skilling' than a 'de-skilling' model. It resembled Japanese labour practices (then beginning to impact upon global markets) which required all factory managers to be adept on assembly lines, while workers contributed new ideas for improving productivity. Its superiority to English 'science' was rooted in the mature relationship between Dutch players and coaches, compared to the antediluvian class distinctions between the British 'Boss' and his 'lads'. Although the Dutch produced some 'crack' players (notably Cruyff) the majority acquired a basic technical virtuosity that enabled them to play anywhere.

Giulianotti's point is that the British system effectively diminished the skill levels of their players, compared to the Dutch system which developed and liberated players.

Applying Giulianotti's theory, this would effectively put Charlton into a coaching tradition that seeks to de-skill players so that managerial orders can be followed all the better and this is precisely the reason why skilful players, such as Ronnie Whelan, Liam Brady and David O'Leary, all fell foul of the Charlton system: their high skill levels posed a serious threat to the functional purity of his long-ball game. Their troublesome talents would always be likely to surface and disrupt Charlton's devotion to the all-important system that contained players but admitted no individuals.

This is what Dunphy meant when he said Charlton was 'confused by talent'. Talent, for Charlton, was the uncontrollable quantity, source of the unknown, and unpredictable in its very essence. Charlton just could not accommodate it into his ultra-simple conception of football. Consequently, excellent players were wasted under Charlton's management and not just at international level. At club level, before managing Ireland, Charlton had already found it difficult to incorporate talent into his conception of football. An example of this occurred in his single season of tenure at Newcastle United when Charlton clashed with a young, future England international.

The player was Peter Beardsley and Charlton singles him out for special criticism in his autobiography, claiming that the player's major failing was his inability to follow direct orders. Charlton tells of his exasperation at trying to persuade Beardsley to rein in his attacking instincts when the team were ahead in games. He pleads with Beardsley, 'When we are ahead, keep possession, kill time, be negative', but to no avail. Beardsley routinely disobeyed and continued to create goal-scoring chances. After one such incident, Charlton describes giving Beardsley the 'bollocking of a lifetime'. He tells him: 'You nearly cost us the fucking game ... why don't you ever listen?' Why does Beardsley not listen? The answer is, probably, because he had nothing to learn from Charlton. Beardsley was one of the most talented players of his generation, who went on to have a memorable career at Liverpool, Everton and later at Newcastle again, earning 59 caps for England, which he also captained.

By opposing Charlton, Beardsley remained true to his abilities and went on to flourish at Liverpool in a way that simply could not have occurred under Charlton. It is not credible for Charlton to suggest that the player somehow needed 'correcting', and nor can we swallow the suggestion that the problem lay with Beardsley and not with Charlton. To use Dunphy's phrase, Charlton was simply confused by talent. He did not know how to use Beardsley and what should have been a gift to the Newcastle team rapidly became a problem in Charlton's eyes. The conflict between Charlton and Beardsley here reflects the more fundamental rift between the en-skillment and de-skillment dichotomy already highlighted. Their tumultuous relationship was a classic example of a communication breakdown between two very different worlds of football strategy: one was naturally expansive, the other instinctively conservative.

In the context of the Irish team, John Aldridge was another case of a wasted talent. He could not hope to emulate his club form at Liverpool with Ireland, with Charlton ordering him to do nothing but chase 'flick-ons' into the corners of the pitch. Is it any wonder that Aldridge failed to score in his first nineteen international games?

These were players trained to think on their feet, trained to do the unexpected: sacrilege as far as the Reep/Hughes model was concerned, and Charlton was nothing if not a model pupil of that school. Charlton's de-skillment approach was hopelessly unsuited to such gifted players who needed encouragement, not discouragement. It is arguable that some of the players under his management could have even regressed were they not receiving a more progressive daily education at club level.

If we look more closely at Charlton's tactics, we can see that the de-skillment ethic that he sought to enforce is really an approach that is suitable at the lower levels of the game, and becomes progressively redundant the closer you move to the highest level of the game. This explains why Graham Taylor achieved so much in his early years, when he took Lincoln City and Watford up through the lower divisions using the Reep/Hughes system. However, the strategy collapsed when Taylor took Watford into Europe and most famously when he failed as England's manager.

Essentially, the worse a player is, the more strictly the manager needs to control him. A bad player cannot be trusted, and so he should be given simple, rigid orders in order for him to perform a function for the team, and bad players are precisely what you find in the lower divisions. However, asking hugely talented players, at the highest level of the game, to follow a basic game plan, without deviations of any kind, is simply not going to work and will inevitably alienate the manager from the more gifted players. This, of course, is exactly why Charlton fell out with Brady, Whelan and O'Leary. It is instructive to note, and no accident, that Charlton explains how he first began forming his philosophy while watching an English fourth division game.

In *Jack Charlton's World Cup Diary*, he describes how his eyes were opened by watching Northampton Town on a wet Saturday in January. He claims to have discovered proof here in this lowly Fourth Division match that going over teams with long balls was preferable to attempting to pass through them. Of course, there are few other lessons to be taken from a Fourth Division game other than this banal truth. Invariably, players are not good enough to play an incisive passing game at this level, and a long-ball style is generally all you will see if you attend such a match. However, to think that this principle could be lifted out of the Fourth Division and applied in the higher divisions and in international matches represents a serious gap in Charlton's logic. A damp Saturday afternoon in Northampton is hardly an incubator of ideas for coping with the challenges of international football.

It was this tactical mismatch between manager and player that led Dunphy to controversially claim that Charlton was effectively transforming the Irish squad into a pub team and not allowing them to be the world-class players they were.

What alternative, though, was Dunphy offering us? What did he mean by contrasting Charlton to his previously mentioned man of vision? Presumably, Bob Paisley, the great Liverpool manager, would have matched this description, because Dunphy had campaigned for Paisley to get the Irish job before the FAI selected Charlton. The revealing point here is that it exhibits very clearly Dunphy's own football philosophy and allegiances. By opposing Charlton's appointment, and supporting Paisley, Dunphy was aligning himself with the famous philosophy of the Liverpool boot room, which first introduced the continental style of play to English football.

First, under Bill Shankly, and later under Bob Paisley, Liverpool conquered England and Europe, by adopting the short passing, possession game favoured by the top continental European teams of the time. It was Shankly's vision that diagnosed the failings in the British game; namely that it showed insufficient respect for the twin arts of passing and possession, and that major success in European competitions could be achieved only by realising this and modifying a team's tactics accordingly.

The key to the passing game lies in the fact that prolonged possession alters the formation of the opposing team by shifting the ball between your own players. When an opening does eventually arise, you then make a decisive move and capitalise on the space created. Bill Shankly, quoted in Jonathan Wilson's *Inverting the Pyramid: The History of Football Tactics*, describes this theory in the following terms: 'Get the ball, give an early pass, then it goes from me to someone else and it switches around again. You might not be getting very far, but the pattern of the opposition is changing. Finally, somebody will sneak in.'

This is the subtle but potentially devastating efficacy of the passing game, and, essentially, the reason why Dunphy called for a different style of play to that offered by Charlton. The crucial point here is that the passing game turns out to be far more pragmatic than the much-vaunted pragmatism of the long-ball game. The ball, and not the player, does the running, while the opposition team is forced to expend energy trying to win back possession. This more nuanced approach to the game also recognises that a sideways or backwards pass can be a progressive pass in that it is reshaping the formation of the opposing team, thus allowing for an eventual opening to occur.

Understood in this way, passing sideways and backwards is far more dangerous to the opposition team than the constant, hopeful, long forward passes that Charlton demanded, a point proven most effectively by the 2012 Barcelona team, which has mastered the art of the short pass to great effect. The unarguable logic here is that the ball does not have to be constantly going forward for progression to occur. However, in a confused display of machismo, Charlton always dismissed the passing game as somehow a sign of unmanliness, something irreconcilable with that very British tradition of always elevating the physical above the technical in football matters. Charlton's root obsession was that no team of his would engage in wayward niceties in the centre of midfield. Charlton's teams would get up and at the opposition, give them a battle to fight, and if you didn't win the game, at least you knew you had won the physical battle and could go home with pride intact.

This undercurrent of machismo has been ever-present in Charlton's attitude to football. It comes directly from that outmoded British conception of the game, which emphasises all the battling values, to the neglect of the artistry of the game. Simon Kuper and Stefan Szymanski in *Why England Lose & Other Curious Phenomena Explained* have referred to this malaise in the British game. They characterise the British accent on heroic physicality as being trapped in a kind of recurring effort to recreate the spirit of Dunkirk, the idea being that the most important battle is the physical one: anyone can play pretty football, but only the British can do it in a suitably manly fashion. Charlton is based squarely in this tradition, which finds its raison d'être in England's 1966 World Cup triumph, of which he was an integral part.

Dunphy, then, in his promotion of Bob Paisley and with his preference for the passing game, was continually asking for Charlton's removal, since as long as Charlton was in charge, the Reep/Hughes model would obtain and the Irish players would degenerate further.

In the final analysis, it can be said that Dunphy's basic point about Charlton had strong merits. Ireland did have the players to play a better brand of football than the Charlton way and a passing game could have brought greater success. This would have been particularly true in major tournaments, where Charlton's 'hold what we have' approach effectively guaranteed nothing more than respectable exits from major tournaments. Far too often, it seemed that Charlton did not know where a victory would come from, and was frequently left clinging to the limited hope provided by penalty shoot-outs.

I have already pointed out how impressive Charlton's statistics are as Ireland manager. There is another statistic that is equally telling. Ireland managed only 75 goals in 93 games under Charlton. This tells its own story. Although Ireland, under Charlton, was a formidable opponent and was feared by just about every international team, scoring so few goals placed a definite limit to the level of success that could be achieved. There were just too many heroic drawn games which could have been victories had Charlton been able to show more adventure in his style of play, as Dunphy had repeatedly demanded. For example, in the nine World Cup matches over which Charlton presided, Ireland managed only one victory in normal time – the other victory being achieved via a penalty shoot-out against Romania at Italia '90 – and scored a meagre five goals. The Irish did tellingly, however, manage five draws in that same group of games.

Worse still, Ireland seemed to celebrate these kinds of draws as victories, in an attitude that betrayed limited ambition and low self-esteem as a football nation. Conor O'Callaghan, once more, has brilliantly described the alarming frequency of, and Ireland's peculiar fondness for, 1-1 draws. He describes the strange phenomenon in the following terms:

> We are the one-all specialists, the Brazilians of the moral victory. I can think of no other instance in which a footballing nation has patented and fetishised a particular score line. It has become

the bequest of the Charlton/McCarthy years to Irish football. It has become Irish football's contribution to world football. The pattern is almost always the same. They take an early lead. We show great character. We refuse to lie down. We eke out an equaliser, and leave it at that, point proven. There are no more chances between our goal and the final whistle. We raise our arms aloft, embrace. We go down to the end at which a sea of green is singing 'You'll never beat the Irish' and kiss our crests. The opposition have long since disappeared down the tunnel. Next day, they are pilloried in their tabloids, and we are lauded by the editorials of our broadsheets.

A perfect example of this pattern was the pair of 1-1 draws Ireland shared with England in the 1992 European Championship qualifiers. In both cases Ireland out-played England, especially in the away game at Wembley, but Charlton's limited tactics helped to ensure that they would hold out for no more than valiant draws. A victory in either of these matches would have seen Ireland finish top of the group and playing at Euro '92 instead of England.

These are the fine margins with which we are dealing when we debate the Charlton era and Dunphy's critique of it. Charlton brought us very far, farther than ever before, but it became apparent that he could not take us beyond a certain point. This is where Dunphy's man of vision becomes relevant. A manager who believed in an expansive style of play, encouraging great players to express themselves, instead of tying them to a dogmatic system, could have brought Ireland even greater success. Such a manager could have defeated England in both those qualifying encounters in 1990 and 1991 and posed a more serious threat for Italy in the quarter-finals of Italia '90, and even Holland in the second round of USA '94.

Yet there could be no dissent. Charlton had established early in his tenure that he would tolerate no debate, constructive or otherwise, about his chosen methods. The tactic of walking out of press conferences, honed to perfection during those ten years, let the press know very clearly that their access to exclusive interviews and much-needed headlines would dry up quickly if they did not toe the party line. Moreover, he was domineering in his behaviour towards journalists, making interviews a dicey affair for anyone who wished to test his wrath. According to Dunphy, who had first-hand knowledge of Charlton's manner in press conferences, he was possessed of a 'fiery, intemperate rebuke' that had journalists walking on egg-shells.

This was why Dunphy stood out from the flock of journalists covering the Irish team during these years. He did not shun pariah status, standing up to Charlton, and he remained a vocal thorn in Charlton's side. His criticisms were all the more effective for him being an outsider.

In a piece written for *The Independent* in 1995, some days after Charlton's last game in charge of Ireland, Dunphy attempted to sign off on the Charlton years. Ireland had just been beaten emphatically 2-0 by the Dutch at Anfield, in a match that both ended Ireland's chances of reaching Euro '96 and drew down the curtain on the Charlton years. Dunphy was hugely critical of Charlton's defensive line-up, selecting as he did two full-backs as wingers, in a move that Dunphy described as 'absurd', 'cowardly', and which 'reeked of fear'. Attempting to summarise

Charlton's shortcomings, Dunphy highlights his 'mistrust of originality', his 'narrow mind' and his 'fearful spirit' in accounting for the unfortunate end to Ireland's qualifying campaign.

Although Dunphy was shocked by Charlton's defensive formation, which saw two full-backs, Terry Phelan and Jeff Kenna line up as wingers, it was the logical conclusion of Charlton's era. With no new players of note coming through, and major injuries to Staunton and Keane to contend with, Charlton retreated into himself by choosing an even more extreme version of the norm. It was just defend and hope, little more than that. The fundamental truth revealed here is that Charlton's tactics, successful as they were in their time, never evolved during his tenure as manager. He kept trying to impose the same basic game, regardless of the teams and players that he was facing. In fact, Charlton himself tells us in his autobiography that only once in ten years did he adapt his tactics, when Ireland played England at Euro '88.

Such stagnation was hardly good for the Irish game. Charlton did not have anything to bequeath to the next regime. He had adopted short-term tactics to maximise results, without paying attention to players' development. This was obviously not good for the future of Irish football. In order to improve the game, a more detailed, long-term approach would have been required.

Dunphy, it can be argued, established valid arguments against Charlton's management of Ireland. He pointed to the shortcomings of the long-ball game, to the careless and unprofessional preparation, to Charlton's lack of regard for talented players, to his lack of a concerted vision for Irish soccer, and to his damaging manner of stifling all possibilities of constructive discussion about the national team. Dunphy showed that though Charlton could deliver results, he could not deliver even passable football. As Dunphy has argued consistently, possibly the greatest generation of Irish players was asked to play beneath themselves and, as a result, the development of Irish football was damaged.

There is a weakness in Dunphy's position, however, and it springs from his propensity to gravitate towards the extreme. Had he conceded the positives that Charlton had brought to the Irish game, his basic criticism of Charlton's pragmatic football may have been taken more seriously, as it rightly should have been. By maintaining such trenchant opposition to Charlton's every move, Dunphy perhaps made it too easy for fans and journalists to dismiss him as a reckless renegade, bent on promoting controversy wherever possible. Dunphy's taste for personal attacks on Charlton left him vulnerable to the *ad hominem* charge that he simply did not like the man. This detracted somewhat from the main thrust of his argument, which was that Charlton's football philosophy was the major concern and not simply Charlton the person.

It is interesting to note, however, that Dunphy did not always oppose the Charlton regime. There were some cooling-off periods, most notably before USA '94, when Dunphy professed himself much happier with the Irish style of play. He noted that the football had improved and he was even generally supportive of Charlton's management. It was, however, a short-lived phenomenon because the drudgery of USA '94 rapidly brought Dunphy back to his familiar opposition to Charlton.

Charlton's Ireland achieved, to a point, spectacular results, but was the cost worth it? This is the question on which Dunphy's and Charlton's opposition hangs. Pragmatists align themselves behind Charlton, idealists behind Dunphy. Charlton, it should be noted, has experience on his side. He actually attained serious success by using his utilitarian methods, while Dunphy's calls for the passing game remain a hypothetical, a tantalising, 'what if?'. However, the foregoing analysis, has, I believe, established that the passing game, when properly employed, is superior to the long-ball game and that, consequently, Dunphy was right to call for more from Charlton as Ireland's manager.

Disbelieving critics of Dunphy might ask what more could you want from a manager who delivered so much success. Dunphy's short answer is the World Cup. Dunphy, speaking on Newstalk before the 2010 World Cup, reiterated his view that Ireland could have won Italia '90 had the players been led by a different man. He reasoned that, given that it was such a poor tournament, with one of the worst finals in recent memory, Ireland, with more ambition, could have gone all the way. This was the 'more' that he demanded of Charlton, and the source of his near-constant criticism of his management.

Could that generation of players, which included Brady, Lawrenson and Whelan, have achieved more with the ball at their feet? Could they have won a World Cup? We shall never know, but Dunphy's analysis has presented a compelling and thought-provoking case for that possibility. The fact that the passing game has worked for so many other nations remains an undeniable piece of evidence to support his claims.

Whether one is of the aesthetic or practical mind, there surely remains a valid lingering doubt, unvanquished by Charlton's results and arguments, that something truly great could have come from that generation of Irish players who signed off at Anfield in 1995, if a more cultured and open-minded manager had been in charge.

Chapter 4

'The Sergeant-Major too Eager for a Commission': Dunphy and Mick McCarthy

Eamon Dunphy's views on Mick McCarthy are possibly surpassed for notoriety only by his famous and long-running criticisms of Jack Charlton. It is a close contest, however. McCarthy is the man whom Dunphy once described as 'the boil on the arse of humanity' and for whom he has repeatedly shown little but contempt, both as a player and as a manager. McCarthy first played for the Republic of Ireland under Jack Charlton and then went on to succeed him as manager in 1996. Dunphy has had plenty to say on both topics.

We first look at Dunphy's analysis of McCarthy as a player. Although McCarthy was a central participant in many of the Irish team's most successful years under Charlton, for Dunphy he was the major weakness in the set-up. McCarthy – who in his long club career, from 1977 to 1992, represented Barnsley, Manchester City, Celtic, Olympique Lyonnais and Millwall – won his first cap for the Republic of Ireland on 23 May 1984 in a match against

Poland at Dalymount Park, during the managerial tenure of Eoin Hand. Subsequently, under Charlton, he became essential to the team, ultimately receiving the captaincy and leading Ireland into the 1990 World Cup in Italy. In total, he played 57 times for his country between 1984 and 1992, scoring two goals, and captaining the team on 22 of those occasions. Throughout his international career, McCarthy enjoyed practically unqualified support from the Irish fans and media, so why did Dunphy campaign so energetically for his removal from the squad?

In the summer of 1988, when the Irish were taking part in their first international tournament at Euro '88, Dunphy used his column in the *Sunday Independent* to undermine the public's belief in their 'Captain Fantastic', as McCarthy had affectionately come to be known.

In football terms, Dunphy did not rate McCarthy as an international defender. He argued that he lacked pace, positional sense and the crucial skill, especially at international level, of being comfortable on the ball and hence capable of playing out from the back when possible. For Dunphy, he was a slow, ungainly, kick-it-anywhere defender; a no frills, 'put it in Row Z' kind of stopper you might witness at any lower division game on a Saturday afternoon. Writing in May 1988, in a piece assessing the strengths and weaknesses of the Irish players who were about to fly out to Germany, Dunphy targeted McCarthy as the team's Achilles' heel. Where others perceived a tough, take-no-prisoners, leader of men, Dunphy saw a lumbering centre-half, an all too willing foot soldier hacking aimlessly at everything – ball and man – that ventured within the radius of his flailing limbs. He wrote: 'McCarthy is not my idea of an international defender. He is painfully lacking in pace and far too impetuous. He is a bit too gung-ho for my taste, the sergeant major too

eager for a commission', and he concludes by expressing the fear that McCarthy and Ireland could be horribly
exposed by his limitations in the coming tournament.

Returning to the topic in a piece published on 26 June,
after Ireland had been eliminated from the tournament
at the group stage, Dunphy laid much of the blame at
McCarthy's door, referring to him mockingly as 'Jack's Man
of Oak', who 'does not possess the instincts of a good
defender nor the discipline of mind that is required to do
the sums good defenders need to do'. Speaking disparagingly of McCarthy's major attributes – his heading and
tackling skills – Dunphy rounded off his analysis by noting that 'Good defending is about far more than crunching
tackles and mighty leaps to head the ball'. As evidence, he
pointed first to the way in which McCarthy's lack of speed
and positional sense had invited 'Gary Lineker's sacking of
our defence' in the first group game against England, and,
secondly, to the fact of McCarthy being woefully out of
position for the Soviet Union's equalising goal in Ireland's
second group game. Although Ireland achieved excellent
results in both these games, beating England 1-0 and earning a highly creditable 1-1 draw against the Soviets, it was
clear that something was seriously wrong with the team's
defence. In the England game Gary Lineker broke free of
his marker, McCarthy, enough times to ensure what would
have been a cricket score in England's favour had he been
able to beat Ireland's inspirational goalkeeper on the day,
Packie Bonner. The result was a thing to celebrate, but
the alarming frequency with which England breached the
Irish rearguard was something to worry about, as Dunphy
rightly points out. Similarly, McCarthy left his defensive
partner badly exposed for the goal that saw the Soviet
Union equalise, being some 20 yards behind Kevin Moran
when the ball was played in behind them both.

Although Dunphy was no fan of McCarthy as a footballer, it was more than an instinctive dislike of the man that drove his criticism. The real reason lay in the fact that he wanted David O'Leary promptly returned to the heart of the Irish defence instead of McCarthy. O'Leary was a player for whom Dunphy had great admiration. In the same article, he was emphatic in his praise, noting that 'O'Leary is one of the best central-defenders in Europe', and he pointed to his 'pace and ability to read the game' as qualities evidently lacking from McCarthy's repertoire. Although most saw O'Leary as an automatic selection, Charlton did not agree and the player, falling out with Charlton almost immediately after he took control, found himself overlooked for the first two-and-a-half years of the manager's tenure.

When Charlton took charge of his first game, against Wales, in March 1986, O'Leary could already have been described as a veteran of club and international football. At club level, he had been a regular in Arsenal's defence since 1975. Additionally he had 40 caps for the Republic, receiving his first in a 1-1 draw with England in 1976 and had become a mainstay in its defence, with his classy style of defending bringing poise and confidence to the team. After playing against the Welsh, O'Leary withdrew through injury from the next scheduled friendly match against Uruguay in April of the same year, a withdrawal that did not seem to sit well with Charlton but was demanded by his employer's at Arsenal. O'Leary had feared this very response, remembering Charlton's unsettling pronouncement before the Welsh game that players, if selected, must always present themselves to play. He told his players: 'Even if you are struggling with injury, I expect you to get over here [Republic of Ireland] and report for international duty.' This was borne out by the fact that O'Leary was not selected for Ireland's subsequent friendly tournament played in Iceland at the end of May, a decision that the player learned of only through third-party sources. Charlton had not contacted him.

O'Leary, stung by Charlton's lack of communication, subsequently refused the manager's eleventh-hour attempt to include him in the squad as a replacement due to a number of last minute withdrawals. O'Leary, believing his summer to be free, had arranged a holiday with his wife and children and, when Charlton rang, he explained that he could not make the trip. In different circumstances, perhaps O'Leary would have unquestioningly cancelled his family holiday in order to play for his country in Iceland, even if the occasion was an unimportant pre-season tournament. However, in his autobiography *David O'Leary: My Story,* the player cited Charlton's lack of respect as the primary reason for his decision. Of Charlton's phone call he says:

> He telephoned again on the following Monday morning ... I thought there and then to ask why I had been left out in the first place. Deep down I was furious. I knew he was using me... I felt very hurt by the way he had gone about things. I hadn't heard a word about why I had been dropped. Now, suddenly, he needed me. I wasn't going to be his lackey.

The phone went dead and O'Leary's two-and-a-half-year absence from the Irish squad had begun. Was this stubbornness on Charlton's part or simply a football decision? According to Dunphy, writing, once more, in his 26 June column piece for the *Sunday Independent,* it was always a footballing decision on Charlton's part – his preference for brawn over brilliance – that had led to O'Leary's exile. But, he argued, Charlton was happy, instead, to conceal this unseemly truth by seizing upon O'Leary's apparent lack of loyalty to justify leaving him out of subsequent squads. In Dunphy's mind, there was no reasonable football argument that could make sense of choosing McCarthy ahead of O'Leary, so Charlton had to look elsewhere for an acceptable reason. According to Dunphy: 'Jack Charlton has never expressed his preference for Mick McCarthy in terms of his own conviction about O'Leary. Instead, he has chosen to cast doubt on O'Leary's loyalty to Ireland's cause.' Elaborating on the point, and with evidently little regard for McCarthy's feelings, he dismissed Charlton's loyal captain as 'the price you pay for stubbornness soured into prejudice'.

Was Dunphy right? Were there really no compelling football arguments for McCarthy's inclusion ahead of O'Leary, and was it a vendetta on Charlton's part that saw him overlook O'Leary for so long? Not according to Charlton. In his autobiography he denies holding any grudge against O'Leary and presents his own reasons for preferring McCarthy. While acknowledging the former's undoubted ability, Charlton gave the following assessment of O'Leary's play:

> Essentially he was a drop-off defender. He didn't believe in getting tight on his opponent, preferring instead to rely on his pace to pick up the bits and pieces. I'd been to see his brother Pierce play at Celtic, and he was exactly the same. And, to be brutally frank, they didn't fit my game plan. I needed centre-backs who would compete with the players in front of them, push them out, deny

them time and space to turn with the ball. David O'Leary didn't do that, at least not consistently – so I left him out.

In contrast, McCarthy fit Charlton's requirements perfectly with his 'strong, aggressive' and 'exceptionally competitive' style. Where Dunphy saw an awkward, inelegant brute, Charlton saw an inspirational and fearsome athlete, complete with the no-nonsense style that he expected of defenders. Conversely, with O'Leary, where Dunphy witnessed a composed, continental-style defender capable of bringing the ball under control and starting passing moves for his team, Charlton could see only an expensive luxury fannying about with the ball on the edge of his own area. For Charlton, a centre-half's role was to get the ball clear as quickly as possible and not to linger on it under any circumstances. McCarthy did this job for him; O'Leary, on the other hand, could never play this way and so was not going to feature in Charlton's plans, a fact that he was made aware of on his very first meeting with the man. In his autobiography O'Leary tells us that he soon realised that Charlton 'didn't want defenders who thought about the game' and he recounts his inability to understand the man's true colours:

> The first time I met Charlton was after he had picked a squad to play Wales at Lansdowne Road. We all got together in Dublin 24 March 1986. It was a day I am unlikely to forget. One of the first things he said was, 'All my life I have never regarded defenders as being able to play. You get the ball – and you get it away.' This from a man who was a centre-half himself! I wasn't his sort of player – that was obvious.

McCarthy, then, ticked the boxes for Charlton when it came to his playing style, but why did Charlton go one step further by making him captain of the Irish team, and even describing him in his autobiography, along with Paul McGrath and Andy Townsend, as one of the top three international players with whom he has worked? It was more than just football. It was about loyalty, and this is what made McCarthy so odious in Dunphy's eyes: he was Charlton's ever so dependable yeoman of the guard, his on-field proxy, who ensured that the letter of the Charlton law was observed, clause by clause. Charlton makes it clear that McCarthy was pivotal to the success of his game plan, and in particular, by playing the role of enforcer for his tactical plans: 'I could say my piece in the dressing room, but once they got on the park, it was down to the players themselves. And McCarthy made certain the instructions were carried out to the last detail.' Charlton then gives an example of his captain carrying out this role:

> Before the England game in Sardinia, [the Republic of Ireland's first group game at the 1990 World Cup in Italy], I had warned our fellows to beware of Peter Beardsley... To minimise that threat, we had to get to him quickly, to force him to go in the direction we wanted him to go, not the other way around. And the game was only a couple of minutes in progress when I saw McCarthy charge through a forest of players, friend and foe alike, to light like a wasp on Peter. The casual onlooker may have missed it, but in that moment, Mick was laying down the benchmark for his team.

Given the controversial nature of Charlton's direct tactics, as discussed in the previous chapter, he obviously felt that he needed an on-field presence to make sure that his more talented players would not lose the run of themselves by starting to play football, instead of just following his simple game plan. McCarthy was this man and so Charlton made him captain. Is this enough, though, to justify captain status for a player? Should unswerving loyalty, alone, be deemed sufficient to receive this accolade?

When managers choose their captain there are a number of factors for them to consider. Firstly, loyalty is a valid consideration. As a manager, you want to select a player who agrees with your understanding of the game and who, more importantly, follows that game plan unerringly on the pitch. In this sense, a captain is the manager's right-hand man, someone he can always trust on the pitch and, also, someone with whom he can privately confer on team matters when necessary. Instinctively, managers know how tenuous their authority over a squad can be. Although they are in charge, they cannot insinuate their way into the private sphere of the footballer's world. There is a shared experience amongst the players that has the latent potential to break out in dangerous cliques and dressing room revolts, something a manager is often powerless to resist once it has been set in motion. This is especially the case with a group of experienced players, who may have already seen a handful of managers come and go, and consequently, with a well-honed cynicism, will often only be a hair's breadth away from writing off their newly appointed taskmaster as a spoofer. Hence, the need to have your own man, working diligently for your cause, on the inside, both on and off the pitch.

For Charlton, there was no one better than McCarthy to play this role. As one of the more limited players at Charlton's disposal, he would have felt more grateful than others to be selected for his country; hence his willingness to please Charlton at every turn.

If loyalty is an essential factor in choosing a captain, then ability is every bit as important. If the leader of the team can inspire only by undying commitment to the cause, by always obediently following his managers demands, then not every player is going to be impressed. It is a weak manager who selects his captain on this basis alone. A captain, should also, where possible, be the best player on the team. The resulting composure and confidence that such leaders give to the players around them is more effective than the loyal and well-meaning, but often aimless, never-say-die attitude of McCarthy types. It is clear that Charlton favoured McCarthy for just these battling qualities and was, as a result, happy to overlook his obvious deficiencies as a footballer.

It seems that it was this close partnership between Charlton and McCarthy that Dunphy could not abide. He viewed it as a two-man conspiracy against what he regarded as the proper direction for Irish football; a plan orchestrated by Charlton and facilitated by McCarthy, the servile henchman. If we leave the captaincy issue aside and focus on Dunphy's criticisms of McCarthy as a defender, we can see that there is some substance to his analysis. Charlton, as we have noted, said that he favoured McCarthy to O'Leary because he was the type of centre-half who, rather than dropping off his opponents, got tight to his man when the ball was played into the 18-yard area. This style of defending, although uncomfortable for the forward receiving the ball, is in fact a high-risk strategy. It means that a centre-half is continually committing himself to risky encounters where sometimes he will succeed but at other times, particularly against skilful forwards who can cope with receiving the ball under pressure, he will also fail. This is why defenders who do engage in this kind of play will often have blistering pace, a quality that compensates for their rashness by rescuing many dire situations. Pace, however, was conspicuously lacking in McCarthy's game and this made his gung-ho style all the more incongruous and unreliable. By typically coming to meet his man immediately, McCarthy was leaving dangerous space in behind him, space that he did not have the pace to deal with if a forward turned him or ran onto a ball that was played in behind the defence.

From a tactical perspective, this is what happened to McCarthy against Gary Lineker in the opening match of Euro '88, when the forward exploited the room in behind McCarthy at will. Alternatively, if McCarthy, in the mould of a player like O'Leary, had been able to read the game better, he could have dropped off Lineker and led the forward away from goal and down the side channels where little damage could have been done. This is how all good defenders who are short on pace play their game, and it is also why the older a defender becomes, the more he begins to rely on his savvy and less on his legs. The onset of age introduces a new tenet to defensive philosophy: prevention, not cure. The ability to read the game, to see danger before it arises, rather than becoming embroiled in dicey challenges with younger and faster attackers, becomes an imperative.

Paolo Maldini was living evidence of this fact, playing in exemplary fashion until age 41 at the centre of AC Milan's defence. To the end, his faultless positional sense ensured that his defending was invariably calm and controlled. He did not seem troubled by forwards, as a rule, whether they possessed great pace or not, in a subtle style of defending that was almost unfathomable in its quiet efficiency. Further evidence can be gleaned from the exceptional career of another luminary of Italian defensive excellence, Fabio Cannavaro, who, while not the fastest, strongest and certainly not the tallest of defenders, received the World Player of the Year award in 2006 for his performances at the World Cup of that year. In a series of brilliant displays throughout the tournament, captaining the national team to its fourth World Cup success, he showed the world that defending, as much as attacking, was an art form.

In light of the above, Dunphy's issues with McCarthy's style of defending make sense. O'Leary, when he played for Ireland, brought an intelligence to the base of the team, his short passing out of defence providing a platform for consistent possession of the ball. McCarthy, on the other hand, although superficially impressive with his capacity to clear the ball from the danger area with the minimum of fuss, was in fact helping to pile pressure on the Irish team. His dramatic clearances were counterproductive: they usually sent the ball directly back to the opposition, enabling renewed attacks to begin. Understood in this way, such Herculean feats of strength rapidly lose their sheen. This was a style of defence that trapped the Irish players in a yo-yo-like struggle of siege warfare: you attack, we clear it, then you attack again. This need not have happened and it wouldn't have if O'Leary had been selected instead.

What, though, did McCarthy think of Dunphy's public campaign against him? In his autobiography, *Captain Fantastic: My Football Career and World Cup Experience*, written after Italia '90, it is clear that he was genuinely hurt by what he saw as Dunphy's personal attacks against him. McCarthy also claimed that he was not alone in being unable to fathom the reasons for the angry tone of

Dunphy's writings, and other squad members also considered the controversial journalist to be an enemy:

> Eamon has upset many of the players down through the years. At first we thought that his knowledge of the game would give him a better insight into the problems that professional footballers face. He also knew the set-up within the Irish squad as a former international player ... we all felt – well, he's one of us, he knows the problems and we could expect somebody to write intelligently without all the hype.

As a professional, McCarthy surely would have been accustomed to receiving some criticism from journalists, but Dunphy's comments perplexed him. Speaking of a condemning piece that Dunphy wrote in his *Sunday Independent* column after Euro '88 – an article that Charlton tried to hide from McCarthy in order to spare his pride – he noted: 'It was, as I expected, a very personal attack. All Eamon left out was that maybe my father should have been excommunicated and thrown out of his native Waterford!' McCarthy does have a point. Dunphy's attacks had an unwarranted personal dimension, as if McCarthy had committed some truly awful crime of which the rest of us were unaware. His intense dislike for McCarthy seemed to go well beyond a simple football preference for one defender over another. Why was this?

The probable cause was that McCarthy became caught in the middle of Dunphy's campaign against Charlton and his arguments for the return of David O'Leary to the Irish team. Naturally, these are things that McCarthy need not have concerned himself with. So long as the Irish national manager selected him to play, he was going to continue doing so, and, consequently, the claims of other players or the opinions of irate journalists were not relevant. Dunphy, however, with his personal comments against McCarthy, seemed to almost suggest that the player should have had the decency to admit that he was unfit to wear the Irish jersey and hand it over to O'Leary. It seemed that he could not cope with the fact that McCarthy, rather than being contrite in any way for his alleged sins against Irish football, in fact, revelled in the role of 'Captain Fantastic'.

There was also a nasty streak to Dunphy's caricature of McCarthy as 'Charlton's Man of Oak'. The allusion was to a low-intelligence player, a hired-hand eager to please by performing Charlton's dirty work on the pitch. The truth, however, is that McCarthy was not Charlton's lapdog. He played his own game. It just so happened that he was Charlton's kind of defender and was rewarded accordingly. He did nothing wrong by accepting this state-of-affairs and grabbing with both hands the chance to play for and captain his country at international tournaments. If an analyst does not rate a player, then he must confine his analysis to footballing arguments. Anything else is hardly credible and certainly not germane.

Although Dunphy's assessment of McCarthy's limitations as a footballer holds merit, it is too extreme. McCarthy was not world class, but he was an able defender. The problem, so often with Dunphy's approach, is that he will make a good point but then shower it in rhetoric in order to persuade his audience of its truth. Dunphy, through some insightful thinking, succeeded in showing us that Captain Fantastic, was, well, not all that fantastic, but by then taking it a step further and casting McCarthy as an absolute imposter in green, Dunphy was going too far. Furthermore, the manner by which he additionally sought to personally undermine and embarrass the player in his writings added nothing to his analysis.

If Dunphy was critical of McCarthy as a player, this, however, was as nothing compared to the hard line opposition he adopted once McCarthy became the manager of the Republic of Ireland team in February 1996. Out of a shortlist that included Liam Brady, Kevin Moran, Joe Kinnear, Dave Bassett and Mike Walker, the FAI selected McCarthy. Although relatively inexperienced at managerial level – between March 1992 and February 1996 McCarthy had managed Millwall in the old Second Division – his candidacy was undoubtedly assisted by his recent services as captain of the Irish team and not least because Charlton had strongly recommended him to the FAI as his successor. For Dunphy, the appointment was little short of a disaster. He had spent much of the previous ten years trying to oust Charlton from his throne only to look on powerless, as the irresistible machinations of palace politics saw a seamless transition of power to the dreaded 'Captain Fantastic'. What private contortions Dunphy must have experienced, with Charlton seemingly having the last laugh, securing his legacy by helping his favoured son to climb to the top of Irish football.

Although it is fair to say that Dunphy never supported McCarthy as Ireland manager, his most intense opposition to him surfaced only in 2002, when the Irish manager, at a pre-tournament training camp in Saipan, sensationally sent Roy Keane, the Irish captain, home from the World Cup for insubordination. In this national fiasco, Dunphy passionately supported Keane, while condemning McCarthy for what he saw as his dire incompetence. Briefly, the events that led to this unhappy ending for the Irish team were as follows.

The odd idea for the team to spend a week on the small Japanese island of Saipan had been McCarthy's. His vision was of the Irish players relaxing and doing some light training in relative obscurity before moving to mainland Japan where the real preparation for the World Cup, co-hosted by Japan and South Korea, would begin. Keane was unimpressed from the start. Leaving a crowded Dublin Airport, without VIP-standard privacy, and being forced to sit in economy class, while FAI officials enjoyed business class, was not Keane's idea of professional treatment. Worse still, unlike their English counterparts, for example, there would be no direct flight to Saipan. The Irish would take the scenic route, changing flights in Amsterdam and Tokyo to satisfy obligations to their sponsors, KLM, thus ensuring a longer and more circuitous path to their destination. Matters degraded further when it was discovered that the players had arrived at their Pacific frontier outpost in advance of their footballs, training gear and medical equipment. This meant that the first day of training was carried out in the same tracksuits the players had worn while hanging around the hotel.

When, subsequently, the necessary gear did arrive, the theoretical 'training pitch' turned out to be an unwatered, rutted and sloped surface, unfit even for amateur football. Injuries picked up by Lee Carsley and Steve Finnan were testament to its unsuitability for anything resembling sporting activity. Apparently, there had been a mix-up. Local sources had assured the FAI that the pitch would be re-laid but, instead, it remained in pristine awfulness awaiting the Irish players' grand arrival. When the players did train on it, they reported it to be pockmarked with stones and as hard as concrete. The groundsman charged with the task of keeping the pitch irrigated, according to Keane's testimony, insisted that he had not been told which day the Irish squad would be training so he had not watered it. He informed Keane, understandably: 'We could have watered it if anyone had told us you were coming down.'

For Keane, with ten years of FAI disorganisation under his belt, this was one farce too many, and he decided he had had enough. On 21 May he told a stunned McCarthy that he was going home, citing personal reasons as the decisive factor in his decision to walk away from the World Cup. McCarthy implored Keane to stay, but the player stood firm. McCarthy, needing a replacement for Keane, immediately phoned the young Celtic midfielder Colin Healy — a fringe player who had failed to make the original squad of 23 — asking him to prepare to fly out to Japan. In the meantime, Mick Byrne, the Irish kitman, who was particularly close to Keane, had persuaded him to change tack and stay after all. McCarthy came to Keane's room and accepted him back, but he told him that he was none too pleased with the player's to-ing and fro-ing. He said he had just told Colin Healy to join the squad, but he would now have to let the player down by informing him, once more, that he would not be needed; a conversation that was obviously not going to leave McCarthy looking very smart.

Keane was stung by the swiftness with which McCarthy had sought to replace him and once more objected, stating that he was definitely quitting this time. He felt, after his years of service, that he had deserved more time to consider his options.

The next day, 22 May, as McCarthy was scrambling to fax his new player list to FIFA in time for Colin Healy to be made eligible to play at the tournament, FAI president Milo Corcoran unexpectedly advised him that Keane, owing to the FAI's frantic overnight intervention, was now staying. But it was too late. The fax with Colin Healy's name on it had already gone to FIFA headquarters. Now, with the deadline for final squad registration looming, McCarthy had to send yet another fax to once more include Keane in his official tournament squad. But McCarthy's panic was in vain; the FAI had faxed FIFA a player listing with Keane's name on it a full thirty minutes earlier. McCarthy was livid with his employer's high-handed behaviour but relieved that his captain was finally on board and believed, mistakenly, that the crisis was averted.

On the very same day, Keane gave two controversial newspaper interviews, to Tom Humphries of *The Irish Times* and Paul Kimmage of the *Sunday Independent* where he made public his grievances with McCarthy, the FAI and his fellow players. The next morning, 23 May, a furious McCarthy read the interviews and decided that showdown talks with Keane were needed. He called a squad meeting for that evening, brandished the offending article and entreated Keane to raise his concerns publicly. Initially Keane would not take the bait, but when McCarthy unwisely intimated that the player might have faked an injury to avoid the World Cup play-off match against Iran, he could no longer take it. 'Suddenly I snapped. All the fuck-ups and bullshit I and every other Irish player had put up with for ten years flashed through my mind ... And here he [McCarthy] was playing fucking Big Boss in front of people who knew the story, who'd been there, gone along with this farce.' Keane let loose. 'You're a fucking wanker. I didn't rate you as a player, I don't rate you as a manager, and I don't rate you as a person. You're a fucking wanker and you can stick your World Cup up your arse. I've got no respect for you.' Keane knew the game was up, and where previously he had flirted with leaving of his own volition, McCarthy now settled the matter by sending him home, thus bringing the matter to an end.

Keane flew home on 24 May and the Irish squad travelled to Izumo on mainland Japan without their captain. Back in Ireland, attempts grew to broker a deal that might see Keane make a shock return to Japan. McCarthy, as he revealed in his World Cup memoir, *Mick McCarthy: Ireland's World Cup 2002*, did not want Keane back but bowed to public pressure on 28 May by making a conditional offer of peace: if Keane would personally phone him to apologise for his behaviour, then he would consider taking the player back. The next day McCarthy was told to expect a call from Keane at 10 a.m. local time to apologise, but, instead, he awoke to find a note left under his door by the FAI's chief executive officer Brendan Menton telling him that Keane had issued a public statement saying he would not return to the World Cup. This time it was definitely over, and with FIFA rejecting McCarthy's late request to include Colin Healy again, the Irish went into the World Cup with only 22 players.

Throughout all these events, Dunphy was hypercritical of McCarthy's management abilities and directly blamed him for destroying Ireland's World Cup hopes. He, like Keane, believed that McCarthy was personally culpable for the organisational nightmare that was Saipan, and he argued that his decision to expel Keane from the squad was a huge error. Speaking on RTÉ in May 2002 he said: 'I think for all of us who love football, the tournament has been ruined by this. This is an incredible mistake. It really is. To do this to your greatest player in these circumstances ... is an act of monumental folly.' Dunphy's reasoning was that special players need special treatment and that only truly great managers can handle them properly. Comparing McCarthy unfavourably with Sir Alex Ferguson, Dunphy argued:

> Great players just aren't like anyone else. Every football manager in the world would love Roy Keane to be playing for them – except one. Roy Keane is the captain of Manchester United. Sir Alex Ferguson, who is the most renowned manager of our time, gives Keane the respect and the freedom to speak his mind and we all know that he does. And there's no problem there. But McCarthy is a figure of much less stature who owes a lot to Roy Keane. If this is the way he has chosen to repay him in order to establish his own bona fides as a manager, then he is a fool.

Dunphy, heavily relying on the 'difficult genius' argument, contended that Keane was too big a player for the inexperienced McCarthy to cope with and manage properly, and that his insecurity led him to invariably feel threatened by the Corkman's substantial presence. He argued that McCarthy was a small-time manager who was very lucky to benefit from having at his disposal a great player like Keane. He saw it as an unearned inheritance on McCarthy's part and, to illustrate the gulf between the two men, he sought to remind the world of McCarthy's managerial inexperience. Writing in *Ireland on Sunday* on 26 May 2002, Dunphy wrote of McCarthy as 'Another mediocrity drawn from the pitiful ranks of perpetually harassed hang-on-in-there Nationwide League Managers' who also 'possessed no record of managerial achievement' and 'wouldn't have got a sniff of the England job' but yet 'was good enough for Paddy [i.e. the Football Association of Ireland]'.

In Dunphy's mind, McCarthy, through his ineptitude, firstly with the logistical problems and secondly
with his bungled team meeting, had engineered a situation in Saipan whereby Keane would inevitably confront
him and effectively force McCarthy to send him home.
Dunphy even claimed that McCarthy, by bringing a transcript of Keane's first interview to the meeting, was using
it 'as a pretext to rid Ireland and the World Cup of our
great player'. He viewed it as a blatant act of provocation,
akin to holding a red rag to the proverbial bull, designed
to facilitate the volatile Keane in ending his participation
in the World Cup.

This is an extreme viewpoint on McCarthy's role in
Saipan and is tantamount to suggesting that what Dunphy
contends is Keane's undeniable greatness and McCarthy's
blundering just could not live together, and so Ireland
ended up being deprived of their captain the week before
a World Cup.

What does McCarthy say in his defence? As a coun-
terpoint to Keane's hugely successful autobiography,
Keane, which presented his version of the incidents on
Saipan, McCarthy released *Mick McCarthy: Ireland's World
Cup 2002* in order to offer his side of the story.

In his account of the fateful events, he accepts that the
fact of inadequate training facilities and the late arrival of
essential equipment was not good enough, but he insists
that Keane's reaction was excessive because he failed to
understand the reason for the squad going to Saipan. It
was no boot camp. It was only meant to be an unwinding
process, a chance to acclimatise in a Pacific Island retreat,
with some moderate exercise before the full glare of the
World Cup began on mainland Japan. Keane took it too
seriously and so overreacted when the location proved
to be thoroughly unsuitable for footballing purposes; it

was still idyllic and the perfect place to let go, and, in any case, the world-class facilities awaiting the players at Izumo would make good any deficiencies that were identified in Saipan. It is clear that McCarthy took his Saipan stopover very seriously and viewed it even as an integral morale-building exercise. Where Keane saw interminable barbecues and lazy golfing sessions as whittling down valuable training time on the island, McCarthy saw crucial motivational exercises designed to encourage bonding. There is one frankly bizarre moment in his memoir where McCarthy describes his vision of Saipan being realised perfectly. In the midst of all the turmoil, and as he is about to summon his players to a showdown meeting with Keane, he is suddenly arrested by an emotional moment. With a lump in his throat and, lacking only the sentimental accompaniment of strings, he recounts:

> I enter the team's private dining-room and the sight in front of me is almost enough to bring tears to my eyes. There, twenty-three players are singing along with the resident band. The room is hopping as the band leads my players through a medley of South Pacific sing-alongs. I stand back for a second and watch my Saipan dream come to life in front of me. The lads are relaxed, they are having a good time, they have embraced what Saipan is all about.

Time and again, in his memoir, McCarthy stresses that everything will be alright when the squad gets to Izumo in what amounts to a not very subtle ruse: a process by which he hopes to gloss over the disaster that was Saipan. And in his column for *Ireland on Sunday*, which appeared on 26 May 2002, he expresses the same idea: 'Roy, unlike the other players, never understood the purpose of Saipan. We were not there to fine-tune the World Cup bid. We were there to sweat a little, play a little and bond a lot. The hard work would follow as it has done in Izumo, in a state of the art training facility.'

This is not convincing. If the squad really were not on the island to 'fine-tune their World Cup bid', then the experience could only have amounted to a distraction. If everyone's mind is not on the World Cup at this stage, then it is somewhere else, where it shouldn't be. Likewise, McCarthy's explanation of the organisational mayhem that was Saipan reads like an account from a man who is less than ready to shoulder full responsibility. He adopts a not very credible 'what can I do? I've been let down by those FAI numskulls yet again' type-attitude when faced with the grim realisation that the squad had arrived before their training equipment. What McCarthy fails to realise is that there is no one else who can take responsibility, if not him. Perhaps the FAI was letting him down again, but it was up to McCarthy to confront the organisation in the previous six years of his tenure to make sure that these problems would not arise. This he failed to do and so helped to precipitate the crisis that unfolded. When your players arrive before their training gear and your chosen playing surface is a joke, then you have lost the battle long ago. The hard part is beating Brazil, the easy part, you would imagine, is getting your preparation right. On this count, Dunphy's charges against McCarthy are correct.

What about Dunphy's claims that McCarthy lacked the experience and man-management skills to handle someone of Keane's stature and the resulting conflict that developed on Saipan? McCarthy, to his credit, throughout the events, does not claim infallibility. On discovering that his captain wants to go home, and attempting to digest the depth of shock, he says in his memoir:

> I have to be honest, I do not know what to do for the best here. I understand the enormity of the issue at hand but I am not trained to deal with it. I have never been through this sort of crisis before, no manager has. How could any football coach prepare for the day the best midfielder in the world tells you he wants to quit the Irish team on the eve of the World Cup finals.

Fundamentally, McCarthy is right. There is no coaching manual for reliably dealing with extraordinary situations like this. They are the kind of pressure situations that occur so rarely that when they do happen, their intensity easily exceeds your normal abilities for coping. McCarthy was left in an intolerable mess, with his captain repeatedly changing his mind about whether or not he wanted to play any part in the World Cup. Keane was certainly guilty of a prima donna moment, expecting that McCarthy and the rest of his playing colleagues would wait for him to finally make up his mind on a matter of such urgency. This is an obvious weakness in Keane's position that Dunphy tries to conceal, tamely offering the argument in his *Ireland on Sunday* column that McCarthy might have 'cut Keane some slack if, for no other reason, than to honour this player's incredible contribution to Ireland's cause.'

If anyone needed to be cut some slack, it was McCarthy. Once Keane made it clear that he was departing, he was faced with managing, in a very short period of time, a contingency for which no manager could possibly have planned. McCarthy did make some mistakes, but understandably so. We cannot apply the benefit of hindsight from a position of leisurely analysis. To fully appreciate the decisions available to McCarthy, you would have to think from within the maelstrom, not on the fringes where the right options may seem obvious. For example, McCarthy arguably acted rashly in immediately phoning Colin Healy after Keane had first said he was leaving. It would have been wiser to wait longer and trust that Keane could be persuaded to come around. This is just what happened. Keane did turn, but McCarthy's subsequent revelation that he had already contacted Healy as a replacement sent Keane over the edge again, proclaiming that he was leaving once more. McCarthy was in a classic 'fog of war' situation where the complexity of the challenge before him overcame his ability to step back and coolly assess the available options. Yet, to counteract the sense of helplessness, he felt he had to do something, and so McCarthy rang Healy, being the only option that made him believe he was at least tackling the crisis head-on. Sometimes, the hardest thing is to do nothing and just wait. McCarthy did not do so but, as I have argued, he can hardly be criticised for this. Dunphy, in his hurry to apportion blame, fails to think from McCarthy's perspective and presents a one-sided view of the affair.

It is cases like these for which the phrase 'armchair critic' was invented; if you are not in the situation, then you do not understand it fully. Dunphy, in blaming McCarthy alone for the outcome of events in Saipan, exhibits a thorough inability to sympathise with the plight of managers. This is a trait that Dunphy has always shown, even back in his Millwall days when he failed to grasp the difficulties faced by his under-fire manager, Benny Fenton. In this sense, Dunphy remains 'the selfish footballer', a point of view that routinely finds its way into his football analysis. Why is this? The obvious reason is that Dunphy has never managed a club. Although he did manage London University in the British Universities Sports Federation tournament, during his last season at Reading, this could not be considered to be a high enough level to count as relevant experience.

More questionable yet is Dunphy's claim that McCarthy deliberately sought to provoke Keane by bringing a transcript of his first newspaper interview to that fateful meeting. This is a difficult theory to swallow. McCarthy was, at this stage, entitled to be exasperated by his captain's behaviour. Safe in the belief that the conflict was over and that Keane would play in the World Cup, he was outraged to find Keane dredging the whole unsavoury affair up again, and this time in public. Dunphy, unconvincingly and with no little amount of understatement, argued in his *Ireland on Sunday* column on 26 May 2002 that Keane had merely 'fulfilled a previous commitment to talk to *The Irish Times*', and that 'there was nothing unpleasant or inflammatory in the article'. This was a triumph of hope over reality. Patently it was an incendiary article and intended to be so.

McCarthy could do little else but bring a copy of the interview to the meeting and ask for Keane's opinion in order to understand if matters were settled or not. Keane had spoken dismissively of his colleagues in the interviews by insinuating that they accepted low standards, so why not talk openly to them now in a team meeting?

If Keane truly wanted to remain and play for Ireland, then he would not have given these controversial interviews. Instead, in a monumental have your cake and eat it too moment, he sought to rubbish his manager and fellow players and then line up next to them a week later against Cameroon without batting an eyelid. He knew this could never happen, and in his condemnatory interviews, he was already pushing himself towards the exit-door in an act of concealed self-destruction. Keane was bitter, and, if form taught us anything, it was that he was hardly known for going down quietly. Rather than settle for the calm that had been restored, Keane preferred to talk to the press and have his pound of flesh. The price of that was an early flight home.

Both Keane and McCarthy were culpable in bringing about the unfortunate end that saw Keane play no part in the 2002 World Cup. To claim that one party alone should shoulder the blame, as Dunphy has done, is to succumb to bias.

After Keane had gone home, the sting in the tail for Dunphy was that Ireland performed admirably well without their missing captain. At the first-round stage they qualified from a difficult group that included Germany and Cameroon, and in a close encounter, they were unlucky to lose to a talented Spanish side in the second round, going down via a penalty shoot-out.

The next step for Ireland was qualification for the 2004 European Championship, with McCarthy remaining at the helm. However, after a poor start, with Ireland losing their opening two games, McCarthy resigned as manager in November 2002. He had reportedly suffered five months of hell since the trying times on Saipan, with constant calls for the recall of Keane to the international panel. For Dunphy, this was not a time for pity, but simply the beginning of the return of Keane now that the obstacle of McCarthy was out of the way. Subsequently, Brian Kerr replaced McCarthy and persuaded Keane to make a brief comeback to international football in April 2004, with the player making a further nine appearances before retiring in 2006 in order to prolong his club career.

Although Dunphy has on occasion noted with approval the work McCarthy performed at Wolverhampton Wanderers while managing them from 2006 to 2012, he has remained unswerving in his damning appraisal of McCarthy's role as Ireland manager. He could not bring himself to admit any positives about him and yet there were many. McCarthy blooded numerous young players at a time in Irish football when new options were badly needed. Charlton before him had been slow to bring through new talent, but McCarthy bravely and successfully introduced new players to international football, such as Shay Given, Ian Harte, Gary Breen, David Connolly and Kenny Cunningham. Furthermore, he surprised many by favouring the kind of attractive passing game that was conspicuously absent from the Charlton era – something Dunphy had repeatedly called for. Another relevant statistic is that, in terms of results, McCarthy has the better record of the two managers, and although he qualified only for one major tournament, the 2002 World Cup, he came very close to leading Ireland into the 1998 World Cup and the 2000 European Championship, losing, respectively, to Belgium and Turkey in play-off matches.

Dunphy, however, was blind to these facts and forever remained unfairly opposed to McCarthy's tenure. He was never able to shake off the Charlton connection and so McCarthy would always be guilty by association. In truth, McCarthy was very much his own man and easily rebutted the argument that he was little more than Charlton Mark II. It is a common theme in Dunphy's analysis that his ability to reason is sometimes overshadowed by his likes and dislikes. His views on McCarthy as a manager fit this description and so must be seriously doubted.

Chapter 5

Where 'driven bastards' dare: Dunphy and Roy Keane

Since the sensational events of the 2002 World Cup in Japan and South Korea, when Roy Keane, the Republic of Ireland captain, was sent home before the tournament began, Eamon Dunphy has said much that has come to define him as a journalist. No other figure in the sport of football has invoked such a passionate response and such extreme views from Dunphy. Since 2002 his opinions on Keane have ranged from practical hero-worship during Saipan and later when Keane was released from Manchester United, to a new stance in the last five years that has sought to characterise Keane, the manager, as an unhinged maverick chronically unsuited to the rigours of football management. Dunphy has changed tack in his attitudes to Keane so radically that it will be the work of this chapter to trace this path and, in the process, to try to understand how and why this has happened.

First, we look at Dunphy's views on Keane during the events of Saipan in 2002, and his later reaction in 2005 to the player's unhappy departure from Manchester United, situations upon which Dunphy staked his journalistic credibility, so intense was his support for this controversial footballer. Finally, we examine Dunphy's critical views on Keane which began to form in 2006 when the former player began his management career with Sunderland.

Though Saipan principally concerned a falling-out between Roy Keane and Mick McCarthy, Eamon Dunphy was undoubtedly the next most important participant in a fractious incident that saw Ireland send home their captain and most important player on the eve of a World Cup. As soon as the news first broke on 21 May 2002 that Keane would play no part in the Irish campaign because of his sensational confrontation with McCarthy in a prickly team meeting, Dunphy lost no time in assuming the mantle of Keane's spokesman, defender and even advisor. With his popular radio show *The Last Word* essentially becoming operational headquarters for the Keane cause, Dunphy quickly became inextricably identified with the destiny of Ireland's beleaguered captain. His role in Saipan is exceptional when we consider that Keane actually consulted Dunphy on numerous occasions throughout the crisis. In one instance, Dunphy even stated that he had been talking with Keane only twenty minutes before going on-air with his radio show.

Like a man possessed, he fought Keane's corner whatever the cost and no matter what lengths he was compelled to go to. During this emotionally charged period, his irascible presence was everywhere, with Dunphy in great demand from numerous media outlets. He clashed with John Bowman, the chair of *Questions & Answers* one of the major Irish current affairs programmes of the time, who dared question the wisdom of Keane's extreme actions. He found himself in an early morning spat with Ray Stubbs, the one-time presenter of BBC's

Football Focus, who suggested that Dunphy's assignment as ghostwriter of Keane's autobiography compromised his objectivity. He even made an appearance on BBC's *Newsnight* in an interview with Jeremy Paxman and was scheduled to appear on *Breakfast with Frost*, until Dunphy's late cancellation left David Frost without his guest. He even managed to fall out with his life-long friend, John Giles, who argued that McCarthy was right to send Keane home from the World Cup.

Looking back on those events now, it is remarkable to note how partisan Dunphy was in Keane's cause and just how vexed he became by the incident. In a series of caustic articles throughout May and June of that year printed in *Ireland on Sunday*, Dunphy fêted Keane the hero and lambasted what he termed 'official Ireland'. For Dunphy, the alignment of allegiances behind McCarthy or Keane disclosed an important truth about the state of Irish society. It represented a line that separated greatness from mediocrity. If you did not wholeheartedly follow Keane, then you were mired in mere commonness, a member of the same stultifying mass that caused, Dunphy argues, no less than Samuel Beckett and James Joyce to flee Ireland and pursue greatness in some distant, but appreciative, place of exile. For Dunphy, this was the patriotic choice facing the Irish people, and Keane in his determined challenge to the FAI was the catalyst for this rending in two of Irish society. Keane, in Dunphy's thinking, was the initiating force precisely because of his heroic stance. He alone was strong enough, brave enough and of sufficient nobility of character to rail against the status quo, even if it meant taking the ultimate step: departing the World Cup in a sacrificial act of shame so that the Irish people could glimpse the festering reality beneath 'official Ireland'.

Dunphy was intrigued by Keane's delicious obstinacy, arguing that the Cork man 'glowed with high purpose'. Here was a true man taking a stand against ordinariness wherever it may appear in Irish life. In Dunphy's hands, Keane was almost a purifying force, with his 'unflinching gaze' come to arrest our slide into drab, second-rate existence and provide ablution for those already trapped in the clutches of humdrum Ireland. In what must be the peak of Dunphy's eulogising, he paints an image of Keane that casts him in the light of a lonely but inspirational figure, drenched in language that conjures up all the pathos of some timeless mythological hero of almost Homeric proportions. 'Isolated now, he stands more magnificent than ever before. He belongs with the greats of world sport, in the pantheon alongside Ali, Woods, Schumacher, Aidan O'Brien and Michael Kinane.' With such unabashedly epic language, Dunphy is a mere figleaf away from outrightly branding Keane as something of a modern-day William Wallace, a depiction that Ray Ryan, writing in *The Guardian*, has dubbed Keane's 'final ascension into a lonely realm of greatness'.

While such an account makes for undeniably entertaining reading, it leaves the reader with the unmistakable feeling that Keane and the import of events surrounding Saipan are being significantly exaggerated. Dunphy has gone too far. His overblown language is inappropriate; we are talking about a footballer after all. Infusing the Keane story with all the drama of a Greek tragedy was never going to be conducive to maintaining a healthy perspective. It is certainly clear that Keane had an arguable case and deserved to have his actions interpreted in a positive light. He departed as a protest against years of FAI neglect, and Dunphy was correct to stand in Keane's corner and try to articulate the player's motives to the

Irish people. However, to do so with such exceptionally emotive language and wide-ranging, speculative claims was making a gift of ammunition to his willing critics.

Though Dunphy certainly endured a difficult month following Keane's departure from Saipan, he was, nonetheless, occupying old and familiar territory: that of hate-figure, being reviled by some in the media and by members of the public for being so unpatriotic at a time when devotion to the national team was regarded as a basic index of being Irish. It was Italia '90 all over again, practically a case of déjà vu for Dunphy, with the chronically out-of-step football critic feeling the backlash from his proud pronouncement that he preferred Ireland to lose rather than see them succeed without their courageous captain. To prove his point, and with no little hint of the provocateur's impishness, Dunphy sported a fetching Cameroon-coloured tie when Ireland met the West African nation in their opening game of the World Cup and professed himself to be an ardent Cameroon supporter for the next ninety minutes of football. Following this incident and his subsequent stark admission that he also hoped Ireland would lose against Germany in their second match, the complaints rained down on RTÉ, with the broadcaster receiving a record 3,000 calls from irate viewers. The demand was uniformly for Dunphy to be dismissed and the RTÉ hierarchy found themselves in an awkward dilemma. Should they remove Dunphy from World Cup coverage and risk a serious drop in ratings or distance themselves from the out-of-favour analyst?

In the end, Dunphy made the decision for RTÉ, showing up the worse for the wear, after a heavy night of drinking, for coverage of the first round game between Russia and Japan in early June. He visibly slurred his words and appeared to be unfit to carry out his work.

He was duly suspended, providing RTÉ with a convenient solution to a seemingly intractable situation. With
Dunphy at perhaps his lowest ebb, the vultures circled.
Writing in the *Irish Independent*, Jerome Reilly and Liam
Collins blamed the journalist for poisoning Keane with
his advice and imagined him holed up in Lillies Bordello
– a favourite Dublin nightclub of Dunphy's – on a series
of guilty drinking sprees that effectively amounted to an
inability to soberly bear the truth that the Irish nation was
firmly behind McCarthy and the Irish team. This is a fan-
ciful notion from two writers with their own axe to grind.
It is clear that Dunphy has never lacked courage and is no
stranger to alarming dips in public popularity. His isolated
stance took its toll on him, but that, in itself, is no admission of defeat. As for the idea that Dunphy nefariously
swayed Keane and fatally damaged Ireland's chances of
World Cup success, we need only remind ourselves that
Keane has always shown himself to be perfectly capable
of making up his own mind and would not be easily influenced by anyone, even if he did consult Dunphy.

As regards Dunphy's act of incitement, supporting
Cameroon rather than cheering on Ireland minus Keane,
he reasoned that by refusing to follow Ireland, he was
simultaneously refusing to legitimise the years of neglect
propagated by the FAI. It was a protest designed to highlight the shambles that had prompted Keane to walk away
from the greatest football tournament in the world. In
characteristic fashion, Dunphy chose to elucidate the
rationale behind his obdurate position by quoting what
E.M. Forster wrote in *Two Cheers for Democracy*. 'In the spirit
of E.M. Forster, I supported Cameroon yesterday ... "If
I had to choose between betraying my country or betraying my friend, I hope I should have the guts to betray my
country." ' For Dunphy, behind the treasonous views, the

words of Forster and the strategically multi-coloured ties was a simple logic: 'The sooner we lose Mick and get Roy Keane back – and a functioning administration in FAI headquarters at Merrion Square – the better. To that end I hoped Ireland would do badly at these World Cups.'

Although it may seem easy to ignore Dunphy's analysis of Saipan, dominated as it was by passionate and, at times, by bombastic invective, we need to look at the wider context to understand just why Dunphy became so infuriated in the summer of 2002. His primary aim was not to support Keane, but rather to expose the rot in Irish football that he was so tired of tolerating: the 'administrative fools' in residence at 80 Merrion Square, the FAI's Dublin headquarters, who had been determinedly keeping Irish soccer in the doldrums for as long as Dunphy could remember. And that is quite a long time. As Dunphy revealed in his *Sunday Independent* column in June 1988, just before the Irish team flew to Germany for the European Championships, the sub-par organisation and glaring ineptitude of the FAI was at play as far back as 1965 when Dunphy earned his first cap for the Republic of Ireland. The Irish were set to play against Spain in a play-off to decide who would go to the following summer's 1966 World Cup in England. Dunphy recounts his disgust at how, from the very start, the FAI's small-mindedness hampered the team's chances. The game was initially scheduled by FIFA to be played at Highbury, Arsenal's old ground, thus handing Ireland's mainly English-based players an important advantage over the Spanish. However, the Spanish Football Association approached the FAI with a tempting proposal: play the match in Paris and the FAI could retain the entire gate receipts, income that normally would have been shared between the two associations. The FAI agreed and, as

Dunphy puts it 'traded the prospect of glory for the few bob.' The net effect was that the Irish players now had to face a fiercely partisan crowd of 30,000 Spaniards packed into the Parc des Princes in Paris. Dunphy describes the pre-match scene:

> As we sat nervously in the dressing room listening to [Johnny] Carey's [Ireland's manager from 1955 to 1967] team-talk, the sound of 30,000 Spaniards baying outside was a reminder of the overweight our Merrion Square masters had forced us to carry.

The 1-0 victory for Spain saw them qualify ahead of Ireland for the 1966 World Cup. According to Dunphy – in passages that will strike a chord with anyone who has sympathies for Keane's defiant stance against serial FAI disorganisation – 'Paris was a typical adventure – a week in the life of an Irish soccer team that travelled hopefully without any real conviction.' Dunphy elaborates, claiming that a party atmosphere, rather than any serious will to succeed, abounded amongst the Merrion Square officials and the journalists who accompanied the players on the flight to Paris. The FAI and press contingent had left Dublin an hour before the English-based players joined the plane at London. Dunphy outlines the carnival that unfolded on the plane and continued later that night in Paris:

> The flight this band of sporting mercenaries joined at London Airport had set off from Dublin an hour before. The FAI officials and Irish journalists on board were well into the booze by the time we took our seats. The atmosphere resembled that of a lounge-bar half-an-hour before closing

time. Paris was not to be so much a crucial international football match as an inebriated junket,
in that officials, journalists and players had a ball
while the fans at home waited anxiously for the
scoreline. That Monday night, forty forbidden
pleasures of Paris nightlife. My memory of that
first trip is of the Folies, the smell of Gauloises
and the sight of gross Irish officials getting drunk
before 10 o'clock at night.

It is against this background of long-term FAI neglect
that we need to interpret Dunphy's excessive response
to the events of Saipan. By the time Roy Keane publicly
highlighted important deficiencies in the FAI support
structure in 2002, Dunphy had already witnessed nearly
forty years of the same infuriating blundering. Dunphy
erupted with such venom during Saipan because he was
a man at the end of his tether, for whom this last cack-
handed attempt at organising a World Cup campaign was
a step too far. In an interview with Michael Walker that
appeared in *The Irish Times* in October 2007, Dunphy
offered this very explanation for his impassioned outbursts in the days when the Saipan issue was still raw. Of
his controversial appearances on RTÉ during this time,
he said:

> What I do on TV has to be seen against this
> backdrop – soccer people of my generation, like
> [Johnny] Giles, we've lived with the FAI's inepti-
> tude all our lives. As players, as fans, as journalists,
> mistake after mistake after mistake. Therefore
> you are forced into a position where you appear
> to be cynical, appear to be just controversial, say-
> ing the unsayable.

After the initial furore of Saipan had diminished somewhat, with Ireland performing surprisingly well in the World Cup without their captain, the Keane-Dunphy axis turned to print to argue their case against the Irish football establishment. *Keane: The Autobiography* was published in the summer of 2002, instantly becoming a bestseller and one of the most talked about football books in decades. Old wounds and fracture points were reopened for extended examination by the beleaguered comrades-in-arms, with Keane providing the ammunition and Dunphy the pen. Together they would write the alternative history of modern Irish football, a brilliant revisionist handbook that sought to offer the true perspective on the major talking points in Irish football.

Depending on your point of view, Dunphy as ghostwriter was the best or worst option for Keane. No one had been closer to Keane at this time and no one was more sympathetic to the Keane corner than Dunphy. Yet, equally, Dunphy's partiality – sharing Keane's agenda note for note – was under question. What book would he write? The one Keane wanted him to write or the book that would force this footballer to question and analyse himself and find some level of insight beyond the mere settling of scores?

Such was the coincidence of convictions between these two men that the latter outcome was always unlikely to win the day and, instead, for the most part we get an extended diatribe against mutually despised enemies, including, but not limited to, Jack Charlton, Mick McCarthy, the FAI and various overpaid, celebrity-bloated Premiership footballers and, of course, the not-to-be-overlooked, jingoistic masses who have supported and helped to legitimise the above figures over many years. Although such an account inevitably becomes one-sided to a degree, the shared anger and bitterness that Keane and Dunphy express proves to be a powerful force for delivering some home truths. With the exception of the hazily defined masses and with some qualifications attached to his views of McCarthy, the other causes of Keane's ire are legitimate targets and receive an overdue slating in his autobiography.

An important note should be added, however. As compelling as the book is, making it an outing for Keane and Dunphy to set things right ensures that it is perhaps less interesting than it could have been and represents, to some extent, a missed opportunity to challenge and draw Keane out of himself more. In its unrelenting determination to even the score on so many issues, it is sometimes more reaction than thoughtful account. Although this is what lends the book its raw power, it equally ensures that it becomes more a work of self-justification than reflection. Many critics have taken up the point, arguing that Dunphy was simply too close to Keane to provide anything more than a marathon session of axe-grinding across three-hundred-odd pages of print. Ian Ridley, writing in *The Observer* in August 2002, has suggested that Keane and Dunphy deserved each other and, in their shared bias, had produced an engrossing but seriously unbalanced work of football writing. He writes:

> Keane has found a kindred spirit in Dunphy, essential for any good partnership on a book. Both have a rage, fuelled in the past by alcohol as petrol on an already burning fire, which has led on occasion to bad decisions. Both are honest, outspoken men but it is an honesty born not of clarity, rather distorting resentment.

The point is well made and has merit, but only to a degree. There is much clarity to Keane and Dunphy's views, even though they may couch their delivery in tones of deep animosity. The book's passages on Saipan and the Jack Charlton years say plenty that is unquestionably true. Both Charlton and McCarthy were repeatedly guilty of failing to confront the FAI on the shambolic set-up that let down so many Irish players and clearly did nothing to help the team's chances on the pitch. Yes, the accounts provided are not entirely objective – Keane by giving two public interviews on private team matters to Paul Kimmage and Tom Humphries played his own part in forcing the Saipan issue to end as it did – but this hardly robs them of all value.

Considering the proximity of Keane and Dunphy, and Dunphy's obvious personal agenda, it must be asked to what extent does this ghostwriter overstep the mark and become effectively a co-writer? In this respect, many commentators have criticised Dunphy for failing to observe the boundaries of his role as ghostwriter, arguing that his insistent voice can be discerned throughout its pages. Conor O'Callaghan has suggested that whole paragraphs are heavily inflected with Dunphy's own preoccupations, an experience he likens to 'being hectored through frosted glass', and, he concludes, 'you hope it's a meeting of minds, if only to suppress the suspicion that our great warrior has become the ventriloquist's wooden dummy mouthing someone else's wooden lines.' Making a similar point, Joyce Woolridge writing in *When Saturday Comes*, and referring to Dunphy as 'Keane's Boswell', writes that 'a ghost stalks the pages of Roy Keane's autobiography: the unquiet spirit of professional Irish malcontent, Eamon Dunphy' and she concludes that Dunphy leaves a far greater mark on the text than is appropriate for a ghostwriter. In a process that could be described as 'literary hijacking', Woolridge suggests that Dunphy's vaunted 'good pro' is inelegantly crowbarred into the text wherever possible before being awkwardly dressed up in Keane's ill-fitting clothing. She argues that Dunphy's unhealthy fascination with the Cork ınan stems from his belief that Keane is the ultimate incarnation of the 'good pro', a figure who, for Dunphy, stands for everything that is virtuous in sport.

If we look to examples, we can see this process occurring throughout Keane's book. The 'good pro' is the inspiration for Dunphy's football memoir *Only a Game?*, which was also dedicated to the self-same figure. Throughout *Only a Game?* we are treated to a constant refrain that intimates how professional football separates the men from the boys, where only the toughest minds and spirits can survive what is essentially a remorseless world of endeavour. This very same theme repetitively winds its way into Keane's autobiography like a displaced, restless motif struggling to find definitive expression. Although it can be partly explained by a meeting of minds between writer and ghost, the remarkable frequency and insistence of the message across the book shows us that Dunphy, at strategic junctures, surely relished applying considerable pressure to Keane's raw material.

So with Dunphy's willing assistance, we are presented with Keane, the battle-hardened warrior who lives steadfastly at a dizzying, even punishing, level of intensity unknown to lesser mortals. Where other players are merely highly motivated, Keane everywhere exudes double-strength-passion, with a generous side order of steely-eyed determination to round it off. This is gale-force potency. Time and again, the art of football is described in fanatical, harsh tones where nothing less than a painful, superhuman effort is required to survive as a professional in what is a man's world dominated by 'bullshit' (mentioned 19 times) and 'bollockings' (ten times), according to reviewer Ray Ryan's count. Describing footballers as 'men-at-work' and himself as a 'driven bastard', Keane says of football that it is 'savage, cruel, relentlessly punishing', 'hard, sometimes dangerous' and 'invariably exacting' where, unsurprisingly, considering the foregoing, 'there are no free lunches.' This is an all-or-nothing world where 'Family life comes second. Social life is non-existent' and 'Football is all-consuming'. Furthermore, one must live perpetually in a paranoid state of combative tautness where the ever-present dangers of complacency must be warded off by reminding yourself that you dare not 'look back ... or forward, beyond the ninety minutes ahead of you. Start thinking about records and for sure you'll fail to concentrate on the task at hand. History is for anoraks.' Even the closest family and friends can become a function of determination of this magnitude when you are Roy Keane. 'Without my family and friends', he informs us, 'I wouldn't be able to enjoy what I'm lucky enough to have ... It makes it easier to go to war, which is what I do for a living.' This is such a melodramatic, and unnecessarily self-lacerating account of being a professional footballer that Matt Dickinson has been moved to characterise it in *The Times* as the 'exhausting job of being Roy Keane'.

Although expressed in torturous tones, there is a palpable sense of submerged pleasure behind these words of strain and it has all the hallmarks of Dunphy's over-egging of the material. Keane is going to play the role of the 'good pro', whether he fully realises it or not. In these moments, we can imagine Dunphy pausing and luxuriating in the brutal world that Keane struggles through so gallantly, a world that resembles more a tour-of-duty than an account of professional sport. This is such a grim, spartan vision of the game that one could be forgiven for believing that the only motivation for becoming a professional footballer springs from some form of acute and untreated masochistic urge. The excess of expression here is directly proportionate to Dunphy's nostalgia, for, when we read these passages, we are back in 1973 in the forbidding surroundings of The Den, struggling with Dunphy through another ninety minutes of character-defining hard graft. We are in the world of *Only a Game?* where only truly 'driven bastards' succeed.

What can we make of all this pain and suffering? The beautiful game was not supposed to be this bleak. Is there no room for the happiness and the freedom of the game? Surely there is, but to see it, we need to shake off the considerable shadow Dunphy and Keane evoke. It is fairly obvious that there have always been, and still are, many examples of consummate professionals in the game, yet they have not seen the need to create the kerfuffle that Keane has in his book. Consider Paolo Maldini and Zinedine Zidane, players who were undoubtedly model professionals, yet chose to wear their credentials lightly. Other current players of note, such as Ryan Giggs, Lionel Messi, Xavi Hernández and Wesley Sneijder, all similarly and quietly express the qualities that are declared from the rooftops in Keane's book. In fact, the account offered in *Keane* would gladly have us believe that he, the lone-warrior, single-handedly invented, registered the patent, and wrote the handbook – *Professionalism for Dummies* – on über-professionalism, before dispensing it with withering indifference to those who dare to strive towards his perfect level of achievement. Where Dunphy might have been a restraining influence on Keane, winnowing out these excesses, instead, the button is jammed even harder with Dunphy becoming a willing conduit for another man's delusions.

Although it is abundantly clear that Dunphy's notions of professionalism heavily inflect the text and over determine Keane in the process, what is less obvious is the degree to which Dunphy applies the devices of artistic licence in rendering Keane's thoughts in print? The issue specifically arose in relation to the infamous passages of the book concerning Keane's horrendous, career-ending, tackle on the former Manchester City midfielder Alf-Inge Haaland. In the offending section (now removed after an FA inquiry into Keane's comments), Keane appeared to transparently evince a premeditated desire to injure Haaland out of revenge for an earlier confrontation with the Norwegian player that had led to Keane rupturing his cruciate ligament:

> We had a Saturday game away to Leeds and I was in no shape at all. I had the nightmare I deserved. Five minutes from time, I lunged at him [Haaland] in desperation. I knew it would mean a booking but fuck it. As I slid in, my studs caught in the turf and I heard my cruciate ligament snap ... Some years on, I still haven't forgotten him. Now it is Manchester City at home, his new club fighting relegation. I waited until five minutes from the end. I fucking hit him hard. I think the ball was there. 'Take that you c***.' I didn't even wait for the ref to show the red card. I turned and walked towards the dressing room.

Subsequent to this passage being printed, in an interview with *Observer Sport Monthly*, Keane seemed to compound the suggestion that he had acted with malice afore-thought in his encounter with Haaland. When he was asked whether or not he regretted the incident, he stated: 'I had no remorse. My attitude was, fuck him. What goes around, comes around. He got his just rewards. He fucked me over and my attitude is an eye for an eye.'

After the threat of legal action and an FA ban loomed for Keane, Dunphy went public to declare Keane's inno-cence in the whole matter, protesting: 'I am as much responsible as the writer ... There is artistic licence.' Keane's legal team had even prepared a defence that rested on the notion that Dunphy had effectively misquoted Keane on the Haaland passage, so great, apparently, was the extent to which he took licence with the material. Some com-mentators seized the opportunity to question Dunphy's handling of the situation, arguing that his admission of taking artistic licence was 'reprehensible'. Ian Ridley, writ-ing in *The Observer*, suggested that Dunphy had exceeded the limited remit of a ghostwriter: 'The skill of the ghost is in probing the subject, aiding his memory, structuring the work. Not, however, to embellish the work.'

This view, I suggest, is fantasy, a fiction maintained by writers who wish to persuade themselves that a ghostwriter can wade into the life of a footballer with-out leaving any significant imprint in their wake. The act of ghosting an autobiography, while not giving a licence to become co-writer, of necessity, involves an extensive re-imagining and re-casting by the ghost of the often-colourless material they are presented with by the subject footballer. If there is a price to pay for this arrangement, namely some excessive leeway with the chosen language, then it is worth it. The alternative is autobiographies written by footballers: creations so short of imaginative literary expression that they can often descend into being a tedious list of things that happened. Worse still, without the creative embellishment of the ghostwriter, a footballer's account, although honest and direct, can be little more than a banal, blow-by-blow description of events. Observe Geoff Hurst's version of England's 1966 World Cup triumph, highlighted by Simon Kuper in his article 'Sporting Fictions' as an apt example: 'And then we won the World Cup final. I was lucky enough to score the winning goal, so it was a great day all round.'

Whether or not Dunphy's taking of artistic licence led to the Haaland passage appearing in its original controversial guise we shall probably never know for certain, but to suggest that he should have restricted himself to simply lending structure to Keane's thoughts is disingenuous. Without Dunphy's substantial contribution, *Keane*, though flawed, would not have been the engrossing book that it is.

In the years after *Keane* was printed, Dunphy's campaigning for Keane went into something of a lull. Only an appearance in October 2003 by the player on Dunphy's short-lived Friday night programme on TV3, *The Dunphy Show*, would break the pattern: an event that was more of a tribute show to Keane than anything resembling a proper interview. The calm, however, would only be an *interregnum*, a chance to catch one's breath before the next round in the battle against mediocrity began. The occasion was 2005 when Keane was sensationally sacked by Manchester United for giving a highly critical interview to Manchester United Television (MUTV), an interview judged nasty enough to be shelved by Alex Ferguson before going on air. Keane, the inspirational captain of Manchester United, it turned out, was dispensable, a fact made brutally clear by Ferguson's decisive and unsentimental action. Keane's interview showed a frustrated man assuming unheard of powers within a squad, deigning to publicly criticise his fellow players, including a number of his younger colleagues for failing to live up to his own exacting standards. There was only one realistic option for Ferguson and he took it. Keane was released, and Dunphy, as expected, raged at this last and most grievous injustice against the player.

The ensuing debate on RTÉ Sport, including the usual panellists, John Giles, Liam Brady and Dunphy, provided perhaps Dunphy's most extreme and at times outrageous outburst against the forces that sought to diminish Keane's name and achievements. Never before had he been so uncompromising in his support for a player. The catalyst for Dunphy's eruption was Liam Brady's suggestion that Keane had behaved in a 'mercenary' manner by publicly agitating for a new contract at Old Trafford through the medium of a few select journalists. Brady concluded that Keane's implosion on MUTV arose from the obvious frustration that Manchester United had failed to respond to his overtures and would not be offering him a new deal.

Dunphy's response, which made for gripping viewing, was astonishingly impassioned and at times scattered, even by his own occasionally immoderate standards, but it was not without merit if we can extract the substance from the subjectivity. Certainly, it was a rant, but that doesn't mean that some truths were not tucked away in the midst of the red mist.

In his fury, with all the darkest memories of Saipan resurfacing, Dunphy first dismissed Niall Quinn – someone he has never forgiven for failing to support Keane in Saipan – as a 'creep', an 'idiot' and a 'Mother Teresa figure', who, unlike Keane, lacked credibility because his chief concern in life was exhibiting his charity work to anyone who would listen. In contrast, he cast Keane as a genuine man, 'who doesn't showboat like Niall Quinn. This is a man who actually goes and sees sick children in hospitals'. He said that Keane was 'a gentleman, a rebel, and a class-act'.

Although he was reprimanded by O'Herlihy for disparaging Quinn's good name, Dunphy was essentially right about Quinn: a contrived personality who has always extracted maximum cachet from a carefully managed nice-guy persona that you have no choice but to admire. No better example was the poisoned olive branch he extended to Keane in the months after the events of Saipan. Quinn and Keane had not spoken since the previous May, after the former had publicly supported Mick McCarthy at a press conference in Saipan, called to announce Roy Keane's departure from the World Cup. The aggravating incident occurred in the autumn of 2002 in an encounter between Manchester United and Sunderland when he presented his hand in peace just after Keane had been sent off. Quinn, a substitute, was readying himself to enter the action for Sunderland as Keane walked past him on the way to the dressing room. Predictably, Keane told him where to go and Quinn was left looking – as planned – like the jilted martyr who had been grievously spurned for no greater a sin than trying to make amends.

Matters, however, reached a climax when O'Herlihy thought it would be helpful to introduce Rod Liddle's words into the debate, the *Sunday Times* journalist who had written the previous Sunday that Keane did not deserve our pity because he was little more than a thug. Dunphy was beside himself with indignation and responded furiously. He dramatically removed his microphone in what looked like a prelude to walking off the set, before

suggesting to O'Herlihy: 'If you are going to start quoting gutter journalists calling Roy Keane a thug, you can
do it on your own.' He then referred to Liddle as the 'guy
who ran away and left his wife for a young one', in contrast to Keane, whom he described as a 'family man with
five children who was a credit to his country'. Although
Liddle's knee-jerk reaction journalism is probably most at
home in the gutter and O'Herlihy was well off the mark
in quoting him, this cannot hide the fact that Dunphy has
a lot of work to do to persuade us that such tangential
insults are at all relevant to the issues at hand.

The only way to make sense of it is to reason that, for
Dunphy, personal qualities count for everything. His argument appears to be that if you possess true greatness, you
earn the right to be more controversial and outspoken,
while if you are lacking in character, as he thinks Liddle
is, you consequently lack any foundation upon which to
offer sweeping statements. This is, in fact, the defence
that Dunphy put forward for Keane's ill-judged comments on MUTV. Dunphy claimed that Keane's twelve
years of unrivalled service to Manchester United entitled
him to an opinion, no matter how extreme it was. Since,
through more than a decade of self-sacrifice, Keane had
built up sufficient credit to legitimately deliver an unsparing assessment of his United colleagues. His greatness
gave him the liberty to speak.

Although an unusual notion, there is some truth in
Dunphy's idea given that Keane, in alliance with Alex
Ferguson, worked harder than any other player in order
to ensure that Manchester United's high standards were
met season after season. Moreover, even though he,
like many others, gained enormous wealth, at no point
did he succumb to the crassness that so many Premier
League players became consumed by, once large wages

were standard in the late 1990s. He remained refreshingly normal and down-to-earth, the way he had been when he first entered the game. He had mostly kept to himself and avoided making any controversial statements. Keane did his work on the pitch and that was generally more than enough. On a moral level it might be possible to agree and sympathise with Dunphy's opinion, however, in the day-to-day world of running football clubs, Keane's comments could not be tolerated and Ferguson simply had to pull the plug on his Manchester United career. No player, no matter how important, can assume the right to publicly undermine his manager's authority by criticising his fellow players. Clubs cannot function in this way. Obviously, Keane knew the game was up and decided that, having little to lose, he would call a spade a spade one last time. He was in the dying dinosaur category: large, dangerous and on the way out.

It is no surprise that Dunphy should have supported Keane's controversial outburst, no matter how desperate the cause may have seemed. Central to Dunphy's views on football is a player-centric perspective that invariably leads him to back the player in any dispute he may have with the various levels of the football hierarchy. For Dunphy, there is a line, with the honest and virtuous footballer on one side and the vice-ridden forces of the football establishment on the other, whether they be managers, club directors, agents or representatives of football associations.

This is a belief clearly expressed in *Only a Game?* where Dunphy spends much of his time struggling to accept, and condemning the rules of a business that hands so much power to non-player elements such as managers, agents and directors. Although the game is played by footballers, it is controlled by another power, a state of affairs with which Dunphy has never been able to reconcile himself. For him, the footballer is the innocent party in the whole complicated business of modern football. He, the player, just wants to play football, if only the powers that be would leave him alone for long enough to do just that. He is the gifted artist who neither understands nor cares for the machinations of business. His sole objective is simple and pure: to live the dream of professional football and give joy to the fans on a Saturday afternoon. Everything else is a distraction.

The pattern emerged again in October 2010 when Dunphy chose to portray Wayne Rooney as the aggrieved party in his unseemly stand-off with Manchester United over contract negotiations; an impasse, which, in the end, appeared to have been more about a wage increase than any genuine concern for his football career. For Dunphy, everyone but the player was to blame, even though it was Rooney who had agitated for the move in the first place, only to change his mind some days later.

It is interesting to note that, although Dunphy stood unquestioningly beside Keane the player through everything, he very rapidly lost patience with Keane once he became a manager. Not nearly as much latitude was extended to Keane now that he had become part of the establishment. He was no longer beyond reproach, moving out, as he did, from beneath the protective shield that Dunphy seems to reserve only for the decent and straightforward professional footballer honestly plying his trade.

The end of Keane's playing career with Celtic in 2006, and the beginning of his management career with Sunderland began a process whereby Keane's hitherto untouchable status started to decline in Dunphy's eyes. Although Dunphy was initially enthusiastic about the idea of Keane taking his talents into the dugout, he would come to view him as a failure as a manager and a figure of fun. On Keane's first season with Sunderland in the 2006/07 Championship season, Dunphy commented on RTÉ Sport's website that the good results Sunderland were achieving did not surprise him at all, considering the innate managerial ability of Keane:

> Keane is doing a marvellous job and I'm not really surprised at how well he's done. I thought he'd be an outstanding manager ... He's always been a very savvy guy with a good sense of humour, great knowledge of the game and shoulders broad enough to cope with almost anything. I think he's got all the qualities to cope with almost anything.

However, in 2008 when Keane's Sunderland began to struggle badly in their second season in the Premier League, Dunphy's tone changed markedly. He highlighted the number of questionable signings Keane had made and the amount of money he had wasted in the process. He also reasoned that Keane had entered management too soon and lacked the experience of learning 'the business of management' in the lower leagues to prepare him for the rigours of the Premier League. He argued that Keane was out of his depth and 'in a fog', and he further believed: 'Everyone gets there at some point in their life, when things get too much for you. You don't know where the levers for the controls are and he's making some really silly decisions.' Given that Keane had resigned from Sunderland in 2008 when the pressure was upon him at the wrong end of the Premier League table and subsequently failed to impress during his troubled 20-month spell as Ipswich Town manager, Dunphy's analysis seems to have merit.

Specifically, Dunphy argued that Keane lacked a detailed knowledge of players by virtue of the fact that he could not have developed a substantial network of scouting connections in the short time since his retirement as a player. This is a valid point when one considers the nature of Keane's signings at Sunderland. The sheer number of former and current Manchester United players he either signed or took on loan betrayed a lack of deep knowledge of the transfer market. On this busy list are players such as Andy Cole, Dwight Yorke, Paul McShane, Danny Higginbotham, Jonny Evans, Phil Bardsley, Danny Simpson, Liam Miller and Kieran Richardson, while other signings such as Stanislav Varga, Ross Wallace and David Connolly came, respectively, from Keane's experiences with Celtic and the Republic of Ireland team.

Keane was relying on what he knew by signing players with whom he was personally acquainted at either club or international level, an approach that is reasonable for a young manager to adopt. The only problem is that Keane knew very little when it came to players. He did not have access to the kind of up-to-date scouting knowledge that more experienced managers possess and, as a result, he signed a disproportionate number of what were effectively Manchester United rejects and nearly-men.

However, when Keane did stretch beyond his previous experience to buy players he had not played with, he displayed questionable judgment both in the money he paid and the kind of player he chose.

Dunphy has highlighted the vast number of players and amounts of money Keane spent as further evidence of his unsuitability for management. In total, he spent approximately £80 million at Sunderland in what George

Caulkin, writing in *The Sunday Times*, has rightly described as a 'scattergun approach to signings', with expensive acquisitions such as Anton Ferdinand (£8m), Michael Chopra (£5m), Craig Gordon (£9m) and Greg Halford (£2.5m), all failing to justify their price tag, while more bizarre signings, such as Rade Prica (£2m), did not even start a game under Keane. With such a record, Dunphy is correct in questioning Keane's judgment and, if we look to some of Keane's own comments about player recruitment, we can see some clues as to why this may be.

In an interview with Tom Humphries of *The Irish Times* in April 2007, Keane spoke of his first season at Sunderland and discussed some of the players he had bought. Keane twice mentions the primary importance of character in his assessment of potential players, but fails to highlight any of the other major qualities needed in a new signing. Was Keane obsessed with character, being excessively focused on finding players who exhibited the requisite levels of moral courage in order to satisfy the Roy Keane personality test? What else could explain signings such as Andy Cole and Dwight Yorke, two players significantly past their best upon arriving at the Stadium of Light. Of Cole, who was loaned out to Burnley after only seven games and released at the end of his first season, Keane specifically noted that the purpose of signing him was that he would be a good character to have around the dressing room. Does this mean that he was not really signed in order to play football, but, rather, just to emanate morale-boosting levels of the right kind of professionalism in the general vicinity of younger upstart players, who were presumably in danger of getting above themselves? As far-fetched as the notion seems, it remains a compelling explanation in the absence of any footballing justification being readily available,

Dunphy signs his autograph for young Millwall fans c. 1970. His eight seasons at Millwall, during which he made 303 first team appearances, constituted the most important part of his career as a professional footballer. All of his 23 international caps for Ireland came during this period. (Hulton Archive/Getty Images)

Jack Charlton overseeing his Republic of Ireland team in 1989 and looking every bit like the traditional 'Gaffer'. Charlton was an old school British manager, versed in a physical and pragmatic style of play, inherited from both Alf Ramsey, his World Cup winning manager of 1966, and the former Football Association (FA) coaching director Charles Hughes, under whom Charlton studied. (Courtesy of Inpho Photography)

Mick McCarthy, with Jack Charlton, pictured during a Republic of Ireland training session in 1990. Dunphy was a sustained critic of McCarthy's involvement with the Irish team both as a player and a manager. In particular, McCarthy's close ties with Charlton, who first made him captain and subsequently recommended him to the FAI as his successor, has never sat well with Dunphy. (Courtesy Inpho Photography)

The RTÉ soccer panel (above), minus Liam Brady, prepare to go on air at RTÉ, the Irish state broadcaster. Much behind the scenes research goes into making the show work, with the parties arriving at the studios hours before going live, in order to discuss the match in hand. (Courtesy of Inpho Photography)

The usual line-up of analysts on RTÉ football, with Liam Brady positioned, as if symbolically, between John Giles and Eamon Dunphy where he provides an essential counterpoint to the consensus that often forms between Giles and Dunphy. On his introduction, in 1998, Brady surprised the other panel members with his knowledge and independence, making an instant impact. (Courtesy of Inpho Photography)

Roy Keane, pictured in June 2008 during his term as manager of Sunderland FC, complete with his trademark brooding intensity. Dunphy, although a staunch supporter of Keane the player, markedly changed tack once Keane moved into management. Dunphy has performed a surprising about face, dismissing the once untouchable Corkman as being unfit for the rigours of football management. (Courtesy of Inpho Photography)

Giovanni Trapattoni in animated form while attending a press conference in his capacity as Republic of Ireland manager. The Italian has brought his usual iron discipline and tactical single-mindedness to the Irish squad, but some detractors, most notably Dunphy, have disapproved of his defensive style and lack of adventure and his obvious reluctance to select the more skilful players at his disposal. (Courtesy of Inpho Photography)

Dunphy holds court at RTÉ's 2010 World Cup coverage launch in his characteristic forthright manner. Although critics have rightly diagnosed a troublesome lack of consistency in his views, Dunphy's place as a pivotal figure in Irish football journalism has never been in doubt; his hold on the Irish public's attention, after more than three decades, remains as strong as ever. (Courtesy of Inpho Photography)

and it suggests that Keane's capacity to judge players was imbalanced.

Interestingly, Dunphy has made the tangential point that Keane is not alone in his failure, and that he, like many great players, has struggled to prove himself as a manager, citing Bryan Robson and Bobby Charlton as other notable failures in the manager's chair. It is enlightening to examine just why so many successful players, such as Keane, cannot make the transition to being effective managers, while many ordinary players seem to excel in the post, but there is indeed some substance to Dunphy's theory. Consider Alex Ferguson, Arsène Wenger, Arrigo Sacchi, Helenio Herrera, José Mourinho, Rafael Benítez, Gérard Houllier and David Moyes, all of whom were at worst poor and at best perfectly mediocre professionals in their playing days or, as in Mourinho's case, did not even play football, yet they have all enjoyed highly successful managerial careers.

On the other side, however, consider the alarming number of former leading players who have failed miserably to make the grade in management. Barney Ronay, writing in *When Saturday Comes* and elaborating on Dunphy's point argues: 'It is a footballing axiom that great players rarely make great managers. No swag-bag of playing honours, no bulging armoury of international caps can prepare a middle-aged footballing man for the vertiginous leap into management.' Ronay then enumerates some instructive examples of this unusual pattern. Sir Stanley Matthews, in his first and last managerial post, relegated Port Vale to the old Third Division. Other former greats have fared little better. Bobby Charlton took control of Preston North End in 1973 but was powerless to halt the club's slide into the Third Division the following year. The same ignominious end awaited another

England legend, the imperious Bobby Moore. The former England World Cup-winning captain started his management career at Southend United in 1984 but presided over the team's relegation to the Fourth Division in his first season. The following season he resigned after only a few games played, with his charges lying bottom of the table.

In the Premier League era, the trend has continued, with Keane merely being the most recent in a long line of former legends to realise that playing and management are two very different jobs. The following examples also fit the pattern: Ray Wilkins at Queen's Park Rangers; John Barnes at Celtic; Gianluca Vialli at Watford; Brian Kidd at Blackburn Rovers; Bryan Robson at Middlesbrough. The disparity displayed here between playing ability and managerial talent is remarkable, but if we look more closely at Keane, what is it in particular that connects his extraordinary playing career with his decidedly unspectacular managerial career?

It is fairly clear that there is no necessary connection between on-field excellence and managerial acumen, but is it possible that there are even qualities in great players such as Keane that obviate against them succeeding as managers? In an insightful moment, Helenio Herrera, the former Inter Milan manager of the 1960s, argued forcefully that great players are at a definite disadvantage when it comes to management: 'Big-star players are monuments of presumptuousness when they become managers. They do not know how to teach someone what they naturally did with so much grace.' When we consider the relatively low-level of player with whom Keane has been forced to deal at Sunderland and Ipswich Town, compared to the world-class footballers he routinely played alongside during his playing career, there could be truth in the suggestion that he did not find his own high standards being met and consequently foundered on the attendant sense of frustration.

Taking this point further, David Bolchover and Chris Brady argue as follows in their exhaustive study of football management, *The 90-Minute Manager: Lessons from the Sharp End of Management*:

> Too much ability as a player can surely sometimes be a disadvantage when that person becomes a manager. If something comes naturally to a person, it can be difficult for them to convey how they do it to someone who does not possess such innate skill. Moreover, a talented individual can find someone with lesser ability frustrating to deal with. When the legendary Stanley Matthews eventually retired from football he had a short-lived job as manager of Port Vale, the club he had first played for. One player observed that when he was unable to perform a particular technique, Matthews would step in and demonstrate, perfectly, the required technique. 'That's what I want. Now you do it', he would demand. He simply could not understand or empathise with the plight of less talented individuals.

While Keane's relationship with his players may not have been as poor as the example Matthews sets, it is evident that the former became progressively frustrated with his Sunderland players as matters deteriorated on the pitch. This is illustrated by the numerous occasions on which he publicly criticised his Sunderland team, a pattern that was likely to alienate rather than motivate players who were already critically lacking confidence. Perhaps as Bolchover and Brady point out, Keane was one of those extremely talented individuals who, in making the transition to management, ran up against the limits of the possible, finding it just too difficult to reconcile himself to the mundane level of the players at his disposal. Dwight Yorke, for example, has revealed in his autobiography, *Born to Score*, that Keane, while at Sunderland, would often join five-a-side matches in training and rain down abuse on anyone who happened not to control one of his passes. Yorke reveals that it reached a stage where players hoped they would not end up on his team for fear of the predictable eruption of anger if a mistake was made.

According to Dunphy, many Sunderland players have told him in confidence that Keane was a remote and intimidating figure, ruling by fear rather than through respect, and that many in the squad were glad to see him leaving the club. Fear, as Dunphy rightly points out, is a very limited means of motivating players and eventually is likely to reduce performance levels, rather than improve them. A number of players, including Richard Sadlier, Tobias Hysén and Dwight Yorke, who worked under Keane at Sunderland, have publicly stated that because of Keane's reputation players were too afraid to even talk to him and that, consequently, he had no relationship with many of them. According to Yorke, Keane's management style 'was leadership by inspiring fear', and he further claims that the Sunderland players' reaction was, as Dunphy has claimed, one of collective relief, rather than regret, when Keane walked away from the club.

Motivating players is surely about achieving a mean between paternalism and the instilment of fear. If you become too familiar with your players, they may begin to relax their standards and put in a sub-standard performance. On the other hand, if you remain aloof, and rule by fear alone, you will almost certainly undermine players' self-confidence, which will certainly lead to poor results. Management by terror succeeds only in inhibiting younger players' development because they will likely stop taking risks in an effort to avoid incurring the manager's wrath. As for the senior players, they will just become alienated, being unmoved and unimpressed by crude fear-tactics and, consequently, are likely to fall back on their own devices, thus creating further divisions in the squad. Authority through fear is a hollow leadership strategy, and is as nothing compared to the far more durable player-manager relations that result from authority through respect. An atmosphere of terror is easily created. Respect, on the other hand, has to be earned and leads to a style of authority where players want to play *for* you, and consequently, do not need to be constantly reminded of who the boss is. With genuine respect in place, duress should be an ever-diminishing factor in player-manager relations. However, by remaining distant and enforcing a draconian regime, Keane, it is arguable, failed to obtain true respect from his players and, consequently, presided over a fractured and paranoid squad in the final weeks of his tenure at Sunderland. In the simple vernacular of football, he had lost the dressing room – typically the prelude to the final act in any manager's lifespan at a club.

Effective motivation of players requires a combination of talent and experience. Keane had neither in sufficient quantities. Perhaps it is the case, then, that Keane is another instance of Bolchover and Brady's theory: his immense reputation preceded him, looming large over the less-talented individuals he was forced to nurture. Keane tried but failed to inculcate his own high standards in lesser players.

Aside from purely football matters, Dunphy has also questioned whether Keane even has the required temperament to cope with the pressures of management, arguing that he had effectively 'lost the plot' near the end of his Sunderland tenure. Similarly, Dunphy has satirised the rambling press conferences that Keane began to specialise in during his term as Ipswich manager, suggesting they were further evidence of a man lacking the required mental makeup for management. Keane, it must be admitted, readily took the invitation from gleeful journalists to wax lyrical on an assortment of topics that had little or no relevance to Ipswich Town. Mockingly, Dunphy labelled these meandering, weekly press conferences as Keane's 'state-of-the-nation addresses' and claimed that he was fodder for headline-hunting journalists intent on drawing controversial quotes from him.

> I know Roy well and the one thing he hated when I knew him and when we were working on that book [Keane's autobiography] was the bullshit that was part of manager speak and part of player-speak ... But now he holds these lengthy press conferences every week in which he anoints David O'Leary to be the next Ireland manager, anoints Terry Venables to be the next Ireland manager. He talks about how wonderful it is for the Premier League to play games abroad and he's just become rent-a-quote. It's quite extraordinary ... This is a sharp, smart, outstanding human being and he's just been sucked into that awful Premier League vacuousness. It's sad to see Roy Keane bullshitting.

Although Keane may lack the required personality traits for management, it is plain that Keane, the player, suffered from no similar deficit, being a genuine leader of men on the pitch. Such leadership qualities constitute a necessary component of successful football management, but they are patently not enough on their own to guarantee success. Keane may have been a force of nature in his playing days, the driving-force of Manchester United's midfield for over a decade, but without the other equally essential traits of good management, he was never going to make a great manager. To succeed in management, dispassion is as important as passion, with a sound, strategic mind having to be wedded to leadership ability. As Bolchover and Brady correctly acknowledge, to excel as a player you do not have to be a thinker or even observe an awful lot about the game, you just have to apply yourself properly and do what comes naturally to you:

> To be considered a great player, you do not need the intellectual ability to conceive of a long-term strategy, to be able to communicate effectively, to motivate others so that they realise their full potential. You simply need a high level of ability and a determination to succeed.

Though Keane was hugely influential as a player, often bringing out the best in those around him through sheer force of will, it is arguable that the cerebral aspects of management – the less obvious elements that manifest themselves in grasping the minutiae of tactical detail and understanding player psychology – may have exceeded Keane's capacities. We can think of other genuinely inspirational players who failed to become successful managers for perhaps the same reason, Bryan Robson, being a case in point. Robson achieved the very same hero status that Keane enjoyed as a player by captaining club and country in a career that expressed all the fearless, battling qualities necessary to inspire others. In words which could comfortably be applied to Keane's career, Bobby Robson, the former England manager, described the awesome effect of his namesake's on-field personality in an interview in Pete Davies's *All Played Out: The Full Story of Italia '90*: 'You could put him in any trench and know he'd be the first over the top ... he wouldn't think, well Christ, if I put my head up there, it might get shot off. He'd say, "C'mon, over the top."'

As impressive as such acts of daring may be, when it came to management, this was not enough for Bryan Robson. Despite being backed heavily in the transfer market, he could not achieve any serious success at Middlesbrough, being unable to halt the club's relegation in 1997 and ultimately leaving in the 2000/01 season, albeit with Premiership status being restored, but without matters having improved significantly on the pitch. This all points to the unavoidable conclusion that there is no necessary link between on-field success and managerial talent, and, in the case of some players, that success can even prove an impediment to effective management. Although Keane and Robson may have been the first out of the trenches as players, undoubtedly winning unrivalled kudos in the valour category, there are far more battles than this to win as a manager. Once more Bolchover and Brady's analysis is relevant:

> It is easier to be a great motivator and leader when you do not have to make the necessary unpopular decisions incumbent on a manager. It is one thing being vociferously domineering on the pitch, but quite another to be coolly dispassionate in your appraisal of a situation and to be tough with those who do not accept your authority. Moreover, to

be successful as a manager, leadership qualities
need to be allied to other attributes, such as strategic insight and vision.

Arsène Wenger is an excellent example of a modern
manager who clearly excels at these more nuanced, rational aspects of football management, yet, as a player he
was barely noticed. In an undistinguished career, his highest achievement was making three appearances for RC
Strasbourg in Ligue 1 in the 1978/79 season. Before this
he had played for a succession of French amateur clubs.
However, while others simply played, ghosting through
their professional careers, Wenger was also watching and
learning. Bolchover and Brady have noted how Jasper
Rees, Wenger's biographer, describes him as a player: 'He
was never a joiner-in anywhere. He was not, to use a male
approval word, clubbable. His default setting was silence,
watchfulness, a certain distance, a mistrust of those he
did not know.' As further evidence, Bolchover and Brady
present the testimony of Paul Frantz, Wenger's manager
at the French amateur club Mulhouse, who stated that,
although an average player, Wenger had an enviable football brain.

> As a player, he was a fine tactician ... There was
> a sort of imbalance in him, in that, on the one
> hand, he had remarkable perception and analyti-
> cal abilities, but, on the other, he wasn't always
> perfect when it came to putting it into practice.
> There was this discrepancy between the concep-
> tualising of a situation and the realisation.

We are a long way from Robson and Keane's glorious
trenches, but who would you prefer in a crisis: the one

with the tactical nous to calmly suggest constructive options or the other, whose solution may simply be to beat the drum and demand yet more effort?

When we consider the above analysis, Dunphy is accurate in suggesting that Keane just does not have the correct personality for football management.

Dunphy's point is further substantiated when we consider some of the antics that Keane became involved in at Sunderland. Former players have indicated how Keane would alternate between launching training equipment around the dressing room at half-time and, on other occasions, just sitting sullenly in silence for the full, allotted fifteen minutes. Sometimes he slapped players, at other times he told them they were nothing. In a particularly questionable incident, recorded by former player Richard Sadlier, one brave Sunderland player showed his unhappiness with being left out of a practice game and was promptly pinned against the office wall and invited to dare to be the first one to challenge Keane's authority. On another notable occasion in September 2008, with his team trailing 1-0 to Northampton Town at half-time in the Carling Cup, Keane left the players alone in the dressing room to sweat for a few minutes before calmly emerging from the toilet. He courteously requested the kit-man to erect the tactics-board, indicating the spot where it should be placed, and then proceeded to launch a running kung-fu-style kick through the board. For an encore, he proceeded to slap his captain, Dean Whitehead, across the head before launching into a hail of abuse. This, as Dunphy has argued, amounts to a man who had lost control of himself and was displaying a painful inability to cope with the challenges of managing other men. Incidentally, as if to prove that practice makes perfect,

Keane got through another tactics-board a month later, reprising his earlier kung-fu-style manoeuvre.

Allied to this wayward personality is a further troubling issue. Keane seems to hold most modern footballers in serious contempt, yet by assuming a managerial role he threw himself into intense proximity with some of these very same infuriating creatures. How was it ever going to work? A browse through his autobiography reveals a litany of insults aimed at his fellow professionals, with Keane venomously condemning them for lacking the requisite heart and dedication to be worthy of their privileged positions. He variously brands them 'bullshitters', 'bluffers', 'conmen', 'whingers' and 'moaners', who are 'content to wear the badge of professionalism without meeting the standards to justify that status' and, he contends, they are more concerned with 'blondes, golfing and shopping' than putting in the hard graft. According to one reliable account of his final days at Sunderland in November 2008, reported in *The Guardian*, Keane reached a critical level of disillusionment with his modern players' fashionable lifestyles. This led him to derive an almost perverse pleasure from guiding young academy players around the first-team dressing room, warning them with mock solicitude: 'Be careful not to trip over the hair-gel containers.'

When we consider Keane's short managerial spell at Sunderland, it seems to have something almost manic about it, punctuated as it was by bizarre bouts of physical and verbal rage. *When Saturday Comes*, in an article on Keane's failure at Sunderland, captures the comic side of Keane's escapade well. They write: 'In the end, he lost trust in his players, vilified them personally, slapped his captain, kung-fu kicked tactics-boards across the dressing room and eventually walked out of Sunderland to take his dogs for a stroll.'

Although Dunphy is surely guilty of spinning myths around the figure of Roy Keane, he is not the only Irish journalist who has succumbed to this. Tom Humphries has proved to be every bit as adept as Dunphy in this regard and has repeatedly appeared excessively beguiled by Keane in his writings. These daft lines appear in Humphries's book, *Laptop Dancing and the Nanny Goat Mambo: A Sportswriter's Year*, concerning an occasion when he had interviewed Keane after the player had just received an honorary doctorate from University College Cork in 2002:

> What fascinates me most about the conversation is a digression he makes to speak about how uncomfortable he felt in University College Cork recently on the day he was presented with an honorary doctorate. I mean to return to the issue, but he wanders off to other areas and I forget about it till it's too late. As soon as we wrap up, I start to regret not exploring the issue of why millions of pounds and the captaincy of Manchester United still can't close the gap for Roy between Mayfield, where he grew up, and UCC.

Dunphy gave us the myth of Keane as warrior-hero and now, with Humphries, we have Keane the enigma, the guru of Mayfield wandering abroad – in his graduation gown? – nonchalantly tossing aphoristic phrases over his shoulder for the eager initiate to gather up and scrutinise. Evidently, what are apparently random throwaway remarks to the rest of us are in fact hidden gems of wisdom to those in the know.

What is missed behind all the false significance of this absurd caricature of Keane is the unremarkable truth.

As a professional footballer, this is a man who has spent the best part of fifteen years on training grounds, mostly clothed in a limited wardrobe of shorts and/or tracksuit bottoms. Why would he not feel uncomfortable wearing an odd-looking gown in the musty surroundings of a university ceremony? Furthermore, Keane, as he freely admits in his autobiography, is a shy person, with no particular fondness for formal social gatherings. He leaves us in little doubt: 'Dressed-up functions I don't normally enjoy. Too much bullshitting. The blah, blah, blah of idle talk. Every arsehole in the room in your face, invading your space.' The truth is boring, but also refreshingly liberating when set against the silliness of suggesting there are a myriad number of concealed sub-texts in the words of Keane, if only we can discern them accurately.

The 'blah, blah, blah of idle talk' sounds just like another occasion when Keane attended a summer barbecue for players and families at Sunderland. An event for relaxing, some easy socialising, and perhaps a chance to get to know new people? Not for Keane. He reportedly executed a tactically late entrance, made a beeline for the food table, filled his plate, and retired to the far side of a nearby field to digest its contents. He returned, dumped the remains, and departed without saying a word to a single person. Mysterious? Inscrutable? Interesting? No. Just shy and awkward. We noted that the truth is often boring. Sometimes it is downright unedifying. Myths die hard in the face of these mundane realities.

At least Dunphy, in his newly acquired critical tone, has moved beyond adulation and has freed himself from enmeshment in Keane's aura. We cannot, however, entirely exonerate Dunphy. His cooling off towards Keane was, perhaps, a little too sudden for us to accept unquestioningly. In fact, it was more of a plummet in the level of affection, than anything that could be described as gradual. There has been a disconcertingly sudden gestalt switch between the old feverish advocate of all things related to Keane – a man whom Dunphy once described on the late Gerry Ryan's radio programme as the 'perfect human being' – and the new Dunphy, who can now nonchalantly write off the once untouchable Keane as little more than a 'bullshitter', an 'asshole' and a 'media tart'. Dunphy has taken us from extreme to extreme, but without, it appears, any critical middle ground being traversed. This troubling lack of balance has, for example, led some commentators to disregard Dunphy's views on Keane. *Soccer-Ireland.com* has specifically attacked his pro-Keane commentary for being 'astonishingly subjective in tone and content'. In a sustained challenge the website has sought to expose what they view as his damaging extremism. They argue:

> In his pronouncements and interventions on the Saipan affair in general, and on the topic of Roy Keane in particular, Eamon Dunphy has hindered rational debate on the issue. His multi-media self-serving obsequious overtures to Keane have disrupted any serious attempts to draw balanced conclusions on Saipan and Keane ... This multi-media venting of his unbalanced views and opinions has retarded a wider and more rational debate on Saipan and the issues that led to Keane's premature exit from Ireland's World Cup 2002 squad.

Rather than following any kind of moderate process of change, it is arguable that Dunphy has simply grasped the fact that he went too far in his defence of Keane during Saipan, and again when the player was released by Manchester United, and has subsequently decided to draw back from these excesses. There is almost an air of the guilty party about him, belatedly coming to his senses and hurriedly leaving the scene of the crime before he becomes further implicated. Dunphy now seems bent on distancing himself from Keane whenever the opportunity presents itself. This is the same writer who effectively placed the credibility of his career as a journalist on the line through his wholehearted dedication to Keane. Yet where is all the righteous indignation now?

Although it is normal for critics to alter their views over a number of years, with Dunphy, however, the about-face displayed in his new attitude to Keane leaves the reader with the troubling feeling that not enough thought and analysis has gone into the shift. This gives the impression that Dunphy's views fluctuate between opposites all too easily and, hence, lose something of their credibility in the journey. The urgency to change his stance seems to spring from a determination to now set a distance between himself and Keane whenever possible. For instance, writing in his *Daily Star* column in 2009, he accused Keane of being unable to let go of Saipan, berating him for still dining-out on its aftermath in an article entitled 'Saipan was nearly eight years ago, Roy, get over it.'

This kind of abrupt turnaround is difficult to stomach given that Dunphy, more so than anyone else, rightly or wrongly, has single-mindedly devoted his energies to ensuring that this period in Irish soccer precisely cannot be forgotten and that the grave injustice of it all be ever in our minds. Consequently, to alter position and suggest that Keane is suddenly the one who needs to move on is to attempt a sleight-of-hand, whereby Dunphy's key role in the whole controversy is glossed over and thereby strategically diminished. Dunphy can hardly be permitted to simply waltz off-stage with such a blasé swagger. Through his consistent comments and writings in the last ten years he has made certain that Saipan should endure as a live issue and sole responsibility for this cannot be so lightly handed over to Keane. This is one piece of revisionist history that will not wash.

Other comments by Dunphy point to the same troubling pattern in his shifting attitudes to Keane. In 2008 when Sunderland was struggling under Keane's management, Dunphy asserted that his wayward behaviour could be explained by the fact that 'Roy Keane is beginning to believe the Roy Keane mythology'. If there is anything that can be properly called a Roy Keane mythology, then it is chiefly writers such as Dunphy who have created and nurtured it carefully over many years. If Roy Keane is starting to believe in the various myths that have been weaved around his career, then Dunphy needs to examine himself and accept that he generated volumes of the very stuff. He is knee-deep in Roy Keane mythology. He helped to dig the grave that Keane was forced to lie in.

Chapter 6

Drunken Gamblers and Stinky Little Rats: Dunphy and Giovanni Trapattoni

When the FAI finally brought Stephen Staunton's doomed term as Irish manager to an end in 2007, it promised the Irish public that he would be replaced by nothing less than a world-class manager. After a protracted search, lasting nearly four months, the FAI announced that the new manager would be Giovanni Trapattoni, one of the most decorated coaches in the history of modern football.

Given the Italian's pedigree and unrivalled experience, it represented a coup for the FAI to have secured his services. Commentators were universal in their acclaim, believing that Ireland finally had a manager to rival that of most footballing nations. The statistics spoke for themselves. His curriculum vitae included seven Italian Leagues, one German League, one Portuguese League, one Austrian League and several cups, including the Champions, UEFA and Intercontinental Cups. Along the way, he has managed AC Milan, Inter Milan,

Juventus twice, Cagliari, Fiorentina, Bayern Munich, the Italian national team, Benfica, Stuttgart and Red Bull Salzburg.

Dunphy, like most, was ecstatic and effusive in his praise, announcing it as the greatest appointment in Irish football history. Where did it all go wrong then? How did it get to the point in October 2009 of Dunphy once more describing an Irish performance as 'shameful' after the team had secured a draw against the world champions, Italy, at Croke Park?

The story is one of creeping suspicion and disenchantment with Trapattoni's management style, which has strong parallels with Dunphy's famous opposition to Jack Charlton's term in charge. Although Dunphy backed Trapattoni to the hilt on his appointment, citing his wonderful managerial record, he clearly had not taken stock of the Italian with a sufficiently cold analytical eye. As Dunphy would subsequently discover, there was much in this football man that was not to his taste.

Fundamentally, Dunphy has objected to Trapattoni's tactics which are system-based and firmly results-oriented, with crowd-pleasing football a distant consideration. Trapattoni would make the Irish strong again, but at what cost?

True to his managerial form, Trapattoni's fundamental priority has always been to stabilise Ireland by making them difficult to beat. After the extremely poor results of the Staunton era, with Ireland's defence becoming worryingly porous, stability is indeed what the team needed, and under the Italian's guidance Ireland have once more become a feared international team. This can be clearly attested to by very impressive results and performances against Italy and France in the World Cup 2010 qualifying campaign and, of course, by the fact that the Irish have qualified for the 2012 European Championship to be held in Poland and Ukraine.

Before we examine Dunphy's specific grievances with Trapattoni, we should first look at the tactical system and tradition – the Italian *catenaccio* system – that is behind the football Trapattoni employs with Ireland, and with which Dunphy is so unhappy. This essentially defensive formation was first used to substantial effect by the Inter Milan and AC Milan teams of the 1960s managed, respectively, by Helenio Herrera and Nereo Rocco. Translated, *catenaccio* means 'a chain', the idea being that the team's defensive order resembles the tightly interlocked links of a chain. Although it came to be used by major clubs such as the two Milan teams, its use had originally been considered to be 'the right of the weak'. This phrase originated from the fact that less talented teams originally used this defensive system to stifle and frustrate superior teams.

The main tactical innovation of the *catenaccio* style was the introduction of the sweeper behind the central defenders. Its purpose was that if any forwards broke through the defensive line, the sweeper would be there, usually unmarked, to provide an extra line of defence. In practical terms, it often meant that a full-back would move into the centre of defence to act as an additional centre-half, thus allowing the sweeper to either drop off or, when necessary, to double-mark. This tactical innovation, first formulated in Switzerland by a little-known Austrian coach named Karl Rappan, gave birth to that famous figure of Italian football, the *libero*. This new kind of player, exemplified most perfectly by a defender such as Franco Baresi, often developed into a highly cultured footballer, even if he often formed part of an essentially negative formation.

The theory behind *catenaccio* was to allow the opposition possession of the ball and to draw them into the tightly packed defence marshalled by the sweeper. When the opposition's attack foundered on this defensive structure, the idea was to counter-attack as quickly as possible. The reasoning was that as the opposition became progressively frustrated, they would usually commit more players forward, thus becoming more vulnerable to a counterattack.

Conservatism and caution have always been the key words of this system. *Catenaccio* is designed, first and foremost, to obstruct rather than to create, and has been the cause of much revulsion amongst followers of a more open and attacking style of play. Jonathan Wilson, for example, has claimed that its very mention 'summons up Italian football at its most paranoid, negative and brutal'. It is hard to disagree with this, when one thinks of some of the hyper-cautious performances turned in by the Italian national team. Although many football commentators and fans may find it difficult to understand or even accept this style, proponents of *catenaccio* believe it has its own unarguable logic. Gianni Brera, a noted Italian football writer, has referred to its 'perfectly logical reasoning' and has claimed that managers such as Rocco and Trapattoni 'have always built their sides on the basis of the principle that it is easier to concede one goal less than your opponents than to score one goal more than your opponents.'

Like it or not, when the FAI hired Giovanni Trapattoni in February 2008, the Irish public and football team were about to become another chapter in the history of this most infamous of tactics, a modus operandi that Trapattoni obviously inherited from his one-time AC Milan manager Nereo Rocco.

Although the sweeper has long departed the scene in modern football, the structural principles of *catenaccio* remain. The team employing it drops deep, attempts to soak up pressure, and hopes to score on the break or from resulting set pieces. This is how Ireland has always lined up under Trapattoni, but with the added element of two defensive midfielders shielding the back four. Although *catenaccio* is structurally negative, in the manner in which the team lines up, it should not be confused with bad football. Once in possession, the tactic does not put any necessary limits on how a team uses the ball. Merely because a team will use the *catenaccio* style does not mean that they have to adopt long-ball tactics, for example. The Italian national team has frequently employed exceptionally gifted midfield players, such as Bruno Conti, Roberto Baggio and, in modern times, Andrea Pirlo. The presence of these players attests to the fact that *catenaccio* can accommodate attractive, passing football. However, the suffocating effects of this system inescapably places limits on the extent to which these players can express themselves.

What, then, has been the essential thrust of Dunphy's criticism of Trapattoni's management style? In general terms, the broad nature of Dunphy's disenchantment is attributable to his undoubted dislike of the negative tactics at the heart of Italian football, and the subsequent way in which Trapattoni has imposed this system upon the Irish players.

After Dunphy's initial enthusiasm for the Trapattoni era, his admiration began to sour within only eight months of the Italian taking over. The occasions were Ireland's nervous 1-0 win at home to Cyprus in October 2008 and subsequent 3-2 home defeat to Poland the following year. Writing in his *Daily Star* column days after the Poland game, Dunphy signalled his lack of confidence in Trapattoni's ways, labelling him 'The Poor Man's Jack Charlton' and proclaiming, dramatically, that 'we are suffering from Trapattoni's bankrupt football philoso-phy'. He even went further, claiming that Trapattoni's tenure was worse than Stephen Staunton's because Ireland appeared to have no shape or plan in evidence from their performances.

Dunphy's major issue concerned Trapattoni's selection of central-midfield players. In particular, he questioned Trapattoni's choice of Glen Whelan of Stoke City and Darron Gibson of Manchester United as a central pair-ing, given that both were mere bench-warmers at their respective clubs and neither possessed the play-making abilities to provide serious creative options from midfield. For Dunphy, they were simply out of their depth at inter-national level and he, instead, proposed Andy Reid of Sunderland and Lee Carsley of Birmingham City, both of whom were showing strong form in the 2008/09 Premier League season.

A manager's choice of midfielder is always revealing of his tactical mindset and Trapattoni's frequent choice of defensively minded, conservative players to fill cen-tral-midfield tells us that he views these crucial positions as a defensive bulwark rather than as a creative attack-ing force. In Trapattoni's system, the central-midfielder's brief is to sit deep and cut out any passes before they reach the opposing team's forwards. Theirs is a defen-sive role, providing a screening wall in front of the back four, and this priority reduces their opportunities for being a link between attack and defence, thus providing creative impetus to the team. In short, there is realisti-cally no room for playmakers in Trapattoni's Irish team and this is exactly why Dunphy put so much emphasis on the absence of Andy Reid. For Dunphy, Reid is one of the few Irish players who can take command of the ball and dictate the tempo of a game from midfield, yet Trapattoni refused to select him after they allegedly clashed after Ireland's qualifying game against Georgia in September 2008.

Of Trapattoni's treatment of Reid, Dunphy drew comparisons with Jack Charlton's marginalisation of Liam Brady and Ronnie Whelan and his preference for playing Paul McGrath, a defender, in central-midfield. More controversially, when Reid was dropped for the Poland game, Dunphy claimed that Trapattoni was acting like a bully towards Reid and he again brought up Charlton, arguing that it had strong echoes of the way in which Charlton seemed to banish David O'Leary from the international set-up in the late 1980s. Arguing that it had little to do with football, Dunphy called the Reid situation a vendetta and claimed that Trapattoni was being deliberately provocative and unjust in his insistence not to select the Sunderland playmaker. Dunphy's anger is not without good cause when we consider that the falling out between Trapattoni and Reid seems to have been relatively minor.

Interestingly, speaking on *Sport at Seven* on RTÉ Radio One in February 2011, Dunphy subsequently compared the Andy Reid situation to Trapattoni's lacklustre treatment of Wigan Athletic's James McCarthy which led to McCarthy making himself unavailable for selection. The impetus for McCarthy's withdrawal seemed to stem from the fact that he was originally left out of the squad to play Wales in February 2011 and he was only subsequently included when other players had voluntarily dropped out. Realistically, though, the fact that McCarthy had been ignored for many previous squads must have also been a decisive factor in his mind.

Since James McCarthy is Scottish-born, it was widely feared that he would declare for Scotland and end his

Republic of Ireland career before it had even begun. Although Trapattoni came good, personally visiting McCarthy to assure him of his value and including him in the next squad to face Macedonia, Dunphy has interpreted the incident as more evidence of Trapattoni's vindictiveness and his damaging habit of forming vendettas against players, rather than putting the interests of Irish football first. For Dunphy, Trapattoni's intransigence amounts to an inability to put the welfare of Irish football before the whims of his personality. Elaborating, Dunphy openly questioned Trapattoni's judgment, arguing: 'If anyone believes that McCarthy wasn't worth a position in the original squad for this game, they're mad and shouldn't be in football.' In the aftermath of the event, Trapattoni, initially, was recklessly unrepentant, advising McCarthy that he could play for Scotland if he wished and that the decision was his alone. Whether Trapattoni changed direction of his own volition or the FAI gently persuaded him to mend his ways, we may never know, but it certainly did nothing to dispel the suspicion that Trapattoni is, at best, a reluctant believer in the merits of play-making midfielders.

In defence of Trapattoni, it can be argued that he is a manager who knows his mind, and possesses the kind of stubborn single-mindedness that is the mark of many great managers. He cares nothing for public opinion and even less for entertaining the baying masses with exciting football. Trapattoni is a bottom-line manager, his only concern the result at the end of ninety minutes. He does things his way and, at age 69, was not about to effect any radical departure from the methods and routines of a lifetime in the game just because Eamon Dunphy was unhappy.

Trapattoni knows his preferred tactics and as a man-manager, he brooks no dissent, reasonable or unreasonable, and demands total co-operation from his players to bring his footballing plans to fruition. If a player is not in accord with this simple dictum, then he can go elsewhere. This seems to be the Trapattoni way, and it is a matter of interpretation as to whether one sees in this the mark of a winning coach or the signs of a damaging tunnel vision.

In truth, vendetta or not, Reid and McCarthy are not the kind of players for whom Trapattoni is searching. His style demands limited midfielders who will do what they are told and stick to their prescribed task of stifling opposition attacks. Reid, for example, although no world-beater, is clearly a talented playmaker who can pass as well as most and can provide a serious attacking threat. These qualities, however, are mostly lost on Trapattoni and, rather than pursuing a meritocratic approach, which would see players primarily chosen on ability, he has consistently selected his squad for their fitness to purpose: fitness that is, to the *catenaccio* system. Dunphy, on the contrary, adopting a player-centric view, has argued that good management involves taking your lead from the quality of players available. He argues that 'you have to assess the players you have and adapt your tactics to suit them', rather than stubbornly putting the needs of the system first. For Dunphy, an able manager should be able to accommodate talented players in his tactical schema and, if he cannot do so, then it is the manager who has the explaining to do.

Trapattoni has clearly taken the view that Ireland essentially has an average group of players from whom he must extract the maximum results using a tightly controlled plan. In this approach, creativity on the ball and possession are not encouraged, and Trapattoni has forcefully illustrated this point with his repeated preference for defensive-midfielders over ball-playing ones and a dogged commitment to the purity of the system that is bordering on the religious. It goes without saying that constructive midfielders are going to find life difficult in such an arid tactical landscape, for Trapattoni is a manager who, as *Irish Independent* journalist Vincent Hogan has phrased it, 'cherishes the integrity of the co-operative, picking a player to serve the collective, not to adorn it'.

It is this insistence on the collective and its necessary tactical limitations, on the one hand so stable, but on the other so unadventurous, that has riled Dunphy during the Trapattoni era. His point has been that if, in certain key games, Trapattoni could have loosened the shackles a little, Ireland could have pushed on to convert draws into a full three points. A salient example of this pattern was shown in Ireland's pair of games against Italy in the qualifying stages for the 2010 World Cup.

In the away game in Bari in April 2009, Ireland equalised late on to salvage a 1-1 draw against an Italian team reduced to ten men for most of the game. In Dunphy's mind, a weak Italian team with a man down was there to be beaten, yet Trapattoni did not alter his basic tactics to reflect the situation. Ireland persevered with a containment strategy, as if Italy still had a full complement of players on the pitch and, although this earned them a draw, for Dunphy, it was too little. He proclaimed on RTÉ Sport, in the post-match analysis, that Trapattoni was suffering from 'negative football syndrome' and likened the Italian's ineffectual tactical changes to the aimlessness of a 'drunken gambler in a casino'. Dunphy bemoaned Trapattoni's inability to open up tactically and finish off the Italians and considered a draw two points dropped, rather than one gained.

In the second game, at Croke Park in October 2009, the score was different, but the result the same, with Ireland and Italy playing out a 2-2 draw which effectively saw Italy guaranteed qualification, while practically consigning Ireland to the play-offs. Dunphy was even more outspoken on this occasion, claiming that the performance was shameful in that once more Ireland had settled for survival rather than triumph and seemed to view the result as a victory rather than as an opportunity lost. Frustratingly, we had, once more, snatched a draw from the jaws of victory, conceding the lead to the Italians in stoppage-time.

What underlies this criticism is Dunphy's basic belief that so much more is possible for the Irish team, that they can in fact play football to match many of the bigger footballing nations. Is this true or should we side with Trapattoni's conservative, safety-first approach? To judge from the backlash against Dunphy in the weeks after the crucial 2-2 draw with Italy, it is fairly clear that many in the media and in football sided with Trapattoni, with the Ireland winger Stephen Hunt, branding Dunphy a 'stinky little rat' for his apparently treasonous attitudes towards the national team.

Truthfully, however, this debate was settled emphatically in the subsequent World Cup play-off at Saint Denis in Paris in October 2009 when Ireland produced a display of football that left no doubt that a wealth of ability and self-assertion had been concealed by Trapattoni's previously wary attitude. In a do-or-die performance, with little choice but to throw caution to the wind, for most of the ninety minutes Ireland played France off the pitch with exciting and incisive football. Trailing 1-0 from the first leg at Croke Park, closing up shop was not on the table, and Ireland responded by matching anything France could produce in footballing terms, crafting an excellent team goal, something fans had not known was in this team. Structurally, the major change was that Ireland played much farther up the pitch and used the midfield and full-backs to support attacks in a way that the deep-lying *catenaccio* formation had not previously allowed.

Although the post-match commentary focused on Thierry Henry's decisive handball offence, the real football story was just how good Ireland had been and the serious question this left hanging over Trapattoni's managing capacities.

If Ireland could play this well, why were they not encouraged to do so against Italy in Bari or at Croke Park, games that could have produced maximum points and led to the team's automatic qualification? The performance was so out of character for a Trapattoni team that rumours even abounded of a player revolt before the game with some senior figures demanding a more expansive style of play. Revolt or no revolt, this game should not be forgotten and neither should Trapattoni be allowed to forget it. It should be scrutinised and brought forth whenever the notion is abroad that Ireland are a small footballing nation who can at best assume only 'the right of the weak' and hide behind Trapattoni's dour tactics.

This is the kind of attitude that has been adopted by many Irish journalists who have failed to learn the lesson of Saint Denis. The very same writers have criticised Dunphy for demanding progressive, brave football and, instead, seem to propose that the Irish should almost be grateful that Trapattoni would honour them at all by accepting a €2m a year salary for what is basically a part-time job. John Meagher, writing in the *Irish Independent*, has followed this trend, contriving to dismiss Dunphy as a reckless crank whose analysis is punctuated by 'unfocused and seemingly ill-informed ravings', yet Meagher is unable to fashion a single compelling counter-argument to Dunphy's call for a change of plan, other than to suggest that Trapattoni's tactics seemed to have worked so far in his career. It does not follow, however, that they are right for Irish football. The evidence now suggests that Ireland does not have to play such safe football, and that the team achieves far more by trusting to its ability to play open football which takes the game to the opposition rather than retreating into a cocoon. Meagher misses or just plainly ignores this fact with his contention that the Irish should clip their wings and simply be content with subsistence. Saint Denis showed that so much more was possible.

Although Trapattoni has made Ireland impressively solid and certainly difficult to defeat, the evidence of that night in Paris cannot be dismissed by those who attempt to write off Dunphy – and there are many – as an impossible to please, grumpy old codger, who demands unrealistic total football.

It is not just the Italian's tactics that have upset Dunphy, however. He has also questioned the effectiveness of some of Trapattoni's methods, suggesting that his approach does not always mirror accepted best practice for international management. One example is his questionable habit of rarely watching his players perform for their clubs in person, but, instead, entrusting this responsibility to his assistants.

Indeed, this arrangement represents one of the most controversial aspects of Trapattoni's assumption of managerial responsibility because the FAI allowed him to formally stipulate that he would not be expected to attend English Premier League matches to watch his players in action. Trapattoni successfully negotiated a contract that allows him to remain in Italy with his family, departing from this arrangement only for international training and match-day duties.

Dunphy has attacked this cop-out strongly, arguing that the Italian, like all international managers, should be required to watch his players in person. Speaking on RTÉ after Ireland's 1-1 draw with Bulgaria in March 2009, Dunphy was withering in his assessment of Trapattoni's lack of commitment, arguing that a huge salary should come with considerably more responsibilities. Comparing him unfavourably to the England manager, Fabio Capello, Dunphy argued that Trapattoni was just not attending enough matches, did not care enough about the job, and was delegating too much work to his assistants, Liam Brady and Marco Tardelli, who were given a watching brief in Trapattoni's absence at matches. Struggling for words to express his disappointment, Dunphy claimed, 'I feel a sort of despair.'

Is Dunphy's despair justified? Is it acceptable for a national manager to rely on reports and video footage to assess the merits of the players at his disposal? Obviously, the work of competent scouts will provide precise player profiles, and examining video footage of games will tell you a certain amount about your players, but this still leaves gaps in Trapattoni's knowledge. Reports remain second-hand knowledge, no matter how accurate and, as such, are hardly an acceptable substitute for first-hand experience.

As for the use of video footage, it is a limited and even potentially misleading way to assess players' strengths and weaknesses. There are aspects of a player's game that do not readily reveal themselves to this medium. For example, movement off-the-ball is a substantial aspect of the game to which the television camera cannot pay adequate attention, following as it does the passage of the ball and the players immediately in its vicinity. How, for example, can Trapattoni observe the total number of off-the-ball runs a forward makes throughout the course of a game or properly appreciate the positional sense of midfielders, defenders and goalkeepers, all subtler elements of football that are not visible in television footage?

Furthermore, there are mental aspects of a player which also may not be evident through viewing video footage alone. Is the player a talker? Is he vocal enough or is he unusually quiet on the pitch? If he is a forward, perhaps not being so loud is not a serious concern, but if he is a defender or a goalkeeper, is this going to be a problem? Does a player have a suspect temperament or problems with confidence and motivation in adverse conditions? Would not a manager want to see these things for himself before he challenges the player with the rigours of competitive international duty?

It would be easy to overstate Dunphy's point and portray Trapattoni as suffering from a serious deficit of knowledge owing to the level of work he is delegating, but the fact remains that he simply cannot know his players as well as, for example, Fabio Capello would have, who regularly attended two Premier League games on any given match-day: one noon kick-off followed by an evening kick-off. In doing so, Capello was able to watch and evaluate how his players performed in a variety of situations. He could observe how they responded to going behind in games and how they coped with defending a lead. In this way, a manager can get a better understanding of players' habits, good and bad, and plan to improve them in training or adjust his plans accordingly. Obviously, there are countless reasons why a manager should watch his players directly as often as he can, but it is sufficient to say that Trapattoni, by using the methods he does, cannot know his players as well as he should.

In this regard, Dunphy certainly has a point, and discomfort with the situation is compounded by the fact that because international management is effectively part-time work, with large breaks between games, the least such a manager can do is frequent himself with airports, train stations and the Premier League fixture list and clock up some travelling miles in pursuit of a better understanding of his charges. Even club managers travel to watch games, despite having regular 14-hour days at the training ground. Seen in this light, for Trapattoni not to adopt such practices is unacceptable. It is ultimately a negative reflection on the FAI which assumed far too weak a bargaining position when Trapattoni's contract was negotiated. The idea of Trapattoni being excused, as a blanket rule, from having to watch his players in person should not have even been a subject for discussion.

A further aspect of Trapattoni's methods Dunphy has questioned are his man-management skills. Dunphy has highlighted the Italian's conduct of the Stephen Ireland problem as particularly troubling in this regard. The background to this issue concerns Stephen Ireland's initial withdrawal from the Republic of Ireland national squad, days before the game against the Czech Republic in September 2007. The player lied three times to the then manager, Stephen Staunton, before being forced to reveal the true reason for his departure, which, he explained, was because his girlfriend had suffered a miscarriage. Subsequently, in October 2008, after a long absence from the team, Ireland publicly stated that he would not play for the Republic of Ireland in the near future, and to date he has yet to make another appearance for his country.

According to Dunphy, Trapattoni has not done enough to end Ireland's self-imposed exile and bring the troubled player back to international football, claiming that 'management is about managing situations. If things go wrong, you've got to solve problems on the field and off the field.' However, considering the highly unusual circumstances of Stephen Ireland's originally absenting himself from international selection, with the litany of lies he told to Stephen Staunton and the FAI, it is difficult to criticise Trapattoni for his handling of the affair. It is fair to say that the onus was always on the player unequivocally to declare himself interested in playing for his country again, but he has failed to do so.

Trapattoni and Liam Brady personally met Ireland when many might have not done so, and, although the exact nature of their discussion remains uncertain, with Ireland contradicting Trapattoni's version of the meeting, it proved that the Italian was willing to let Ireland's bothersome past lie and give him another chance. It is off the mark, and excessive, for Dunphy to accuse Trapattoni of poor man-management skills because of this incident. On balance, concerning the Stephen Ireland situation, Trapattoni has probably gone as far as a manager can go without compromising his own dignity or that of the Irish team.

On the issue of his man-management ability, Dunphy's point carries far more weight in relation to Trapattoni's awkward handling of the James McCarthy selection issue, and his refusal to acknowledge the claims of Andy Reid and his related failure to find a way of incorporating a player who, it seems, is guilty of no more than a minor moment of insubordination.

Although Dunphy's stance towards Trapattoni is well documented, Trapattoni, true to his self-belief, has rarely deigned to comment about critical journalism, preferring instead to brush aside anyone or anything that does not accord with his own views. On one notable occasion, however, Trapattoni did respond to the probing of a journalist who asked about his views on Dunphy.

Trapattoni, with more than a hint of impish disingenuousness, replied: 'I don't know this reporter, but I wish to speak to him to see if he knows international football and what he thinks about this or the other games.' In words clearly meant for Dunphy's ears, he continued. 'After fifty years I know there are two different types of critic: the one who is balanced and right and we accept, but on the other side, particularly in Italy, they become cynical, nasty and sneaky.'

Behind the diplomatic tones employed here is a very definite attempt to dismiss Dunphy's outspoken journalism, by consigning him to the margins of football criticism, where only extremists with grudges ply their trade. Trapattoni's suggestion is that no one takes such commentators seriously anyway and so neither shall he concern himself with Dunphy's opinions.

It is not a new idea to characterise Dunphy as an analyst who strategically thrives on controversy by adopting typically unpopular opinions. Many Irish journalists share the view. Paul Hyland, for example, writing in the *Evening Herald*, has taken this line, arguing that Dunphy is dependent on promoting a sensationalist and outsider view in order to maintain his prominent position in the public's attention. He believes this is the real reason for Dunphy's opposition to Trapattoni, not any careful and cogent analysis of the facts, and he lampoons what he sees as Dunphy's attempt to 'wrap the flag of football purity around himself' and writes off his demands for better football as elitist and extremist.

Although Dunphy's views may often be expressed forcefully and without the garnishments of diplomacy, they are not the rantings of an extremist and, in fact, in relation to Trapattoni, his thoughts are founded on compelling and objective evidence.

It is a fact that, as Dunphy has argued, James McCarthy, Keith Fahey and Seamus Coleman are all accomplished players on the ball and would improve Ireland's performances if selected, yet Trapattoni has shown an inexplicable and damaging reluctance to play them, preferring instead to rely on ordinary and uninspiring midfielders such as Glenn Whelan, Paul Green and Darron Gibson. The evidence supports Dunphy, for as Ken Early of the Newstalk soccer show *Off the Ball* has noted, McCarthy, for considerable periods, has been the only Irish central-midfielder commanding a regular place in a Premier League line-up. However, in a feat of reasoning that confounds logic, it seems that talented players, such as McCarthy, have a heavier burden of proof to satisfy, compared to patently workmanlike players, before they meet Trapattoni's unusual requirements. In other words, if you are a limited but competent professional, you stand a better chance of representing your country under Trapattoni than an obviously talented player does.

Writing in his *Daily Star* column in March 2011, Dunphy has rightly diagnosed the root of this bizarre tactical perspective by highlighting how for Trapattoni the system is everything, even if it means not selecting the best players. This accounts for Trapattoni's dithering when it came to selecting skilful players like Coleman and McCarthy. He prefers to stand by ordinary players because he knows they can be trusted to do a job for him, unburdened as they are by the unpredictable quantities of talent and initiative elements of the game that Trapattoni struggles to harmonise with his rigid thinking. He insists on the micro-management of every detail on the pitch and demands not individuals, but eleven parts that can be fitted into a whole. This mania for system stems from the belief that the scientific application of simple, fixed principles is more efficient than allowing talented individuals to express themselves.

This is the questionable, negative reasoning, so prevalent in the modern game with which Dunphy takes issue and which has been so brilliantly outlined by Jorge Valdano, the former Argentinian international and one-time director-general of Real Madrid FC. Valdano, quoted by Jonathan Wilson, who has dubbed him the philosopher prince of aesthetic football, argues persuasively in the following terms:

> There is room for all theories but individual expression on the pitch is something I don't think we can give up. The brain of one manager can't compete with the infinite possibilities of eleven thinking brains on the pitch. Ultimately, while the concept of team is very important, you need individuals to go to the next level.

Not content to leave it at that, Valdano attacks the malaise afflicting managers of Trapattoni's hue, who 'have come to view games as a succession of threats and thus fear has contaminated their ideas. Every imaginary threat they try to nullify leads them to a repressive decision which corrodes aspects of football such as happiness, freedom and creativity.' Of this modern breed of negative manager, Valdano, in a separate piece, has tried to link such management styles to the kind of player these men were during their playing days. Primarily, he cites José Mourinho and Rafael Benítez as examples of defence-obsessed coaches, neither of whom was good enough to make the grade as a professional footballer. Valdano's argument is that their failure as professional footballers has led them to 'channel all their vanity into coaching', and he concludes: 'Those who did not have the talent to make it as players do not believe in the talent of players, they do not believe in the ability to improvise in order to win football matches.'

If we apply Valdano's concept to Trapattoni, we can see a strong connection between his playing career and his management style. Trapattoni, in his 12 seasons representing AC Milan from 1959 to 1971 and in his 17 international appearances for Italy between 1960 and 1964, was a tough and uncompromising defender who was something of a specialist man-marker. His achievement of marking Eusebio out of the match, to help AC Milan win the 1963 European Cup Final, is ample evidence of the kind of playing abilities he possessed. Trapattoni was a stopper, a dogged defender who enjoyed making life awkward for opponents, and the way he played the game is also the way he coaches the game. The same could be applied to Jack Charlton, whose unbeautiful but effective style of defending became the blueprint for the way in which, as a manager, he would demand his own teams perform.

Trapattoni has always sought to place order and structural resilience before individual expression, and in this trait his management techniques are at one with those of Mourinho, Benítez and Charlton. Regardless of the number of trophies won and results achieved, these are not the great coaches of the game, and arguably posterity will reflect this. Success and greatness are not the same thing;

any purely quantitative analysis cannot be taken seriously. It must be remembered why we watch football. We do so to be inspired by great players, to witness the spectacle of thrilling spontaneity, to observe the mercurial talents of a Messi or a Maradona: all qualities that managers will never be able to create, nor fully negate with tactics alone. We do not watch football to see games dominated by coaches who are locked in their own private world of chess-like mechanics.

Yet this is exactly what the likes of Trapattoni, Mourinho, Benítez and Charlton attempt to do. They hope to control every aspect of the game in order to win by the application of cautious tactics alone, an approach whose theoretical underpinning is the idea that the team that makes the least number of mistakes will win. This is football viewed through the distorting lens of fear, where footballers cannot be inspired, because fear inspires nobody but, instead they have to be ordered to conform exactly to highly nuanced tactical demands. This management style is heavily inflected with militaristic overtones, where players are kept under the heel of the manager's iron will; where there might be creativity, all we find is a lifeless martial spirit. Trapattoni even likened himself to a hammer for the relentless way in which he instils his message into players' minds, and he tellingly describes his training sessions as instances of 'practical tactical education'.

These coaching techniques have been extremely effective for Trapattoni and others, but we need to realise that such managers are not concerned about the development of football. Their methods are designed to achieve short-term success for themselves and their teams. Obviously, it would be ruinous for football if such controlling tactics became the norm, and so, instead, we need to focus on what is great in football. Here, once more, we can turn to Valdano for guidance.

The former World Cup winner offers an eloquent homage to the beauty and universal appeal of football, a view that chimes with Dunphy's own vision of the game:

> At the heart of football's great power of seduction is that there are certain feelings that are eternal. What a fan feels today thinking about the game is at the heart of what fans felt fifty or eighty years ago. Similarly what Ronaldo thinks when he receives the ball is the same as what Pelé thought, which in turn is the same as what Di Stefano thought. In that sense, not much has changed, the attraction is the same.

Critics argue that such romanticism is all very well, but it is results that are recorded and that are remembered forever, not heroic displays of beautiful football. Trapattoni has said as much, arguing that nobody remembers the performance, but only the result of the game. This, I would argue, is patently untrue. The best footballing teams, the great players, the memorable goals are what we cherish about football and not the mere tally on the score sheet or the trophies collected. Valdano captures this sentiment with feeling and exactitude when he writes:

> What remains in people's memories is the search for greatness and the feelings that engenders. We remember Arrigo Sacchi's A.C. Milan side more than we remember Fabio Capello's A.C. Milan side, even though Capello's Milan was more successful and more recent. Equally, the Dutch 'total football' teams of the 1970s are legendary, far more than

West Germany, who beat them in the World Cup final in 1974, or Argentina, who defeated them in the 1978 final. It's about the search for perfection. We know it doesn't exist, but it's our obligation towards football and, maybe, towards humanity to strive towards it. That's what we remember. That's what's special.

This is a powerful and appropriate riposte to Trapattoni's philosophy of the game. He is a manager whose achievements, in the long-term, will likely be forgotten, while the style and success, of for example, Sir Alex Ferguson at Manchester United and Josep Guardiola at Barcelona FC will be rightly recalled for many years to come as displaying all that is great about the game of football.

It is not just Valdano, however, who has attacked the philosophy that Trapattoni represents. Even from within Italian football, a dissenting undercurrent has surfaced which laments the way the country's national game has become beset by fearful tactics, such as those of Trapattoni. Writing in *The Italian Job: A Journey to the Heart of Two Great Footballing Cultures*, Gianluca Vialli and Gabriele Marcotti attack the paranoia and insecurity that seem to dominate and restrict their national game, describing its character as 'Machiavellian' for its insistence on a cynical and calculating approach to matches. Although the writers correctly indicate that Italian football has become synonymous with *catenaccio*, we should not forget some of her more glorious chapters, most notably Arrigo Sacchi's AC Milan team of the early 1990s which, in its devotion to thrilling football, formed the most powerful counter-argument to those who would have us believe that Italian football has only one path before it.

It is this nightmare vision of fear and crippling tactics, highlighted by Vialli and Marcotti, which Dunphy fights and regards as unacceptable for Irish football. His wish that Irish players be allowed to perform free of the constraints of over-management cannot be dismissed as naive romanticism. Dunphy concedes that 'we are not Brazil', but argues the more moderate point that there is simply a lot more in the Irish players than Trapattoni will allow for.

Further to this point, in his RTÉ post-match analysis for the June 2011 European Championship qualifier against Macedonia, Dunphy called for a change in strategy, pointing out that the 4-4-2 formation has become redundant at international level, a fact shown by the manner in which the fluid midfield of Russia tore Ireland apart in the earlier Euro 2012 qualification match at the Aviva Stadium in October 2010 and once again in the away leg played in Moscow in September 2011. In the latter game, although the result was 0-0, the Russians managed a staggering 26 shots on target, a statistic that should keep any manager awake at night. Dunphy has argued that Ireland should look at employing a three-man central-midfield, which, as other nations have realised, affords you a greater opportunity to control possession and, hence, to dominate games.

It is important to consider what Ireland could achieve with a 4-5-1 formation. In such a line-up, caution need not be abandoned, in that one holding midfielder could still be selected behind two ball-playing midfielders who would support the lone striker. The extra possession garnered by such a line-up could in fact prove the best form of defence. Allied to this, considering the able wingers the Irish possess in Damien Duff, Aiden McGeady and Seamus Coleman, they could combine structural integrity with robust attacking menace. We shall never know if this kind of expansive game is possible for the current Irish team, unless they are encouraged to play in this way, but the performance against France in the qualification play-off for the 2010 World Cup should certainly indicate that it can become a reality.

Trapattoni will not alter his tactics at this late stage of his career and he has had enough success at club level to argue that nothing needs to be changed. At international level, however, his record has one significant failure. His preference for conservative tactics back-fired at Euro 2004 when Italy failed to qualify from its group, managing only a single win against an unfancied Bulgarian side. Although Italy played some excellent football at this tournament, they failed to capitalise, in what was a crunch game, on a 1-0 lead against Sweden, sitting ever deeper and deeper until the Swedes equalised just before the final whistle. Trapattoni appeared unable to have his selected players build upon the goal they had scored and, instead, encouraged the team to retreat in the hope of holding on. Italy went out of the competition and Trapattoni was subjected to a hail of criticism in the Italian press.

It was the same story two years earlier, when Trapattoni's Italy attempted to hold on by defending a 1-0 lead against South Korea at the 2002 World Cup, but instead succumbed to a late equaliser and were subse-quently defeated in extra-time by the golden goal of Ahn Jung-Hwan. The common thread with the 2004 Sweden game was Trapattoni's decision to take off a striker and play an extra midfielder instead, a tactic designed to hold rather than increase Italy's lead. Although Trapattoni's innate conservatism was certainly a significant cause of the defeat, it should also be noted that Italy suffered from exceptional bad luck in this tournament and were on the receiving end of some very poor refereeing decisions.

However, Italy's failure at both these tournaments, which represent the highest stage of the game, suggests that Trapattoni's normally so-efficient tactical machine may not be sufficiently clever or flexible to succeed at this level, and this is a lesson Irish fans would do well to remember. Being one of the smaller footballing nations, Ireland is prone to being heavily influenced by the tenets of the major footballing countries, and, in Trapattoni, they have a manager who is attempting to apply very Italian, defensive principles to the Irish game. They need to be aware of this fact and decide if this is the direction they want Irish football to take, because, clearly, there are other ways. Ireland should have the confidence to fashion its own style of play, but, unfortunately, as a footballing nation, it lacks a distinctive coaching tradition, a situation that has led it to trust wholeheartedly in Trapattoni's ways, however low the quality of football on offer.

Considering that the Irish have qualified for Euro '12 in Poland and Ukraine, defeating Estonia 5-1 in a two-legged play-off in November 2011, it will be interesting to observe how Trapattoni's conservative approach with the Republic of Ireland fares in its biggest test yet. The Irish have been drawn in a forbidding group that includes world champions Spain, Italy and Croatia. Against such high-calibre opponents and with the dull, safety-first style favoured by the Italian, it is very difficult to imagine the Republic progressing beyond this first stage.

Without question, as Dunphy has emphasised, Trapattoni has brought discipline, order and self-belief to the Irish set-up, and has done so not by inheriting a winning team, but by starting effectively from the roots, with a team that had firmly hit rock bottom under Stephen

Staunton. From a group of players who were wandering aimlessly around Europe engaging in desperate and epic struggles against footballing minnows such as San Marino and Cyprus, Trapattoni has made them highly competitive once more and capable of qualifying for major tournaments.

This said, one significant qualification applies. The Staunton reign was so disastrous for Irish football that his successor was always going to appear to be a substantial improvement. No doubt Trapattoni has benefited from his predecessor's term for this reason, but it should not be permitted to conceal his flaws. As Dunphy has frequently stated, there is more in the Irish players than the machine-like efficiency that Trapattoni promulgates. Such proficiency is a vast improvement on Staunton's ramshackle Ireland, but it is not enough. From here, Ireland must open up and learn to play football again.

Ireland should not have to settle for low standards, as some Irish journalists seem to suggest, but should have the self-belief to demand more progressive football, as Dunphy has advocated. The Staunton era has damaged what was already a fragile self-belief; the way to move on is not to reactively settle for a defensive retreat into their shells, but to allow themselves to develop a more positive and expansive game which can build on the foundations that Trapattoni has established. Whether or not the septuagenarian Italian can do this remains to be seen. History tells us that his intrinsic dislike of risk may rule out any such development occurring in Irish football under his tutelage.

Although I think that Dunphy's analysis of Trapattoni is valid and supported by the evidence, it must be pointed out just how unusual it is that Dunphy did not see what was ahead when the Italian took charge in February

2008. At the time, Dunphy professed it to be the greatest appointment ever in Irish football history and was visibly ecstatic at the thought of Ireland having secured such an illustrious coach. Dunphy, however, was wearing blinkers. Trapattoni's footballing preferences had been there for everyone to see over a long and highly publicised career. He was not about to have any overdue epiphany, which might lead him to extol the virtues of fine, flowing football. What Ireland got was a winning coach, with a winning mentality, but the football was never going to be pretty, and Dunphy should have realised this, instead of setting himself up for the inevitable fall.

Trapattoni has never kept his football philosophy a secret. In 2000, when appointed to manage Italy, the Italian sports magazine *La Gazzetta dello Sport* asked him a direct question: Which do you prefer, getting the result or playing well? Citing Fulvio Bernardini's Bologna team of the early 1960s, which played exemplary football but won nothing, Trapattoni made his preference very clear and in a later statement he unequivocally pronounced: 'A beautiful game is for twenty-four hours in the newspapers; a result stands for ever.'

To those of Dunphy's ilk, these ideas are toxic, and that he could not see this to be Trapattoni's true nature indicates that he allowed his footballing mind to be overcome by his heart.

Of course, Dunphy's misplaced elation must be read in the context of what went before. The Staunton reign was such a low point, riddled as it was by amateurism and disorganisation, that Dunphy was ready and willing to interpret Trapattoni's appointment in messianic terms. He made too much of Trapattoni, projecting the kind of idealistic hopes and wishes onto his shoulders that the Italian was not likely to achieve.

It is a truism in football that there are no messiahs, just the unrealistic expectations of beleaguered fans. In the case of Trapattoni's appointment, Dunphy was a fan first and an analyst second.

Chapter 7

Why do 'England expect...'? Dunphy and the English national team

Given his background in English football as a player with Millwall, and his general appreciation for the modern English game, it is understandable that Dunphy has always shown a strong interest in the fortunes of the English national team. At World Cups and European Championships the RTÉ panel and Dunphy in particular, place special importance on the coverage of England's games. Dunphy's analysis, as noted earlier, is refreshingly free from bias, considering that he has a certain distance from the English game. This grants him the dispassion to describe matters in a manner very different to that usually found in the English media, and the results can be both highly educational and entertaining, even if they are not always for English ears. Dunphy enjoys indulging in bubble-bursting exercises when it comes to discussing England's national team, a habit that can lay bare some uncomfortable truths.

Although Dunphy has never excused the English team when it comes to pointing out their weaknesses, it is clear that he is not anti-English in sentiment. When asked in May 2010 before that year's World Cup on Newstalk if the Irish should celebrate England's woes, Dunphy was emphatic that he would never do so. He said that he hoped England would perform well at the upcoming World Cup, and he also suggested, that he, like most Irish people, holds the English players in high regard owing to the intense interest the Irish public have in the Premier League. If Irish people derive any guilty pleasure from the sight of an English team crashing out of yet another tournament, it is a pleasure born of the delight in seeing the outrageous media hype fall flat on its face, rather than being any reflection on the team's players. Dunphy, likewise, rather than having any issue with English footballers *per se*, instead has focused his attention on two points: the negative impact that the English media have on the team's success and the outdated tactics and playing style that repeatedly haunt the English football team at major tournaments.

We first look at Dunphy's often-humorous thoughts on the overblown rhetoric that sometimes emanates from English media sources. His opinion was forcefully expressed in one of his more sparkling moments on RTÉ, while covering England's opening game at the 2006 World Cup in Germany. Dunphy, on this occasion, revealed the manifest daftness of the *Daily Telegraph's* exaggerated take on the beginning of England's World Cup campaign. In the middle of a general discussion on the pre-tournament frenzy surrounding the English team's chances, Dunphy put on his glasses, produced a copy of the *Daily Telegraph* and treated everyone to a lesson in the excesses of a feverish British press:

God is in His heaven, and all is right with the world. Today is such a day: a cloudless June sky, the oxen reposed in the shade of the mighty British Oak, the reek rising from a million barbecues, and England beginning its World Cup endeavour.

Responding to Bill O'Herlihy's suggestion that 'it's the kind of thing that puts you off England', Dunphy with quick wit noted: 'There is no irony in that. The *Daily Telegraph* is an irony-free zone. They think God is English.'

Entertainment aside, one might ask what is the importance of highlighting this media hyperbole? How is it relevant to the performances of the English team? It is significant because of the bipolar nature of the British tabloids, which tend to artificially crank expectation levels up to the maximum, only to savage the very same players when they are eliminated from a tournament for not meeting these unrealistic demands. This all amounts to unnecessary pressure; a burden that all England teams carry into each tournament and one which must have a detrimental effect on their performance. In a more serious moment, Dunphy made the point, in the Newstalk radio debate in May 2010, that England could do very well at the impending World Cup, but not with any assistance from the English media. He argued that the latter's efforts to pile the pressure on before every major tournament constituted a major restraint on England's chances of success. The unfounded ambitions and naked propaganda flowing from tabloid newspapers ensure that England enter World Cups and European Championships without a proper perspective, believing that this time will be different.

When we look more closely, we see that Dunphy's point has merit. Through intense and relentless hype, England begin every tournament at a disadvantage. The players carry around a hulk of an ego hoisted upon them by their own media, with the memory of 1966 serving not as a source of inspiration but a threat: bring home the cup like the boys did in the 1966 World Cup final at Wembley – England's only competitive, international trophy – or you will have failed abjectly. This uncompromising demand robs the English players and management of perspective and leads them blindly into another tournament, whether a European Championship or the World Cup, which usually ends in tears and scandal. It is the classic device of tabloid journalism: build 'em up and knock 'em down. Often, the English players, caught in the middle, perform with lead in their boots, failing to live up to their normal high standards. Where other nations can play with a calming sense of freedom, England seemingly cannot. The difficulty the English players face is not the weight of expectation – all top tier nations have to deal with the same pressure – but the weight of expectation without a corresponding tradition of success. Teams such as Brazil enter tournaments with an arguably even more demanding populace to please, yet they generally perform consistently well because they have authentic self-belief – a belief that has been accumulated through repeated success at World Cups. England, on the other hand, typically, are at best a quarter-finalist but the players are saddled with the unusual idea that they should be winning World Cups. No evidence supports this and so the players simply do not believe it to be true. The victory in 1966 is well in the past and cannot be used as a barometer for the objectives of current English teams. Aside from this solitary World Cup win, the only occasion where England bucked the trend was at Italia '90, where West Germany defeated them on penalties in the semi-final.

The whole thing, however, begins to turn to farce when we consider the yawning disparity between the hype and the calamity that has followed England into most international tournaments in the last thirty years. Dunphy, speaking after England v Slovenia at the 2010 World Cup, cheekily referred to England's regular World Cup hardships as the 'the soap that keeps giving'. This, unfortunately for English football fans, lends a tragi-comic dimension to support of their team. Has any other nation suffered so much drama and anguish from botched penalty shootouts, disputed red cards, and apparently dodgy refereeing decisions? English international football seems trapped in a nightmarish groundhog day of its own making, doomed to live out the same scenario over and over again. Simon Kuper and Stefan Szymanski, authors of *Why England Lose & Other Curious Football Phenomena Explained*, have called this emotional odyssey 'England's elimination ritual' and they have helpfully divided its course into eight distinct phases. They write that every time England enter an international tournament an 'ancient ritual' begins to unfold:

Phase One, pre-tournament: Certainty that England will win the World Cup.

Phase Two: During the tournament England meet a former wartime enemy.

Phase Three: The English conclude that the game turned on one freakish piece of bad luck that could happen only to them.

Phase Four: Moreover, everyone else cheated.

Phase Five: England are knocked out without getting anywhere near lifting the cup.

Phase Six: The day after elimination, normal life resumes.

Phase Seven: A scapegoat is found.

Phase Eight: England enter the next World Cup thinking they will win it.

Considering the scant success that all this hope and drama has brought England, it is worth considering what a little lessening of the expectation levels could do for their fortunes. The next time they qualify for a World Cup, they should try a novel approach. Their aim should not be world domination but simply a place in the quarter-finals and if that is achieved, then they can take stock again. Nothing more is warranted. As Kuper and Szymanski have noted: 'The sad fact is that England are a good team that does better than most. This means they are not likely to win many tournaments, and they don't.' As statistical proof of England's true place in football's world order they note (although strangely overlooking Croatia, which also reached the semi-finals at the 1998 World Cup in France) that 'since 1970, Bulgaria, Sweden and Poland have got as close to winning a World Cup as England have'.

But far from belittling English football, such an acceptance, though painful, could be just the tonic. What a relieving dose of reality this might be for England's players, to enter a tournament with an attitude that says 'we are a good international team and let's see how we can do'. Such an approach would unburden the players of a groundless sense of entitlement and could lead them to reproduce the form they usually show for their clubs in the Premier League and in the Champions League, and lead, whisper it, to perhaps greater international success.

If we look briefly at England's lamentable showing at the 2010 World Cup, we can partly understand why genuinely world-class players like Wayne Rooney, Steven Gerrard and Frank Lampard often appeared unable to control or pass the ball to one another. England, so imperious in the qualifiers, froze spectacularly upon arrival in South Africa, as if to say 'we are at the World Cup now. Let's get worked up and implode again'. They didn't disappoint. In the group phase, they were lucky to hold on to draws against the USA and Algeria, while their laboured 1-0 victory against Slovenia was a blip on the way to being blown away by a youthful German team by 4-1 in the second round.

England, rather than building on an excellent quali-fication record under Fabio Capello, were, in fact, worse than ever before. It was barely believable to watch inter-nationally renowned players trudging through quicksand. What was even more telling, however, was to observe just how little joy the players showed. The English media had wound them up, once more, to breaking point and this brings us back to Dunphy's point: they could have achieved something at the 2010 World Cup, if the English media warhorse had just allowed them some space in which to breathe. They were so petrified of failing that they failed.

Another aspect of the English football media that Dunphy has criticised is the manner in which they exagger-ate the magnitude of English footballers' achievements, despite compelling football evidence to the contrary. In this regard, the former England captain, David Beckham, has been a major target for Dunphy. Writing in *Ireland on Sunday* in June 2002, he proclaimed: 'David Beckham is a good player but a better celebrity'. For Dunphy, Beckham, in his prime, was certainly a good player, but not deserving of the attention and adulation he received in the English media. His argument was that Beckham's huge reputation was not as a result of anything he did on a football pitch, but was in fact a product of his considerable celebrity-status and the willingness of the English press to perpetuate this unwarranted stardom. Dunphy wrote that Beckham has been 'conferred with greatness by the fans with typewriters who write in English newspapers' and he further argued that Beckham had become, even by 2002, more of a 'public relations triumph', 'a hero designed, one imagines, for the pages of *Hello!* magazine' than a serious footballer.

Dunphy, speaking in 2007 in an interview for the 3 Mobile Network, was even more dismissive of Beckham as a footballer and person. Beckham had just announced his surprise transfer from Real Madrid to LA Galaxy, a team playing in the low-level US Major League Soccer, in a deal reportedly worth £128m to him over a five-year contract. From a football angle, by any analysis, the move was difficult to understand. Many players before Beckham had made the move to US football, but usually as a late-career money-spinner once they were sure they no longer had a career in top-level European football. Beckham, however, could have moved to the Premier League, with a number of clubs expressing interest, but, instead, he preferred the allure of Hollywood, where presumably his marketing-machine could explore new and exciting commercial opportunities. Dunphy was scathing of the player's skewed priorities, and painted a picture about a lonely and unfulfilled millionaire-superstar aimlessly whiling away the hours in a vast Californian mansion, cut off from the highs of professional football, an experience he had once routinely enjoyed in the colours of Manchester United and Real Madrid:

I think it's an awfully vacuous way of living. What can you do with money? You can put it in the bank but you can't talk to it. You can't play football with it and you can't make love to it. What good is it to you? You get all that money but you have still got to sit in your house at night in L.A. and you have got to say to yourself 'what are you doing? what is my life about?' And you know your life is a succession of press conferences, of marketing drives, of photo shoots. But what makes football people happy is football, and I would say that at no time in his life will David Beckham ever be as happy as he was playing alongside Paul Scholes, Roy Keane, Ryan Giggs and winning Premier League titles, winning the Champions League and winning FA Cups. That would have been the happiest time of his life. Where he has gone now is a pretty empty place.

Any dedicated football fan can see that the harshness of Dunphy's words is fully justified. Beckham's lucrative transfer to LA Galaxy confirmed what many already believed: his football career had become dwarfed by 'brand Beckham' and was now merely a footnote to his true vocation in the world of showbiz. In an act of desperate cynicism, the deal was driven by the perceived need to bring the David Beckham endorsements-machine to the American market. He had become a commodity primarily, a footballer secondarily, and, as with all commodities, the US market is the one you want to crack. This was a hard-nosed business deal masquerading as a football transfer. If he had long threatened to do so before this decision, Beckham now made it clear to the world that he was not to be treated as a serious footballer. He openly swapped top-flight European football, and jeopardised his place in the England team, and all because he had not yet had his fill of the aphrodisiac of fame. He was happy to gamble away his talents for a tilt at Hollywood: his own personal tryst with showbiz-destiny.

We need look no further than Beckham's own words to show the ludicrous nature of his priorities. When asked if he had considered the pros and cons of the deal before accepting it, he informed the football world that he had asked his good friend Tom for advice. By 'my good friend Tom', Beckham was referring to Tom Cruise, the American actor. It is difficult to know which part is more astonishing: that he sought the counsel of Tom Cruise on the future direction of his football career or that he was capable of voluntarily offering this piece of information to the world with a straight face. Naturally he did not care to consult someone within the game for advice. It was only his football career on the line, after all. Why not seek the wisdom of a Hollywood actor if you're lucky enough to have their ear?

In footballing terms, as Dunphy has rightly empha-sised, Beckham is now a redundant figure, yet he won't go away. Why is he so irritatingly omni-present? He cannot just retire like everyone else. One suspects that Beckham doesn't do retirement. His hold on the world's attention is so superficial that nothing short of constant exposure can maintain his tenuous grip. If he is not being seen, then there is not a lot else to talk about. Hence, his need to stick around knows no bounds. For instance, although not eligible for selection for the 2010 World Cup squad because of injury, he nonetheless managed to wriggle his way onto the flight as 'player-liaison' with unofficial back-up duties as an ambassador for England's bid to host the 2018 World Cup. For those wondering what the role of 'player-liaison' is, that's management speak for 'we're not quite certain what he does, but whatever it is, we're sure it's awfully important'. Proof? An FA spokesman, when quizzed on what exactly Beckham would be doing at the World Cup, responded with revealing vagueness: 'I can't put a label on it'. I didn't notice any other football nations bringing former players with them so that they could just hang around, albeit in an official capacity of course.

Beckham's sole contribution to proceedings was to participate vicariously by looking terribly anxious on the sideline as England faltered against the USA and then some more as England's World Cup progressively fell to pieces. Marina Hyde, writing for *The Guardian* in June 2010, aptly described Beckham as the '24th man – without a job description' and outlined his chief task as 'perfecting his concerned face for the dug-out'. Beckham's ridiculousness was shielded behind the new statesmanlike aura that has been granted to him and he is now spoken of by some British media sources in the kind of hushed, reverential tones normally reserved for members of their royal family. As if to make up for the fact that he has no function beyond the calculated use of his worldwide fame to boost the cause of the day, honorary roles must frantically be created for him. Dunphy, on this point, has rightly pointed to an obsequiousness in British journalism towards the player. Writing once more in *Ireland on Sunday* in 2002, he disapprovingly quoted Paul Hayward, at the time England's Sports Writer of the Year, when he wrote of Beckham: 'This is no Liberace. Behind the great edifice of his celebrity, Beckham is maturing into one of the great sporting Englishmen of his time.'

Coming from a well-regarded journalist such as Hayward, these words are crazy. 'One of the great sporting Englishmen of his time'. Why not Paul Scholes then,

Steven Gerrard or Gary Neville, to name only three: dedicated footballers who did not leave their dignity outside the door many moons ago and who do not require an intravenous link to the limelight to convince the world of their worth. No. Instead, apparently we have to talk about Beckham, national treasure and all that. As one of the few analysts who has been brave enough to see through this smokescreen and puncture the Beckham-bubble, Dunphy is to be commended.

Media hype aside, when it comes to the England team, Dunphy has frequently been critical of their playing style and has argued that their incapacity to adapt to the changing trends of the international game has been another major cause of their poor performances. Analysing England's woes at the 2010 World Cup on RTÉ, Dunphy subscribed to a theory put forward by his colleague John Giles. Giles had suggested that the disparity between English players' performances in the Premier League and their consistently poor form in the national colours was because at club level they had the assistance of technically superior foreign players, while at international level they were cut loose from this support structure and suffered for it. It is clear that England's disappointing showing in South Africa revealed a lack of technique in both the passing and the control of the ball. They could not maintain possession for long enough to set a tempo and so command the game. Instead, as Dunphy noted on RTÉ Sport after their 1-1 draw with the USA, they played without any discernible shape or tactical system. They appeared flustered and clueless, unable to apply their superior skill to the game, and so a supposedly ordinary international team made England appear as the ordinary ones, despite the roll-call of big Premier League names in their line-up.

The paradox is that the very weakness of English football at international level is its greatest attraction at club level. The Premier League enjoys a huge worldwide following precisely because its games are so exciting. At its best, it offers end-to-end, edge-of-the-seat entertainment with a refreshing absence of negative formations. At club level, players such as Gerrard, Rooney and Theo Walcott have all made their names playing in this action-packed style, but with the crucial assistance of such foreign players as Xabi Alonso, Ronaldo and Cesc Fàbergas.

At the 2010 World Cup, however, without this calibre of foreign player to rely on, England, once more, in a process that Capello was helpless to stop, fell back on an old-fashioned, harum-scarum approach that lacked poise, and crucially, possession of the ball. At this level, a measured approach is required; a way of playing that can control the direction of a game, instead of just backing yourself to score more goals than the opposition. Unfortunately, the English national team usually lacks the technical finesse to unite the disparate talents of its players into a concerted effort. They do not play like a team, but like a collection of highly skilled individuals in search of a co-ordinated strategy. This is why England so regularly make such heavy weather of defeating ordinary opposition: teams that may lack star players but who, nonetheless, are able to play smart by adopting a cohesive, possession-based game that makes the most of limited individual ability. Dunphy, in his post-match analysis of England versus the USA, made this very point, pointing out that the Americans had the worse individual players but the better team because they played with a clear system in which each player understood his role.

There is an essential innocence to the English game, an attitude that says: we are out here to outgun every team that sticks its head above the parapet. Whoever runs faster, tackles harder and scores more goals will win the day. Not so, unfortunately. The need to pace yourself in international football is critical. To choose when and how you want to attack and, no less importantly, to know when to close out games. England, typically, will be first out of the traps in a cavalier, charge-of-the-light-brigade rally against the opposition, but after twenty minutes, with the barrage withstood and the air raid sirens silenced, the composure and shape of the other team begin to tell and England appear ragged and shapeless, losing control of the game. They often attempt to attack teams indefatigably, a strategy that sometimes leads to impressive early goals, but for all the pressure will not manifest itself as domination of the game. This is why a two-goal lead for England is never game over for the opposing team so long as they can set the rhythm of the game, something England will not do.

A good example of this pattern was England's opening game of Euro 2000 against Portugal. England began at lightning speed, scoring twice early on, to briefly stun the Portuguese. Portugal, however, won the match 3-2, clawing back the lead by patiently controlling the subsequent flow of the game.

Some nights, of course, the English helter-skelter game will triumph spectacularly, the initial punch being too much for the opposition to bear, but for all their glory, such victories are not obtained by domination of the ball. They tend to be just nights when everything the English players hit goes in and everything the opposition hits does not. The famous 5-1 thrashing of Germany in their 2002 World Cup qualification campaign is the obvious example of everything that is good in the English game working on the night: power, speed and exciting goals.

The point, however, is that this hit-and-miss approach, although entertaining, does not provide a durable platform for success at the highest level. You cannot do the extraordinary without first doing the ordinary: maintaining a shape, a game plan and holding on to the ball. These sporadic, crushing victories do more damage than good for the English game since they immortalise a flawed approach to international football. Simon Kuper and Stefan Szymanski in *Why England Lose & Other Curious Football Phenomena Explained*, noting that England score a disproportionate number of their goals in the first-half of games, only to subsequently fade away, describe this manic football as follows:

> Habitually English players charge out of the gate, run around like lunatics, and exhaust themselves well before the match is over … They don't seem to have thought about pacing themselves. Italians know exactly how to measure out the ninety minutes. They take quiet periods, when they sit back and make sure nothing happens, because they know the best chance of scoring is in the closing minutes, when exhausted opponents will leave holes.

Drawing a similar contrast between the English and Italian games, Gianluca Vialli and Gabriele Marcotti in *The Italian Job: A Journey to the Heart of Two Great Footballing Cultures*, use a boxing analogy to make the point. They compare England to an 'aggressive and direct' fighter:

> His stance isn't dictated by the need to defend himself; rather, it's a point of attack. He keeps his gloves low or wide or forward, depending

on how he plans to land his next blow. Because that's what it's all about: pummelling the opponent. And if he gets hit too, so be it ... It's about being the last man standing and giving everything you have.

Conversely, they portray Italy as a wily and calculating boxer:

For him, too, it's about being the last man standing, which is precisely why he wants to make sure he's covered and his guard is high at all times. He knows that, as long as he is on his feet and has the necessary energy, he has the chance to deliver the knockout blow. That's why he's patient. He's in no rush to win ... He waits for the right moment: the opponent's mistake, the one glimpse of daylight that affords him the chance to land his blow.

The analogy is accurate and reveals the touch of almost cynical nous that the England team often lack. As Dunphy argued, at the 2010 World Cup the English players were at sea without the assistance of this foreign rationality, something to tone down the innate gung-ho tendencies of the English players. Fabio Capello, an Italian coach, admitted to being lost for an explanation as to why players who had excelled in an impressive qualification campaign should collapse so spectacularly at the main event. He had been hired to instil his players with a more disciplined, continental style, capable of succeeding at the highest level, but he was powerless to halt his players' reversion to their old habits. Once matters on the pitch began to deteriorate in their opening game against the USA, the English players panicked and fell back on what they knew: a brave but disjointed type of play without any unified purpose.

It would not be correct, however, to suggest that English football should become consumed by strategic caution and chess-like tactics; its charm, after all, lies in its highly competitive and exciting encounters. The point is simply that in international games a little more guile and a little less honesty of effort could provide England with the ingredient they need to succeed.

The English national team may not have learned its lesson yet, but some of its clubs have already grasped the insight. Manchester United is a prime example when you consider the way in which Sir Alex Ferguson has altered his team's approach to European football. After chastening, high-scoring defeats to Bayern Munich in 2001 and Real Madrid in 2000 and 2003 in the Champions League, Ferguson had been burnt one too many times. His team, generally open and attack-minded in Premier League games, now often line up with a cautious 4-5-1 formation in Europe – especially away from home – with the players adopting a more calculating, wait-and-see approach to winning games. The result has been three Champions League final appearances since 2008, with one victory.

It is not just the English style of play, however, with which Dunphy has taken issue. He has also highlighted deficiencies in some of its star players such as Steven Gerrard whom he famously declared was a 'nothing player' after a poor performance for Liverpool against Barcelona in the Champions League. Although there is an obvious and not inconsiderable rhetorical flourish to this statement, what Dunphy correctly suggested – revealing an important truth about English midfielders in general – is that Gerrard, for all his incredible match-winning feats, is not a midfielder who can run a game from the centre of the pitch. Yes, there are few players more accomplished at scoring 30-yard screamers on order or at launching raking cross-field passes directly to his colleague's feet, but what about the essential, metronomic role of the central-midfielder: receiving the ball over and over again throughout the game, each time finding a man with short, incisive passes and thus ensuring that your own team sets the tempo of the game. In other words, Gerrard is not a playmaker and, in fact, Glenn Hoddle, Paul Scholes and Paul Gascoigne aside, England, as a rule, do not tend to produce playmakers. Currently, in Spanish football you can take your pick from sublimely subtle but equally impressive examples such as Xavi Hernández, Andrés Iniesta, Cesc Fàbergas (Barcelona), Xabi Alonso (Real Madrid), Iker Muniain, Javi Martínez (Athletic Bilbao), Mikel Arteta (Arsenal), David Silva (Manchester City) and Juan Mata (Chelsea), but England's most fêted midfielders are usually Roy Race prototypes: fit, strong and fast; all-action superheroes driving forward at every available opportunity. The crucial difference is that the English players want to come onto the ball at the edge of the box to power home the winner, rather than getting on it in the middle of the pitch where a true midfielder will earn his salt performing the unostentatious role of playmaker.

Consider the list of big-name English midfielders who for all their to box-to-box heroics and set-piece prowess could never be relied upon to set the tempo of a game: Bryan Robson, David Platt, David Beckham, Frank Lampard and Steven Gerrard all come to mind. Modern football is leaving these action-men behind. As Musa Okwonga argued in the English football magazine *The Blizzard* in March 2011, in an article entitled 'Xavi and the Square Pass', going sideways has become the future.

Sticking with the Roy Race theme, Scott Murray, writing in the same issue of *The Blizzard*, pointed out how this famous comic-book character, first appearing in the pages of *Tiger* and later in *Roy of the Rovers*, was unashamedly used to hammer home the merits of a limited but proud English way of playing the game. He describes the suspect football tutorial that Roy Race, Melchester Rover's star forward, provided for adoring, young football fans:

> He was super-talented ... able to belt in goals from all angles, usually thundering home one of his trademark Racey's Rockets in the last minute to save the day. But while his insistence on sportsmanship offered a valuable life lesson for impressionable young readers, his talent for timely goalscoring and pulling irons from fires warped their minds in far more harmful ways ... thanks to Roy Race, English children spent their formative years sat on their arses being taught a very strange lesson: it doesn't really matter what you do for 89 minutes, because a superhero will turn up eventually, welt the ball into the net, and you can all go home with your cups and medals.

For Roy Race, without too much of a stretch, you could substitute Steven Gerrard, scorer of countless late thunderbolts fit for the pages of *Roy of the Rovers*, yet as Dunphy has pointed out, often found wanting when it comes to dominating the midfield across ninety minutes of play. In a wider analysis of the significance of *Roy of the Rover's* message, Murray views it as a reactive, cultural response to the chastening drubbings the English team received in the 1950s: in 1950 England were knocked out of their first World Cup by a part-time team representing the USA; in

1953 they suffered their most famous loss, with Hungary
defeating them 6-3 at Wembley; a year later against the
same Hungarian team, it was a 7-1 defeat in Budapest;
finally, in 1954 they were humbled once more, losing 4-2
to Uruguay in the World Cup. According to Scott Murray,
Melchester's lantern-jawed colossus was designed as an
unequivocal two-fingers to 'Johnny Foreigner': a harsh
footballing lesson delivered by 'Racey's left boot of justice' clearly showing that 'English football was not on the
bones of its arse. That in fact everything was fine, and
would be forever more, so there was no need to worry, or
indeed think, about anything.'

On the evidence of the 2010 World Cup, there is
plenty for the England manager to think about if he is to
learn how to make the best use of his talented individuals at the 2012 European Championship. It is clear that
Dunphy's theory has substance to it. The English players'
reliance on foreign colleagues at domestic level was indeed
horribly exposed on the international stage. There is no
doubt that the sprinkling of stardust that foreign play-
makers such as Luka Modrić at Tottenham Hotspur, Juan
Mata at Chelsea and David Silva at Manchester City bring
to their current Premier League clubs is painfully lacking
in English midfielders. These specialist foreign imports,
coming at a premium, are like expensive guns-for-hire,
plugging a hole in the domestic workforce. Why else did
Sir Alex Ferguson spend most of the 2011 pre-season trying to first lure Luka Modrić and then Wesley Sneijder to
Old Trafford: he realised that a suitable playmaker, someone who can join everything together on the pitch, could
not be found from within the ranks of British players.

A related aspect of the English game that Dunphy
has discussed is its peculiar fascination with suffering and
physical warfare as metaphors for understanding football.

English players are comfortable with the idea of going to war on a weekly basis, intent, first and foremost, on fronting up to their foe and winning the physical battle. Speaking of his playing colleagues at Millwall, Dunphy writes in *Only a Game?*:

> The lads know, especially in the lower divisions, that the one thing that keeps them in the game is their application. Their dedication. The intensity with which they approach the game. Which leads them to this feeling that they have to go out and punish themselves for ninety minutes. This is crucial to players, particularly in the lower divisions. It is one of the most important things in the game at the moment – the idea that you somehow have to suffer ... The one thing about English football is that you have forty-two battles, more or less.

Dunphy strikes a chord with these thoughts. Often in English football, tactical nuance only comes as a secondary consideration; making sure you have the bottle for the fight is your priority. The belief that you have to suffer and strive to somehow add validation to your performances is a factor that lends a manic quality to English football. The battle is glorified and this too has created its own tradition of English hard men. According to Arsène Wenger, this bulldog spirit 'is in the blood of the English. It's the almost military attitude with which they approach everything'; comparing the English players to their continental peers, he notes:

> Here in England, maybe because they are an island, they are more warlike, more passionate.

> They view it [football] like an old-style duel, a fight to the death, come what may. When an Englishman goes into war, that's it, he either comes back triumphant or he comes back dead. But the Italian or the Frenchman is not like that. He will calculate, he will think about things, he will do what he needs to do to protect his own interests.

It is true that you can find a naive element in English football: a traditionalist belief that honest effort and pluck count for more than devious tactical ruses designed to hoodwink the opposition. In the true spirit of the Marquess of Queensbury, English footballers insist on defeating opponents fair and square; gentleman's rules apply and if you get a few battle wounds along the way, that will only make the telling of the tale all the better. Side-by-side with this is a suspicion of too much skill and tactical theory: window-dressing that might only distract from the cut-and-thrust of battle.

However, the fact is that spirit and determination are not always synonymous with self-belief and often, in fact, can reflect a certain desperation. These are qualities that tend to suggest an attempt to compensate for some inherent lack rather than indicating anything intrinsically positive.

Raphael Honigstein has written extensively on this 'blood, sweat and tears' tendency of English football in *Englischer Fussball: A German View of Our Beautiful Game*. Honigstein, viewing the intensity of the game with a neutral's eyes, is frequently shocked at the bruising physicality and relentless pace of English football. He goes back to the origins of the game in Britain in the nineteenth century to discover the root of this attitude. At a decisive FA meeting held in London on 8 December 1863, football received a standardised rulebook for the first time, but not without intense disagreement amongst those in attendance. One major point to be settled was the issue of carrying the ball with the hands. This was ruled out and so football and rugby were separated.

The really contentious point, however, was the issue of hacking. Hacking, essentially, was the act of kicking downwards onto your opponent's shins as you ran forward with the ball. Dribbling, in the early game, was unlike its modern, elegant equivalent. In many cases it involved a head-down, forward-charge through – with the help of hacking – rather than between the opposing players. Do not think of Maradona; imagine a well-built rugby back, cutting a lung-busting swathe through enemy lines and you will be closer to the truth. Although hacking was outlawed at this gathering, it is instructive that one member, F.W. Campbell of Blackheath Football Club, put up such impassioned resistance that he resigned over the affair. In words which would now be laughed at, Blackheath did, all the same, reveal British football's preoccupation with manliness and physical prowess: 'If you do away with [hacking], you will do away with all the courage and pluck of the game, and I will be bound to bring over a lot of Frenchmen who would beat you with a week's practice.' Football, Campbell raged, was not for those 'who liked their pipes and grog or schnapps more than the manly game.'

Honigstein concludes that this cannot be written off as just an amusing story since 'it poses the key question of English football, the one that covertly dominates all others: are you hard enough, or just a schnapps-drinking, pipe-smoking Frenchman?' According to Honigstein, this attitude lives on in the English, with each player having to 'defend himself against the ancient accusation of being too soft'. Although one would not want to push the point too far – all contact sports are highly combative in nature, after all, regardless of what country they are played in – there appears to be truth to Dunphy's and other commentators' suggestion that English footballers view the game as a battle before anything else; an attitude that does not always assist the technical development of its players. To a degree, there is still an unhealthy suspicion that elegant touches and excessive dribbling amount to a great deal of ineffectual activity: so much effeminate faffing around and, worse still, acts unworthy of real men.

Although Dunphy rightly highlights this questionable element of English football, at another juncture in *Only a Game?*, as Honigstein points out, confusingly we find him exulting in the very same attitude and openly mocking the pointless daintiness of skilful play. This is the ambivalent strain in Dunphy's memoir once more announcing itself: the clash of the real and the ideal, with Dunphy's pretensions towards continental-style football becoming submerged in the world of the English Football League. After Millwall comfortably defeated Preston North End by a margin of 5-1 on 22 October 1973, Dunphy responded:

> I hate all that... Every man doing his party tricks. Indulging himself, flicking it here, flicking it there, beating a couple at a time, crossing it, having a shot. Taking it down on your thigh or on your chest... Battle is what the game is all about in the Second Division. And you come to have a taste for it, to enjoy it. And you tend to get turned off by something that is too easy.

In moments such as this, Dunphy succumbs to the 'Are you hard enough?' war cry and cuts an unusual figure: an artist who wants be a warrior.

Regarding England managers, although Dunphy has often been critical of former appointees such as Graham Taylor, Sven-Göran Eriksson and Fabio Capello, his most important views concern Terry Venables, who managed the national team between January 1994 and January 1996.

The reason Dunphy found himself discussing Venables was that the FAI had installed the former England manager as a serious candidate to replace Steve Staunton as Irish national manager in 2007. In November of that year, using his column in the *Daily Star* and his platform on RTÉ Sport, Dunphy delivered a blistering attack against Venables, urging the FAI to distance themselves from someone he objected to in the strongest possible terms. Dunphy cast serious doubt on both Venables' management credentials and character. He claimed that Venables was a 'hollow man' and that if the Irish people had any self-respect, they should object to his candidacy outright.

He argued that Venables' CV as a football manager was 'riddled with failure' and that, at best, 'his managerial record was very average'. As evidence, Dunphy pointed to the fact that he had won only two trophies in thirty years of management and that his last seven jobs had all lasted for less than two years. For Dunphy, it was unbelievable that Venables, who had been sacked as assistant manager of England, along with the manager, Steve McClaren, one week earlier, should now find himself in the running to become the Republic of Ireland's next manager. He suggested that Venables, after this recent failure with England and his similar failure as manager of Leeds United in the 2002/03 season, departing with the club near the bottom of the Premier League, would stand little chance of getting a job in England, so why should the FAI consider him? He also emphasised Venables' poor record as manager of Australia in 1996/97, and the fact that he left Portsmouth in bad condition financially in 1998 where he was briefly chairman. Dunphy insisted that Ireland should look for the best, not just the scraps from England's table who might be seeking a career pick-me-up in the last chance saloon. He viewed Venables as an ambitious but unreliable man eager to secure another big job at the expense of gullible 'little Paddy-land'.

Worse for Dunphy, however, was what he termed Venables' dubious 'extra-curricular activities' in the world of business. He quoted, on RTÉ, the English High Court's 1998 verdict against Venables that disqualified him for seven years from acting as a company director for serious irregularities in the management of four of his companies. The case had been brought by the Department of Trade and Industry which cited incidents of bribery, lying, deception, the manipulation of accounts and taking money that should have been given to creditors. This, to Dunphy, suggested that Venables' character was suspect, his true goal was wealth and so, consequently, 'he could not have the interests of Irish football at heart'.

A further troubling example of this pattern was the fact that throughout his tenure as assistant to Steve McClaren, Venables continued to write a column for the *Sunday World*. This Dunphy considered to be a blatant conflict of interest, especially since Venables embarrassed McClaren in some of his pieces, and, according to Dunphy, again it was all solely for the money.

In the end Venables did not get the job; Giovanni Trapattoni did, and the losing candidate subsequently claimed in an interview with the *Sunday Independent* in March 2008 that Dunphy's rant effectively killed off whatever chance he had of securing the job. A furious Venables, who even considered taking legal action against Dunphy, said he sensed a definite 'change of heart' from the FAI officials once Dunphy had said his piece. Initially, Venables had not known about Dunphy's attack, only viewing the video online a number of weeks later. Once he had seen it, he felt sure this was the reason his application was rejected. He accused the FAI of being intimidated by Dunphy, saying 'amazingly, I think everyone is terrified of him', arguing that when Dunphy intervened 'they shit themselves'.

He then dismissed the FAI, stating that he would rather not work for an organisation that lacked the courage to stand up to the likes of Dunphy: 'I honestly think that if they are not strong enough to take their own decision I am better off not being there.'

As for Dunphy, himself, Venables hit back, asking how someone with such a checkered past could plausibly question his character. 'How can a self-confessed cocaine user who has been banned for drink-driving and driving without insurance lecture me on my character?' Furthermore, Venables claimed that some of Dunphy's facts were wrong and he expressed disbelief that the analyst should still hold such a prominent position in Ireland. 'How can he get away with it and how can people listen to this on a continual basis? You have to laugh ... he shouldn't be allowed to bullshit his way through as he does.'

Venables, although understandably frustrated at not being given an opportunity to respond to Dunphy's criticisms before the FAI had made their decision, is surely overstating Dunphy's importance. He has been a sustained critic of the FAI for over twenty-five years and so it is not likely that the Association would suddenly heed his advice on such an important matter. As tempting as it may be for Venables to see it this way, Dunphy just does not wield such influence.

Were Dunphy's arguments fair? His analysis did gloss over certain facts, such as Venables' notable success with Barcelona and the fact that he had led England to the semi-final of Euro '96, but his basic point held. Venables' record since 1996 was poor and the FAI should have had the confidence to look higher than to recruit a man who had just been released from duty by the English FA. It would have been an appointment that settled for second best; something that the Irish team and supporters did not have to accept. Dunphy's high standards were appropriate.

Chapter 8

It's the company you keep: Dunphy and the RTÉ panel

The relationship among Bill O'Herlihy, Eamon Dunphy, John Giles and Liam Brady has now exceeded its narrow football origins to become something of a celebrated institution throughout Ireland. In its 34 years of broadcasting, RTÉ's coverage of football, with its outspoken and idiosyncratic panel has become a genuine sporting phenomenon. Although Eamon Dunphy has fashioned a very successful and distinct career outside of this context, it is here, alongside his long-term colleagues on RTÉ Sport, that Dunphy became the analyst of football that he now is. This is the domain where Dunphy is best known and is at his best, precisely because it is not the Eamon Dunphy Show.

Although Dunphy is frequently brilliant in his writings, in that solitary medium he does have a tendency to lose control of his judgment. It is an arena where he has unfettered reign over his readership, with no one to interject with a contrary view or a calming influence. On RTÉ, however, Dunphy has had to contend with the views of two very influential figures in Irish soccer, John Giles and Liam Brady. Neither Giles nor Brady suffers fools gladly, and some of Dunphy's most controversial and best moments have arisen from the frequently trenchant and intelligent opposition offered by these colleagues.

Indeed, it is the open-conflict between the panellists, moderated expertly by Bill O'Herlihy that marks out RTÉ's coverage for special noteworthiness. In fact, the ever-present possibility of friction is the key to its success. In an era when television football analysis has become dominated by featureless and anodyne coverage, the level of robust, honest debate regularly occurring on RTÉ's panel is little short of a revelation, in an otherwise barren television environment. It is to RTÉ's credit that the station does not seek to stifle the talents at its disposal. When we watch Dunphy, Giles and Brady in action, we know we are watching a genuine conversation that could go in any direction. The brilliant dynamic is allowed to take its own course, free from the stifling constraints of rigidly rehearsed lines and defined roles. The net effect is a gloriously cliché-free zone, where easily the best television football coverage in the British Isles and Ireland takes place. RTÉ's major rivals on Sky Sports and BBC Sport just cannot match the acerbic wit, careful analysis and brutal honesty of the RTÉ team.

The origins of this television line-up stretch back to 1978 when Eamon Dunphy joined Bill O'Herlihy to cover the World Cup of that year. This first incarnation was a simple affair, with O'Herlihy and Dunphy doing their best to keep pace with the more expensively assembled teams of ITV and the BBC. Over the past few decades, however, the panel has grown significantly to now include nine regular members. Aside from O'Herlihy, Dunphy, Giles and Brady, it also features Ronnie Whelan, Graeme

Souness, Ray Houghton, Kenny Cunningham and Trevor Steven. Although some of the others do make a serious contribution, most notably Souness and Steven, attention here will be focused on its four senior members who are the longest serving and by far the most important components.

When the RTÉ panel debate issues, we are in the presence of the unexpected, an endangered commodity in the world of television. As viewers, we are frequently thrilled by the open-ended and uncertain nature of the discussions. We do not know where it is leading and sometimes the panellists themselves do not know either. This quality puts the RTÉ panel in an order entirely of its own. Brady, Giles, Dunphy and O'Herlihy have true conversations in the sense that their communications are not strangled by being minutely prepared in advance, and hence do not serve narrow agendas, as frequently occurs on the BBC and Sky Sports.

What makes this special dynamic work, though, and how do the various parties contribute to it?

The first thing that should strike a viewer unfamiliar with RTÉ's coverage is the manner in which the interaction is so refreshingly unrehearsed and natural. The exchanges are not restricted or sanitised by the findings of focus group studies or the mandates of television executives. What we get are three experienced football analysts simply engaging in open discussion, moderated by a talented anchor in Bill O'Herlihy. It's not fake, it's not patronising and it's not scripted. It is truthful and direct, and viewers instinctively respond positively to these qualities. The formula is so simple that one wonders why all broadcasters cannot follow RTÉ's excellent example.

Although Dunphy, Giles and Brady obviously provide the footballing acumen, O'Herlihy's role in the proper running of operations cannot be underestimated. It is a strange irony that O'Herlihy may not get the praise he deserves owing to the fact that, for the most part, his talents involve him receding into the background while skilfully allowing the pundits to hold the foreground. O'Herlihy does this by expertly playing the stooge: he is the ordinary man equipped with the questions that the viewer at home wishes to ask. As Dunphy has put it in an *Irish Times* interview, O'Herlihy 'can actually ask the questions that are lingering out there for people who really don't know'.

It is noteworthy, also, just how often O'Herlihy will strike the correct note with his line of questioning, an interrogative process that unerringly allows the experts to shine. Of course, it is axiomatic that if you want interesting answers, then you need interesting questions, the kind of questions that invite original analysis and do not merely encourage yet more hackneyed footballing truths. Furthermore, what makes O'Herlihy stand out from comparable anchors is that he actually joins in the discussion. On football programmes on other stations, such as the BBC and Sky, it is evident that the presenter often stops listening once he has asked his prepared question and just waits for the pundit to finish before asking another. Not so with O'Herlihy. He prods, he probes, he interrupts, he provokes and, most importantly, he is not afraid to incur the wrath of the panel by posing awkward questions.

In the early days it was a two-man show. Although O'Herlihy has always been adept at providing a framework and platform for his long-standing colleague, Dunphy felt after the 1984 European Championships that something was missing from the set-up and he persuaded an initially sceptical RTÉ that John Giles was that missing factor.

Giles joined the panel for the 1986 World Cup in Mexico, and the positive reception of viewers indicated that the change was a popular one.

What Dunphy had realised after the 1984 European Championships was that he needed a voice of sanity to lend focus and a more reasoned legitimacy to his own naturally expansive style. Giles would be the tactics man, having the ability to break down football formations and theories into their fundamental elements, and to offer compelling arguments based on sound principles. Although one would not wish to tone down Dunphy entirely, in that his controversial style of football wisdom is often exhilarating, there is certainly merit in his tempestuous views being channelled and supported by Giles's calmer presence. Dunphy is the firebrand, offering the inspiration and the big ideas, while Giles often provides the groundwork, filling in the tactical gaps and blind spots in Dunphy's arguments. With its whistle-bright clarity of logic, Giles's tactical mind should be the envy of any serious football analyst, a realisation that has not been lost on Dunphy.

In fact, the specific moment when Dunphy decided to bring Giles on board stemmed from the consequences of his much-publicised criticism of Michel Platini, then captain of France and president of UEFA at the time of writing this book. Before the 1984 European Championship, Dunphy famously declared that the attacking midfielder was a good player, but not a great player, and even ventured to announce before one first-round match that it would finally be the day that his play would be found out. Instead, Platini went on to score a hat-trick and Dunphy was left with some explaining to do. To alleviate his soul-searching, Dunphy met Giles and sought a second opinion over a pint. Of the encounter,

Dunphy has said: 'It was kind of wrecking my head, although I wasn't letting on. I said to John, "Am I fucking wrong about Platini?" and he said "No, you're right – but you're an awful gobshite to be saying it on television".'

With this laconic reply, Dunphy realised that in Giles he had a kindred football-mind who would provide greater focus and structure to his larger claims. That Platini was not a great player was a bold hypothesis, and, as such, it needed detailed tactical analysis to lend it credence, and this is precisely the role that Giles has adopted on the RTÉ panel. He lays the foundations for Dunphy, and in the process controls and regulates Dunphy's tendency to become something of a loose cannon. Dunphy has admitted that, on his own, he was just not going to be credible and has praised Giles for his sober approach and for bringing 'gravitas and a depth of knowledge' to proceedings. That he has come to depend on the respected opinion of his peer is still very evident. For example, when Ireland performed poorly against the lowly Cyprus at Croke Park in October 2008, Dunphy seriously questioned Trapattoni's ability to do the job and in mid-speech broke off to earnestly seek Giles's approval: 'John, isn't it outrageous? It means more if you say it. They think I'm mad.'

If Giles's sanity grounds the discussion, though, it is Dunphy who takes the analysis onto a higher level, drawing in social, historical and even psychological aspects of the game. With a formidable intellect and caustic wit, Dunphy has provided some of the best moments of television football analysis one is likely to witness. Of Dunphy's talents, Giles has said:

We have a saying for Eamon – he flies at 5,000 feet, but we're grounded. It's a combination of

everything. Eamon will broaden the discussion –
and this is where he comes into his own – in ways
that I wouldn't be able to do or Bill wouldn't be
able to do.

There are many instances of Dunphy widening and
enhancing the discussion in this way, taking us on illuminating digressions that introduce deeper levels of insight
and fresh perspectives on the topic at hand.

A typical example of this analytical style was shown
during coverage of the 2004 European Championship
when O'Herlihy asked Dunphy to explain why the
Dutch national team is so prone to imploding at international tournaments. It was common knowledge that
the Dutch players had a nasty habit of forming fractious
player cliques which often led to open mutiny against the
manager. In the 1994 World Cup, Ruud Gullit clashed
with manager Dick Advocaat. In the 1996 European
Championship, it was Edgar Davids's turn to challenge
Guus Hiddink's authority, while at the 2004 European
Championship Advocaat again was in conflict with
a leading player. This time it was Ruud van Nistelrooy
who objected to the manager's tactics. Dunphy replied
that the problem with the Dutch was that they were just
too liberal and were possessed of far too healthy a consciousness of their democratic rights. His point was that
the advanced nature of civil and political freedoms in the
Netherlands obviated the possibility of 25 men being
able to accept the dictatorial control of a manager for
the time needed to win a modern football tournament:
approximately four weeks. His response was an exceptional mixture of humour and insight which brought the
analysis to an entirely unexpected conclusion by drawing
in a relevant political dimension.

This ability to introduce extra-curricular and illuminating points to football analysis is also apparent in Dunphy's critique of British football experts. When asked what he felt was wrong with the analytical efforts of certain analysts on the BBC and Sky, he suggested that they were incapable of expressing themselves with any articulation, and accused them of mangling the English language. Introducing social factors to explain their lack of erudition, he elaborated by arguing that they were unwitting creations and exponents of the English Industrial Revolution underclass, which threatened to undermine the dignity and beauty of football. One can disagree with the heavy suggestion of class distinction here, but the ability, once more, is clearly in evidence, to deliver an argument that is bold and rich in possibilities.

If we briefly emphasise the humorous side of Dunphy's analysis, which can be merciless, we see that he can be as entertaining as he can be informative to a degree that other pundits simply do not approach. For example, when dissecting the performance of French forward Djibril Cissé, after a less than impressive outing in March 2006, while playing for Liverpool against Benfica in the Champions League, Dunphy helpfully explained to O'Herlihy:

> Here we have Cissé, right wing, attempts to put in a cross, BANG ... hits the full-back. Again, BANG hits the full-back. BANG ... off the full-back again, and once more, BANG ... smacks the full-back again ... Millions of euro and he can't clear the first man, I mean ... what's he trying to do to the full-back here? Kill him?

In such flashes of biting wit, Dunphy achieves a rare mixture of humour, insight and withering honesty that could not be imagined occurring anywhere except in the RTÉ studio. With a commitment to this at times risky television, and by effectively allowing Dunphy free rein, RTÉ has stolen the thunder of its wealthier competitors in the British market who seem to believe in resolutely non-offensive television at all costs.

Plainly, Giles and Dunphy have a special dynamic, honed over decades of co-commentary, but what is the role and significance of Liam Brady in the panel's success? Brady is the spoiler, symbolically sitting between Giles and Dunphy, and providing an essential counterpoint to the dangers of a cosy consensus forming. He is garrulous, independent-minded and nobody's fool, traits amply illustrated by his many contretemps with Dunphy. Dunphy has even admitted his surprise at the instant impact Brady had on the panel when he joined in 1998, arguing that he 'brought a rigour and a crankiness and an irascibility to it that no one could predict'. Brady himself has indicated, with a touch of humour, that he views his role as keeping Dunphy in his box when necessary and, indeed, when Dunphy has over-extended himself, Brady has usually been on hand to call him on it, bringing his own divergent opinions to bear in a forthright manner.

Their differing views on Roy Keane, for example, accurately show the strong opposition that Brady has brought to Dunphy's views. In the wake of the Saipan controversy when Keane, Ireland's captain, was sent home for his much-publicised outburst against the Irish manager, Mick McCarthy, Brady sided with McCarthy and even argued that the FAI should have banned Keane for life for his rebellious behaviour. Dunphy stood by Keane with undivided loyalty throughout the affair, effectively becoming his de facto spokesman on Irish and British television.

The diametrically opposed views of Dunphy and Brady resurfaced, and with extra intensity when Alex Ferguson sensationally released Keane from Manchester United in November 2005 for giving a pair of highly fractious interviews to Manchester United Television. Brady castigated Keane for speaking out publicly about his fellow players and accused him of cynically using the interview as a means of leveraging a new contract at Old Trafford. Worse still, for Dunphy, Brady claimed Keane had handpicked journalists to do his dirty work; including getting Mick McCarthy removed from the Ireland manager's job. Dunphy was incandescent about Brady's attitude and launched into a fiery defence of Keane, the intensity, and at times even desperation, of which, was largely provoked by Brady's unrelenting resistance.

Brady's immovable presence brought this discussion to life, forcing the burden of proof on to Dunphy by requiring him to justify his controversial commitment to the Keane cause. His resistance did not allow Dunphy to present an uninterrupted tribute to Keane's career but instead moved him on to the back foot and into an, at times, scattergun rant. For the viewer, it was just the kind of grown-up dispute that is now so rarely allowed to occur on television. Brady's combination of experience, knowledge and self-possession generated this and has led to so many other similar healthy debates on RTÉ's football coverage.

When Brady is absent, as he was while acting as assistant to Giovanni Trapattoni's Republic of Ireland team from March 2008 to April 2010, there is a noticeable difference in the panel's dynamic, with replacement panel members such as Ronnie Whelan and Ray Houghton unable to provide strong and astute opposition to Dunphy and Giles. The only exception is Graeme Souness who has shown himself to be a match for Dunphy and Giles, and is comfortably capable of holding his own. He has clashed with Dunphy on a number of occasions, in one instance questioning Dunphy's experience by asking him how many clubs he had managed, to which Dunphy memorably replied: 'I didn't manage anywhere. I've managed to stay alive for sixty-three and a half years, baby.'

As with Brady, Dunphy has developed a history of entertaining clashes with Souness, which have sometimes led to genuine tension and conflict on screen. This illustrates that the panel members understand that their first duty is to call it as they see it, and to worry about hurting fellow panellists' feelings later, an interdiction, which according to O'Herlihy, is made very clear to new panel members before they go on air. Generally the mutual respect between the panel members ensures that such strident differences of opinion pass by without any serious offence being taken.

There was one exception to this pattern, and it is perhaps the best example of the genuine openness of debate on the RTÉ panel. It is illustrated by the major disagreement that occurred between Giles and Dunphy in the wake of the Saipan affair. For fourteen months, the otherwise ideologically inseparable pair were not on speaking terms, yet they were contractually required to work regularly in the same studio. The background to the dispute lay in differing allegiances concerning the events that occurred in Saipan during Ireland's 2002 World Cup campaign. Giles sided with McCarthy, while Dunphy backed Keane throughout and clearly could not understand, or reconcile himself to, the fact that his long-time football companion did not agree with him.

Dunphy was implacable and was adopting a perfectly black and white approach to the Keane/McCarthy debate;

such was his dedication to Keane that he interpreted even a flicker of support for the McCarthy side as opposition to his position. It was a clear case of, 'you are either with me or against me', with Giles's reasonable arguments in McCarthy's favour having no effect.

Undoubtedly, Dunphy was disappointed to be left alone to face the storm at this critical juncture in Irish football. He was accustomed to receiving Giles's rational and much-respected support on most matters, and without it, in the tumult of Saipan, he was left appearing as an unhinged maverick, with a rather unhealthy obsession for all things related to Keane. Indeed, in his autobiography, Giles has said that Dunphy would have expected his support as a matter of course on such an issue. Giles says of Saipan: 'I think Eamon felt this was the same old FAI nonsense that we'd both been fighting against all our lives and, as a result, he may have expected me to support Keane.' The hoped-for support did not come, and the lengthy falling-out which would soon publicly reveal itself, was set in motion.

In an *Irish Times* feature, with sports correspondent Mary Hannigan speaking to Giles, Dunphy and O'Herlihy together, Dunphy has also claimed that he was hurt by what he saw as Giles's accusation that his independence had been compromised by being a ghostwriter for Keane's autobiography. In Dunphy's mind, Giles was effectively accusing him of 'being on the take', and of having literally 'bought into the whole Keane thing'. Although Giles denies ever making such a claim, Dunphy's mind was made up and the groundwork was set for the eventual tipping-point.

The event that cemented the rift occurred on Dunphy's then radio show, *The Last Word*, in August 2002. The topic of conversation was the fall-out from Keane's bold admission that he had harboured a grudge against, and thus fully intended to hurt, Alf-Inge Haaland in the career-ending tackle inflicted on the former Manchester City player in April 2001. Typically, Dunphy backed Keane and suggested as a counter-argument that John Giles had deliberately broken John Fitzpatrick's leg while Fitzpatrick was playing for Manchester United in 1972. Live on air, Dunphy claimed:

> John Giles broke the leg of a friend of mine called John Fitzpatrick who was playing for Manchester United and John [Fitzpatrick] never played the game again. John Giles ... was a notorious merchant for going over-the-top of the ball, which is something Roy Keane has never done in my experience, except in rage.

The implication was blatant: Keane may be violent in moments where his self-control abandons him, but Giles was calculating and deliberate about the infliction of over-the-top tackles. Keane was the misguided midfield dynamo, with an excess of energy sometimes carrying him into dangerous and regrettable tackles, whereas Giles was worse yet: he had malice aforethought. The slight was a step too far for Giles, who subsequently admitted that the only thing binding these once inseparable colleagues was the mere fact of contractual obligation, a fact that required both parties to work together for RTÉ.

In an interview with the *Irish Independent* in August 2002, Giles expressed his deep unhappiness about Dunphy's accusations. Of the claims, he said:

> No, that's totally untrue.... John Fitzpatrick never broke his leg. John Fitzpatrick had damaged

ligaments and didn't come off during the match. He played the rest of the game. I am very surprised Eamon would say that. To elaborate and embellish and even make up things like that is totally wrong and I am upset about it. If you are going to make statements like that, get your facts right. It is quite a serious statement to make.

Interestingly, Fitzpatrick subsequently came out in support of Giles in August 2002, denying Dunphy's controversial claims, and stating that his leg had not been broken in the challenge. He also noted that it was simply a '50/50 tackle and I came off the wrong side of it' thus contradicting Dunphy's claim that Giles had acted deliberately.

Giles and Dunphy's relationship would now be professional and no more, and RTÉ's soccer coverage would face a serious challenge: how to continue a football programme whose vibrancy depended on the open and honest interaction between its two senior panel members, who now were not even on speaking terms.

For better or worse, however, the show continued and the erstwhile friends found a way of masking their private disagreement for the sake of public propriety and contractual exigencies. Though a kind of truce was adopted on air, Giles has stated in his book, *John Giles: A Football Man: The Autobiography* that it became extremely difficult on the programme during this period. He has also highlighted how it was even more awkward for Bill O'Herlihy and the other panellists who were compelled to put on a brave face and pretend that all was well when every viewer knew it to be the contrary. Inevitably, the rapport suffered during these years, with the dialogue between Giles and Dunphy having a certain stilted formality about it, a distinct lack of fluency, and no little amount of icy politeness. For a programme whose major appeal was based on vigorous and free-flowing debate, such a situation could not have obtained for long without something giving way.

In the end, however, time resolved the conflict and for the two Dubliners, who had been friends since childhood, there was no need for showdown talks or dramatic summits. The life-long friendship was strong enough to resurface once the rawness and rashness of Saipan had dissipated. Although the John Fitzpatrick issue had been the precise point of breakdown between the two, clearly Saipan was the underlying source of acrimony, and, as subsequent events would prove, the emotional aftermath of this crisis in Irish football was fading away. McCarthy and Keane shook hands and made public amends, while Niall Quinn and Keane, who had played together for Ireland for approximately ten years before a bitter parting of the ways over Saipan in 2002, became closer than ever, teaming up in 2006 at the Stadium of Light to usher in a new era for Sunderland FC. For Giles, these events showed the absurdity of the rift, and he expresses his disbelief in his autobiography when he notes: 'We had known each other since we were kids, and now it had come to this, over something that happened between other people, on another continent.'

Dunphy's view on the event, typically, is less circumspect than Giles's version. In an *Irish Times* interview in June 2010, he too admitted that he did not enjoy this period of coolness, but he insists that he did not regret it. For him, it was a falling-out between grown men who knew the score. Their job was to regularly provide candid views on controversial football matters and, pointedly, not to concern themselves with whose sensibilities they may offend along the way. Of the conflict Dunphy has said:

> I didn't like it either. It wasn't nice, but I would be much more consumed by passions than John; he's a much calmer person. I just felt, fuck it, that's what I believe; if you don't like it, fuck you. But I'll see you next week. We'll have a drink. If you have a fundamental respect for somebody, it's not going to break on a one-issue thing. We're not politicians, we're people. I didn't regret it. I thought it was full-on combat. Let's go, baby.

In time, however, normality returned. Giles and Dunphy were reconciled, and RTÉ soccer regained its special dynamic, the factor that sets it apart.

The best way, then, to evaluate the RTÉ panel is to assess how they fare in comparison with their major rivals in Britain, the BBC and Sky Sports.

The first point to make is that the panel's discussions undoubtedly benefit enormously from being unburdened by the weight of vested interests. In contrast to their British counterparts, who invariably operate within the ideological constraint of having to promote the Premier League at all costs, the RTÉ panellists always call it as they see it. No player or manager can rest easy with superstar status in their eyes. If someone performs poorly, the fact is not ignored and cushioned with excuses. The party in question will be subjected to the criticism he deserves.

On British television, in contrast, certain sacred cows emasculate genuine debate by prohibiting panel members from crossing rigidly defined lines. A typical example is the almost pathological compulsion to vaunt English internationals when they do anything of consequence on a football pitch and the obverse need to shield them from any form of criticism when they perform below acceptable standards. This wilful blindness reaches its apotheosis when the England football team compete at international tournaments. With the predictable patriotism and 'spirit of '66' cranked up to the maximum, the capacity for objective judgment seems to vanish. In this kind of mood, the British panellists can work wonders, regularly transforming poor England performances into laudable displays of courage and commitment.

On the RTÉ panel, however, the England players receive the dose of reality they deserve when they underperform. To contrast the respective analysis of RTÉ and the BBC can lead to the justifiable feeling that you are watching different matches. An excellent example of this occurred at the 2010 World Cup, in South Africa, during England's final group game against Slovenia. After a terrible start to their group, failing to beat the USA and Algeria, England laboured to a 1-0 win against an ordinary Slovenian side and subsequently squeezed through to the second round. The following sequence, which appeared in Mary Hannigan's column in *The Irish Times* in the days after the game, expertly differentiates the reality gulf existing between the RTÉ and BBC analyses of the game. With the BBC panel fighting a desperate rearguard action and the RTÉ panel ritually disembowelling the England performance, it makes for highly amusing and instructive reading.

The drama began at half-time:

Alan Hansen: 'Once England got the goal, the confidence levels surged. They were excellent.'

Eamon Dunphy: 'They just didn't grow in confidence at all after the goal.'

Gary Lineker: 'The goal really settled them, didn't it? They pushed on from there.'

Ronnie Whelan: 'You'd think they'd have kicked on from when they scored, but they actually got worse.'

Roy Hodgson: 'England's crossing has been absolutely outstanding.'

John Giles: 'Some of the crossing was just awful.'

Alan Shearer: 'Rooney looks more confident. He's getting around the pitch a lot better.'

Eamon Dunphy: 'It's shocking to see Rooney so subdued. He's been reduced to a shivering wreck.'

Alan Shearer: 'They look much more comfortable on the ball. They're passing it with a purpose, with pace, they're closing down – a much better performance. It's encouraging.'

John Giles: 'They're much better than they have been, but they couldn't have been worse.'

At full-time, the interpretative divide, if possible, got even wider:

Lee Dixon: 'A great performance.'

Eamon Dunphy: 'Shocking ... absolutely incredibly bad ... pretty awful stuff.'

Alan Hansen: 'The commitment was there, the spirit was there, the enterprise was there, they passed it better – they could have scored five or six quite easily. Capello will obviously be delighted with the performance.'

John Giles: 'If that's the shackles off, what'll they be like when the shackles are back on.'

Harry Redknapp: 'We played with pace, we got after them, we pressed them, there wasn't a weakness in the team.'

Eamon Dunphy: 'They were astonishingly poor.'

Gary Lineker: 'He looked more like the Rooney we know.'

Ronnie Whelan: 'Rooney is a major worry, his form, his body language, his demeanour, everything.'

Lee Dixon: 'Gerrard was outstanding.'

Eamon Dunphy: 'I can't believe how bad Gerrard was today.'

Harry Redknapp: 'Across midfield we were top drawer.'

John Giles: 'Barry got worse as the game went on. Milner, Gerrard and Lampard the same.'

Harry Redknapp: 'Bring it on! Whoever we play, we'll be difficult to beat.'

Ronnie Whelan: 'If they don't improve, they'll go straight out. It was a very, very inept performance.'

When contrasted in this way, the analysis makes painful reading for the BBC panel, who seem obliged to bend over backwards to find positives about the England team, while the RTÉ experts exhibit all the freedom and comfort that comes from being without a vested interest.

England internationals aside, another pernicious notion of British football coverage is the dogmatic mantra that the Premier League is the best league in the world, a pronouncement made all too frequently to keep count of. Sky Television encourages the idea in order to sell satellite dishes, while the BBC and ITV seem to be just too patriotic to countenance any other possibility. This belief has led to lazy and unthinking football opinions, controlled by recurring themes that typically lead the analysis down predictable, tried-and-tested routes. Of course, the Premier League has arguably been the best league in the world for a number of years, but allowing this fact to cloud and obscure the ability to see its faults is where the problem lies.

A good example of this myopia can be gleaned from the respective attitudes that the RTÉ and BBC panels took towards Ronaldo's playing days in English football. On the BBC, with a panel typically compromising Gary Lineker, Alan Shearer, Mark Lawrenson and Alan Hansen, Ronaldo could do no wrong; the added underlying suggestion was that he must be the best player in the world because he was playing in the Premier League, 'the best league in the world'. Within the confines of this mental framework, to criticise Ronaldo at all was to criticise the Premier League, and such a thing was unthinkable, and so week after week selective editing showed only the better sides of Ronaldo.

To many sober commentators on the game, however, the idea that Ronaldo was the world's greatest player proved to be a difficult sell, despite his prodigious goal-scoring feats for Manchester United.

This lingering doubt was taken seriously and explored by the RTÉ panel and the frustrating package which is the Ronaldo experience was mercilessly laid bare. We saw Ronaldo in all his technicolor infuriating glory. Yes he was, and remains, a phenomenal goal scorer, yet as John Giles is fond of reminding viewers, although the Portuguese impresario may do many things that great players would do, yet equally he does certain things that the great players would never have done. So, in the RTÉ studio we saw the dark side of Ronaldo: the vanity, the wastefulness on the ball, the almost selective interest in games and the prima donna's convenient assumption of being excused from putting in a shift for the team when he was just not in the mood.

In an interview for the 3 Mobile Network, Dunphy has indicated how in one instance on *Match of the Day*, a threadbare highlights package of Ronaldo playing for Manchester United against Middlesborough was used to support the conclusion that the Portuguese forward was 'the best player in the world'. Dunphy expressed his disbelief by highlighting that this was uttered 'on the same weekend when Lionel Messi scored a hat-trick for Barcelona against Real Madrid', and he concluded by noting that 'when you see these clowns trying to hype up guys like him, you have to wonder about the BBC's sanity'.

In an almost one-man mission to puncture this hyper-bole, Dunphy has repeatedly blasphemed against the cult of Ronaldo, variously labelling him 'a cheat', 'a clown', 'a puffball' and 'a disgrace'. We are a long way from the *Match of the Day* sofa, but do we mind when television is this compelling?

Although Dunphy and the RTÉ panel appreciate the Premier League every bit as much as their BBC coun-terparts, the point is that they do not view it through a filter of cheerleading propaganda. They give praise and withering criticism when they are due. This is a league that Dunphy has frequently stated is comprised of four or five top teams and the remainder typically being made up of what he terms 'Ragball Rovers'. This is addictive, entertaining and straight-talking analysis, and if it some-times misses the mark, it compensates by its commitment to the expression of thought-provoking opinions.

In fact, Dunphy has extensively criticised the BBC's approach to football analysis, controversially writing them off as 'spoofers and muppets' for their chronic inabil-ity to get off the fence and call a spade a spade. He has accused them of being 'sycophantic', 'obsequious' and 'bullshitters ... who think their viewers are vegetables.'

Although expressed with characteristic colour, it is undoubtedly true that the BBC contingent of Gary Lineker, Alan Hansen, Mark Lawrenson and Alan Shearer exist in a dreary comfort zone where nothing of conse-quence ever seems to surface between the platitudes and clichés that typically dominate their exchanges. Simply, they seem too safe in their jobs, as if it is enough just to show up on a Saturday night and reel off an hour and thirty minutes of *Match of the Day* on auto-pilot.

Amidst the relentless banter, nobody ever seems to disagree about anything, or if they do, it is never of any consequence, being immediately submerged by an inane quip from Lineker. It is hardly surprising that there are no ripples in the docile tranquillity of the BBC studio. This is a monochromatic world of light-hearted cheeriness, and where there could be committed opinions and ideas, there are only uninformative and bland statements of the obvious, with Shearer in particular excelling in this regard. In fact, the former Newcastle United centre-forward has come in for scathing criticism amongst football journalists for his capacity to do everything but inform. Martin Kelner, writing in *The Guardian*, has posed the question: if 'in all the time the former England captain has been trousering great handfuls of licence-payers' money to put on a nice shirt and sit next to Gary Lineker, has he ever said one single thing that has added in any way whatsoever to the sum of human wisdom?' Shearer, it seems, as soon as his playing days were behind him, was fast-tracked and veritably airlifted into the BBC studio principally because he was a former England captain and general all-round Premier League legend. That Shearer is patently out of his depth at this level did not seem to exercise the minds of the BBC hierarchy. In truth, it is just another victory for style over substance, to the detriment of serious and thoughtful analysis.

On this point, Dunphy has highlighted Shearer and his BBC colleagues for their uncanny ability to say nothing at all. 'They just don't seem to have any conviction about how they make their judgments. Sometimes they talk like they're on sleeping pills and other times they just spout hype, hype, hype.'

It is not just Eamon Dunphy and his colleagues who have picked up on this. There has been a growing contingent in British football media for some years who have questioned the BBC's capacity to provide intelligent and illuminating football analysis. Many commentators have focused on how the BBC's football coverage has lost its edge and has essentially become a harmless forum for light entertainment with the likes of Lineker, Hansen, Lawrenson and Shearer being well-trained proponents of this cuddly art. The panel just get on so well, and how boring this is. We could hope for the kind of coruscating argument and insight offered up by the RTÉ panel as a matter of course, but instead all we get is grating joviality and a repetitive series of pally in-jokes which have been described by Scott Murray, writing for *The Observer*, as the 'inane old boys in the dressing room approach' to football analysis.

This manifests itself in a thoroughly irritating bonhomie that seems unavoidably to say: 'Do we have the best job in the world or what?' Making the point in the English football magazine, *When Saturday Comes*, Paul Doyle has summed up the BBC crew as a 'giggling gaggle of self-satisfied golfing buddies', who 'inform and entertain no one but themselves'. Taking the golfing reference one step further, Martin Kelner has argued that, no matter what the issue under discussion is, the panel always inevitably return to the 'usual cosy 19th hole consensus', as if the matters under examination do not really matter.

It may be fine for Lineker and Co. to pass a Saturday evening in such pleasant and agreeable surroundings, but their anodyne, buddy-buddy exchanges bear scarcely any resemblance to the nuanced and full-blooded debates that take place between football fans every day. As national football analysts, the very least they should aim to achieve is to be tuned into the level of such discussions, and to perhaps contribute something that will encourage, dare I even say incite, further comment and discussion. The truth, however, is that the BBC panel is out of touch.

The panellists' analysis delivers so tame a punch that the viewer is left with little or nothing to respond to. After all, how can you agree or disagree with such meek analysis?

The RTÉ panel, on the contrary, does not pull its punches. The members express reasoned and strong opinions that you might not always agree with but which nonetheless demand a response, and, in so doing, contribute greatly to the football debates of the day. For Dunphy, making this connection with football fans is the *sine qua non* of valid football analysis. He has stated: 'Punditry's supposed to be real and a reflection of what the fans would be arguing about when watching a game.' The RTÉ panel does, more often than not, achieve this connection but the BBC panel seems trapped in its own solipsistic world of stating the 'bleeding obvious', a malady to which very few dedicated football fans will ever succumb.

It is all a matter of priorities. The BBC has clearly chosen to emphasise style over substance, in a pattern that has led to years of neglect in their football coverage, while RTÉ, which may lag behind in its production values, has managed to corner that elusive quarry: substance. With their grey suits and cranky dispositions, Dunphy, Giles and Brady may resemble guests at a country wedding, rather than smooth television personalities, but do we care when they so consistently deliver such high-quality analysis of all football matters?

Sadly, for British football fans, the BBC has taken the other road, making an art form out of a style-driven, glitzy and polished presentation, where everyone near a camera seems to have a fabulous tan, but cannot deliver a single sentence of lasting meaning. This has prompted Taylor Parkes, commenting for *When Saturday Comes*, to write off the beleaguered BBC panel as 'guys under bright lights in differently coloured ties and £200 shirts'.

Although, in a truly unusual state of affairs, the BBC does actually have talented experts on its books, but they are nicely tucked away on either BBC Radio 5 or on their late-night offering on Saturdays, *The Football League Show*, where presumably any strident and thought-provoking point of view will receive limited attention and so do minimal damage. Robbie Savage and Steve Claridge, for instance, fit into this class of talented BBC radio exiles who should really be featuring prominently on their flagship TV coverage.

Even *Football Focus*, the BBC's Saturday morning offering, which, as the title suggests, is nominally their forum for a more in-depth analysis, fails to deliver anything of significance to the viewer. It merely succeeds in adding yet another hour of dreadful banter and colourless opinions to the BBC's weekly output. It does, to be fair, give us weekly interviews with footballers and managers, but these are invariably tepid and pointless exercises, with players being allowed to hide behind the usual gallery of prosaic commonplaces they employ when they want to say precisely nothing. Taylor Parkes, once more, writing in *When Saturday Comes*, has diagnosed with precision and humour the emptiness of these interviews. He writes that they typically return to familiar themes: 'Someone is interviewed on a training pitch and says the lads are all well up for the trip to Southampton; someone is interviewed in a dark room and says he won't stop thumping people because it's part of his game. Focus my arse.'

Although the BBC has its share of shortcomings, they cannot hope to wrest the title of worst analysis from the clutches of Sky Sports, a television behemoth that has been, in equal part, sexing up and dumbing down football analysis for the best part of twenty years.

A Sunday afternoon of Sky football coverage is not a panel of football analysts discussing football; it is a hostage situation, with be-suited, make-up-laden footballers of past and present, visibly harangued into a hard afternoon's work of product promotion. No matter what the level of game, no matter what the quality of player on show, these put-upon pundits are exhorted to read it from the script, and the script never lets us down. No game is so insignificant and lacking in incident that it cannot be given the Sky Sports treatment and transformed into some such variant of 'a cracking match', with the presenter rather unsubtly nudging the panel's thoughts in the 'correct' direction. This is a role that Richard Keys played with great aplomb before his resignation from Sky in January 2011, owing to the overtly sexist comments he made about the competence of young female referee Sian Massey.

If we break down Sky's football coverage to its irreducible components, what we find is a product, the Premier League, which has been progressively commodified by Sky in its twenty years of existence, and, of course the product has to sell and so must always be good. This insidious hyperbole is the fundamental prejudice that derails Sky's analysis and undermines its ability to provide honest and accurate coverage. It ensures that all conversation is rehearsed, stilted and entirely predictable. The product must deliver, so the script invariably mandates that the game be talked up, rather than dissected truthfully. In the end, in this world of incessant, upbeat analysis where everything is always splendid, nothing has any meaning any more. It is a bizarre condition which Barney Ronay, writing for *The Guardian*, has rightly called a 'crisis of diminishing superlatives' where, as he points out, we are subjected to a 'superheated Sky-driven

Premier League where everything is great pretty much all the time', and with justifiable confusion he asks: 'How do you express excitement or even mild approval in a world where the emotional barometer is continually pitched at a level of damp-eyed superbity[*sic*]?'

Obviously, football fans should not be naive. Resistance, naturally, is futile. There is no escape from the machine, with *Sky Sports News* keeping the temperature ticking over nicely in the dead of night by offering a terrifyingly complete twenty-four-hour, seven-day-a-week service to addled insomniac-football-junkies who are unable to wait until dawn for their fix. How can any self-respecting football fan sleep soundly when he knows he may be missing vital 'breaking news' such as Darlington FC moving to a new ground or Bristol Rovers being forced to release three promising youngsters? It is not easy being a football fan in the world of *Sky Sports News*. One has to always be on, just as 'IT' is always on. Even for the innocent couch-dweller hoping to snatch a guilty nap during coverage, Sky has a solution: the futuristic whooshing noises of their graphics as they career onto your screen will promptly arrest your decline into a much-needed slumber and reconnect you to the system once again, open-eyed and ready for further 'breaking news'.

If we could give this uneasy hybrid of melodrama and hype a formula it would be: marketing meets football, bypasses honesty, and equals theatre, and bad theatre at that.

For nothing sums up the exchanges of the Sky Sports panel as well as the designation 'bad theatre'. Each week we are treated to a poorly rehearsed, shoddily acted and unnecessarily long drama which feels more like a party political broadcast than a benign couple of hours of football talk. Unlike the RTÉ panellists, who are refreshingly natural and open in front of the camera, the Sky guests often appear hectored and uncomfortable, as if a part of them resists the pressure to toe the party line, which requires them to endlessly spin positives about the football on offer, regardless of any evidence to the contrary. In Richard Keys's renowned radio interview with *Talk Radio*, when he sought to explain his involvement in the Sian Massey sexism row, he stated that one of his main tasks, as presenter, was to make guests comfortable and encourage them to relax in front of the live cameras. We must thank Keys for this piece of insider knowledge because we would not have guessed it. Any random perusal of the Sky panel on a Sunday afternoon will attest otherwise, and invariably present at least one member who looks as if he would rather be anywhere else but lodged in front of a Sky Sports cameraman.

A very good example is Graeme Souness, who appears taciturn and circumspect on Sky but is a liberated force when he takes his place on the RTÉ panel. This is the man who after only days of beginning work for RTÉ during the 2006 World Cup, labelled Garth Crooks a disgrace to journalism for conducting a fawning post-match interview with the England manager Sven-Göran Eriksson. Clearly, Souness was enjoying throwing off the shackles and could only do so because he saw that nobody else on the panel had shackles on, and that such bracing, open expression was not shocking, but simply the norm. After all, he had just beheld Eamon Dunphy utter the disbelieving words: 'Bill, that's the first time I've witnessed sex between two men on the BBC.' Perhaps, this was Souness's epiphany moment, his coming of age as a football analyst when he was suddenly granted a tantalising glimpse of a world beyond Sky. O'Herlihy has even stated, in what must be a veiled reference to

Souness, 'that certain people, without mentioning names, who have worked for Sky told us that you can't say what you want really because they do not want their games rubbished.' It must be like therapy, expiation even, for Souness to be afforded regular opportunities of penance for his sins on Sky, by firing a couple of salvos across the bows of received myths in the inspirational company of the RTÉ panel.

What further restricts the possibility of insightful analysis on Sky is the panellists' insistence on highlighting and then hammering to death silly angles of the game in question. Rather than engaging in unplanned and intelligent comment, the story is already written before the cameras roll. One week it may be all about the return of a manager to his former stomping ground and what it means to the fans. Another week, it will concern how such and such a team will be desperate to get its first win at such and such a ground in fifteen or so years. It is all so stultifying and unnatural. If by conversation, we mean novelty, surprise and open-endedness in the conduct of a discussion, then we can venture the opinion that no true conversation has ever happened on Sky Sports. All we are a given are a succession of dull, scripted exchanges.

Even the rationale for choosing experts on Sky reveals the station's disinterest in promoting serious analysis and further displays its determination to miss the point. Rather than choose analysts for their pedigree, Sky will often insist on having a former player from each of the teams on display contriving to dispense wisdom. What has this got to do with football analysis? Nothing, and it merely points to the conclusion that Sky has scant regard for the substance of what is being discussed, and view the analysis part of their football coverage as little more than a box-ticking exercise.

When it comes to selecting experts, spectacular proof of Sky's skewed priorities can be evidenced by the arrangement whereby Jamie Redknapp seems to actually pass for a respected analyst. If ever the selection of a panel member was based on purely televisual considerations, then Redknapp's appointment is it. Patently Sky gave him the nod for reasons that had little to do with football, but plenty to do with the fact that he can turn himself out reasonably well on camera and generally can be trusted to display superhuman levels of enthusiasm, no matter how dull the occasion. And to think that Sky apparently headhunted Redknapp from the BBC, such was their determination to have him. In his 'unfathomably tight trousers' and not-so-very-accidental-at-all two-day designer stubble, Redknapp has been rightly described by Dave Hanratty, writing for *backpagefootball.com*, as a 'walking, talking advert for Topman', rather than as someone whose job it should be to expound intelligent thoughts about football games. He is Sky's very own Adonis, a telegenic dream, who comes complete with the full battery of unthinking myths about the Premier League that Sky so loves to sell. Perfect analyst material for Sky, in other words.

Certainly, Redknapp played football at one point in his career, and quite well, but we now know, at least, that he did not spend his plentiful spare time contemplating the minutiae of football tactics. That's one nagging question we can put to rest. Indeed, nothing seems to make sense about this man. He is so eager to get his word in ahead of his more senior colleagues, yet when he speaks, all this well-meaning excitability is perfectly countervailed by his lack of any insight. He is yet another football analyst locked in a desperate and unsuccessful search for a varied vocabulary. Redknapp has one mode of expression, and seemingly only one adjective to help him achieve it. Barney Ronay has labelled it the 'Redknapp Index' for his novel emphasis on and multiple use of the word 'top' to explain just how good Premier League players really are: Gerrard, Lampard, Rooney, with Redknapp's mono-syllabic tour de force, all top, top, top players.

But Redknapp is not alone in this marketing project. Sky presenters generally know how to lead him along, drawing out of him exactly what they require. Richard Keys was adept at this strategy. Although Keys's days as football anchor ended with himself and Sky parting on less than happy terms, he was the most loyal of servants over a twenty-year period, providing the glassy-eyed menace and oh-so-fake laughter to keep proceedings carrying along at just the right breezy tempo. Keys was the ringmaster of this staged world, where, in his pumped-up language, everything was 'LIVE' and where we were frequently terrorised with the exhortation, 'DON'T GO AWAY', in tones that left us in no doubt that something terrible would happen if we dared change channels during the advertising break.

This is all so patronising, and leads to the inescapable conclusion that Sky just does not respect its football audience. The analysis is kept at such an infantile level, with only the genuine quality of Andy Gray – before he was dismissed for his role in the Sian Massey controversy – to sometimes raise the bar, that one can only assume that Sky regards its football viewers as persons of low intelligence. By displaying an astonishing degree of ignorance, what Sky neglects to understand about football fans is that, as Paul Hayward put it in *The Guardian*: 'People who follow football properly spend more time thinking about the game than is probably good for them' and expect, 'from ex-players the kind of enlightenment that is beyond their own musings on the bus or train.'

The RTÉ panellists take this point seriously and treat their audience with respect, knowing that the football public cannot be so easily duped with platitudes and hyperbole. Instead, what they offer the viewer are opinions that are reasoned, nuanced, brave and controversial in a way that excites and generates further argument. The panel does not always get it right, but then the point is not about always being right. It is about providing views on the game that are intelligent and courageous, the kind of views that excite the football community, and in doing so, lead to further enlightening debate. On this point Dunphy has said, 'What we try to do is to be part of that community, which doesn't mean being a smartass, doesn't mean always being right; it means being prepared to go out on a limb.' On the Sky and BBC panels, it is not a difficult task to be always right; sitting tight and refusing to commit yourself to any position of note necessarily affords you the luxury of never being corrected on anything. The unceasing monotony, critically speaking, creates a protective area where nothing of consequence is uttered and so nothing can subsequently be contradicted.

Released from this safe, cotton-wool-coated world, the RTÉ panellists, when they are wrong, are often gloriously wrong and, when right, are gloriously right. Either way, serious football commentary occurs and the well-informed football public acknowledges and appreciates this fact.

Dunphy has specifically attacked Sky on this issue, arguing that the station's view of the football fan is that of a low-intelligence bloke, afflicted with chronic laddishness, who is obviously incapable of constructing anything resembling a thoughtful opinion on the game. Of Sky's errant caricature of the football fan, Dunphy has said: 'For them ... the guy watching is a couch potato. He's got a can of beer in his hand and he's showing off to his mates.' This is the lad culture, so nefariously and needlessly associated with football, yet this seems to be the precise target audience for Sky. Contrasting this conception with the viewers of RTÉ football, Dunphy draws a sharp distinction: 'That's not our audience. They [our audience] are actually interested in the analysis, they're interested in good conversation, honest opinions ... they're not half-cut on the couch looking to be patronised.'

If we examine Sky more closely, we can see this caricature running through all its football programmes. The hype-machine which is *Gillette Soccer Saturday*, with its boisterous cast of likely lads, engaging in mock pub banter for the afternoon, is aimed squarely at the same demographic: the beer-swilling yob who demands much shouting and certainly nothing too cerebral.

Delving further into the abyss, we meet *Soccer AM*, which has been rightly described by Sarah Sands in *The Independent* as 'only a step away from the lads' mags', with each week a female football fan parading around the studio in her tight football top to a chorus of wolf-whistles. Whether or not this is patently sexist is another argument, but such a caper certainly has nothing to do with football analysis.

In plain terms, Sky is dedicated to keeping things dumb, and this can be seen in even the smallest of details. This was evidenced by the way in which Keys, when he was in his pre-resignation pomp, constantly gazed disconcertingly into the camera during conversations, just in case the viewer was unable to keep up with the blistering intellectual gymnastics on show. Sky lives in this nightmare world of viewer paranoia: tormented and terrorised that at any moment the viewer's ailing attention will lead to a changing of the channel.

In contrast, on RTÉ the viewer is not condescended to. Whether it is Dunphy, Giles or Brady holding forth, the viewer is assumed to be someone who has probably spent too many hours pondering the vagaries of football problems and who should be treated with genuine respect.

That the RTÉ panel has created something special and worthy of serious critical note has not gone entirely unnoticed in Britain. The late Alan Ruddock, writing in *The Guardian*, sought to persuade floundering British viewers that there is another way. In an otherwise grey world of fatuous comment, where 'most of what passes for television analysis would not pass muster in a pub', Ruddock lauded what he called 'RTÉ's gang of four' who 'treat viewers as intelligent and informed fans and approach each match they review with a determination to provide insight and provoke response.'

In contrast, Ruddock wearily lamented the state of football analysis on British television, making the key point that 'for too much of the time producers and pundits appear to treat viewers with contempt.' He concluded, 'it is not beyond the wit of the BBC, ITV, Sky or Setanta to recognise one simple fact: fans are not morons.'

Making the same point, and summing up the poverty of options available for the knowledgeable viewer, Paul Hayward has highlighted how football analysis in Britain has become reduced to two modes of television broadcasting: 'shouting into the lug 'ole of the imagined bloke in the pub and cosy-cosy on the sofa for all the family.'

There is another way for football analysis between this unsatisfying dichotomy that Sky and the BBC offer. It need not appeal to blokes only or to the whole family, but to anyone, male or female, who enjoys thinking about football in a rigorous and mind-enriching way.

Acceptance of this fact defines the RTÉ panellists, and has allowed them to venture into unexplored sporting territory, where intellect and football are not mutually exclusive quantities, but can combine to provide frequently thrilling and addictive viewing. The RTÉ panel both edifies and entertains.

Conclusion

'Survival ... without having to kiss anybody's ass'

In order to pinpoint the features that make Dunphy stand out from the burgeoning crowd of football commentators and journalists at work in Ireland and Britain, I will consider the criticisms that some of his peers have levelled against him over the years and attempt to answer those charges. The process highlights what is unique about this veteran broadcaster, both in the positive and negative sense. I will then conclude with some general comments about Dunphy's style of football analysis.

If we are to identify the qualities that make Dunphy's journalistic style distinct, perhaps the most obvious one is his tendency to be controversial. Dunphy does not hold back and has not been unduly worried about whom he might offend along the way. This ability to shock separates him from other journalists and has significantly helped to ensure his prominent place in Irish football commentary over the last three decades. Dunphy, as an analyst, has a knack for adopting the unpopular position, the extreme view that generally flies in the face of consensus. His niche has been carved from this outsider stance: a talent for minting interesting, left-field ideas and then to steadfastly nail his colours to that mast, come what may. This has guaranteed Dunphy periodic pariah-status in Ireland with his fervid opposition to Jack Charlton, Mick McCarthy and Giovanni Trapattoni being prime examples of this, but it has also brought him enormous publicity.

Why are Dunphy's views so intense? Are we always to take him seriously? We might ask if he could, with sincerity, become hot and bothered about so many public issues or if there is something more calculated at play? Does Dunphy, as some critics have suggested, depend on controversy as his career lifeblood? The argument here is that Dunphy has grasped the simple fact that to survive, in a highly competitive multi-media environment, you have to be noticed – and a lot; stir up a little outrage every now and then or you will rapidly become old news.

Can Dunphy's many forthright pronouncements be understood as deliberate attempts to provoke the public's ire so that at least we'll be talking about him, even if we do not like him? Is he a secret advocate of Harold Macmillan's contention that it is 'Better to be reviled than ignored'? An unnamed former colleague of Dunphy's, quoted in the *Irish Independent* in January 2010, has suggested that Dunphy has consciously developed a successful career out of this basic principle of marketing, with Joe Public being the ever-willing consumer. He notes: 'Eamon was the first Irish broadcaster to realise that as long as you are not ignored, if 100 people listen to you and 50 love you and 50 hate you, you are going to have a big impact.' Dunphy divides, for sure, but it is a division from which he can only benefit; people either love him or love to hate him. Either way he is the topic of conversation.

Paul Hyland, writing in the *Evening Herald* in October 2009, during the height of Dunphy's opposition to Trapattoni's management of the Irish team, dismissed the outspoken pundit as 'the nation's most enduring curmudgeon' whose constant objective is to garner attention, at whatever cost. For Hyland, Dunphy contrives to be out of step with everyone by deliberately contradicting the consensus. Michael McMullan, presenter of Today FM's *Premier League Live*, quoted in the *Irish Independent* on 17 October 2009, was even more dismissive of what he views as Dunphy's cynical positioning of himself as the anti-establishment provocateur, ever on hand with a quotable line to fill the headlines. For McMullan, at this stage, Dunphy is little more than a tub-thumping attention-seeker. He further claims that committed football fans, having seen through his act, no longer even consider him to be an important analyst.

> He's box office, that's for sure, but he's no longer relevant for any serious football fan. Anybody with an intelligent, sensible approach to football gave up on Dunphy long ago ... He is a sideshow who is in danger of becoming the main attraction. Everything he says now seems geared towards generating the maximum amount of coverage. It's almost like he thinks 'I haven't been in the papers for the past couple of weeks and I'm going to say something to change that'. He's not an analyst; he's a broadcaster in the style of the 'shock jocks' you get on US radio ... He is a very smart broadcaster in that he knows that in this dumbed-down age people are looking for soundbites. And boy can he deliver soundbites.

Furthermore, the website *Soccer-Ireland.com* has proclaimed that 'Eamon Dunphy has made a very good living in Ireland out of being contentious' and it has sought to call his bluff on what they view as his addiction to sensationalism, arguing that it is not always even possible to be sure if the analyst is being sincere. The site claims that 'with Dunphy it can be difficult to know if he is making a serious point or just giving his controversial persona one of its regular transfusions'. Making a similar point, Conor O'Callaghan, writing in *Red Mist: Roy Keane & the Football Civil War*, suggests that 'Dunphy has styled himself as the begrudger's begrudger, the worm in the fake rose of Irish football glory.'

Is Dunphy's technique so crude? Does he tactically navigate his way towards the extremities, safe in the knowledge that, by doing so, his hold on the public's attention can be perpetuated? Dunphy himself has flatly denied these charges. In his 2009 interview with Ursula Halligan, aired on TV3, he defended his hard-hitting style of journalism when Halligan raised the accusation that it was manufactured:

> If I was that kind of fraud, I would have been found out long, long ago. All I have ever done is say publicly what other people would be saying privately ... People say one thing for public consumption which is called journalism and the other thing they say is when the lights are off, there is nobody around, they are having a drink. Ah, this is the way it really is.

Dunphy then concluded by claiming that he merely says 'what others are afraid to say' and that it was this noble intention to bring searing honesty to public debate that, in the first instance, encouraged him to become a journalist. He believed he could do things differently:

> I went into journalism at the age of thirty-five. I was
> a fully formed human being. I wasn't impression-
> able. I wasn't going to copy any other journalist.
> I thought I could do it in a more forthright way
> and that I wouldn't take any prisoners. I didn't
> belong to any clique, in journalism or out of jour-
> nalism.

According to Dunphy, nothing he says is faked. The passion is real. This is just who he is and the public can take it or leave it. This is a view supported by Glen Killane, RTÉ's head of sport, who disagrees with those who claim that Dunphy is quarrelsome for the sake of it. 'It's a charge that's levelled at him and it's very unfair. He may have a colourful turn of phrase, but he genuinely believes in what he says.' Dunphy also revealed in an interview with Michael Walker in *The Irish Times* on 10 October 2007 that he does not care whom he offends with his strident opinions, stating that his job is not to be liked. 'I just feel the basic position should be that if you have these deep convictions and you want to express them, then don't expect to be loved ... I don't want to be loved. It doesn't bother me.'

True to his word, during his time as presenter of the radio show *The Last Word* from 1997 to 2002, Dunphy never shirked from reading out the less than flattering listener comments that his brusque style attracted. In fact, he positively exulted in airing these jibes in a process that seemed only to make him stronger. Two incidents stand out from the show's output, both of which happened in August 1998. One listener, Dunphy informed us, considered him an 'egotistical bore'. Another, less bashful individual, preferred to liken his commentary to 'verbal diarrhoea'. Where other presenters may have viewed such comments as an unwelcome invitation for some soul-searching, with Dunphy the message was clear: 'bring it on'. It was just grist to his mill.

It is clear that Dunphy's rawness as a journalist, when he first left football, ensured that he was divested of the acquired professional courtesy that might restrain other journalists. He did not grow up in the industry and so he did not respect reputations or rules. If there was any accepted etiquette, he quickly saw to shelving it with his outrageous irreverence and capacity to shock, ensuring nothing less than full-blooded opinions. Dunphy is undoubtedly the kind of journalist who considers that his first duty is to be transgressive, so any fallout arising from this confrontational style must remain largely of incidental concern. In an interview that was published in *Under the Spotlight: Conversations with 17 Leading Irish Journalist*s, a collection compiled by journalist Roger Greene, Dunphy suggested that it was his basic duty as an analyst to deliver the unadorned truth to the public on important football matters. He commented, outlining his beginnings in journalism with the *Sunday Tribune*:

> I started off with a bang ... having been such an avid believer and reader of newspapers, I felt that really people who consume your newspaper, your radio programme, your television programme, are entitled to the real story, as raw as you can give it to them ... I went into it with a determination, which I hope I have to this day, to act in the interest of the person who is turning the dial or buying the paper ... The public pay the piper.

Dunphy then went on to deliver a broadside against the journalist fraternity whom he considered to have failed to meet this calling of fidelity to the public implicit in their vocation. In words that may well stick in the craw of self-respecting journalists and analysts, he claimed:

> Journalists are involved in, basically, deceiving the public, not in a malicious way, but they get sucked into it. They're in the loop. The people are outside the loop and they decide what the people can have. Because if you tell it as it is, you are going to offend those who are powerful and who are close to you, who can do you favours, who can give you stories, who can give you an OBE or just their time to talk to you.

Such austere principles may read well, but without independence they count for nothing. If you have to kowtow to paymasters, eventually your noblest aims will be compromised by grubby realities, and so Dunphy, aware of this danger, has always jealously guarded his right to speak freely, a process he has described as 'Survival on my own terms ... without having to kiss anybody's ass.'

Without doubt, in his early days as a journalist, Dunphy was an upstart. Seamus Martin, Sports Editor of the *Sunday Tribune* from 1980 to 1982, the newspaper where Dunphy received his first breakthrough as a full-time soccer correspondent, alluded to the ambiguous nature of the beast he had unleashed on an unsuspecting Irish public: 'I have created a monster. The Mary Shelley of Irish journalism, that's me.'

Although Dunphy has made an enviable career and a lucrative living out of this no-holds-barred journalism, he has on occasion been brought to book by the laws of defamation. Dunphy's approach is high-risk. He operates on a tightrope, seeking to push the boat out farther each time with increasingly contentious opinions without crossing over into libellous territory. Dunphy has to position himself carefully in this dangerous flirt with the law, knowing that strong opinions are what define him. If he was never at risk of being sued, then he would never be saying anything interesting. That certainly seems to be the rationale behind his style of journalism. He does, in fact, even appear to enjoy the jousting, at times openly offending against basic tenets of decency and provoking the wrath of the law. In May 2002, for instance, when the Keane/McCarthy debate was raging, he entreated listeners of *The Last Word* radio show to continue sending in messages of support for him. 'Keep them coming', he said, 'we'll need them for the libel case'. In another broadcast of his show, aired during the turmoil of Saipan on 4 June 2002, Dunphy was more than happy to fan the flames. He brazenly responded to one listener's questioning of his loyalty to Ireland's cause on the eve of the first round clash with Germany: 'Yes, I will be on RTÉ tomorrow and thanks to those who want me to – as to those who don't, tough shit. As to whether I'll be wearing a German shirt and a swastika, we'll see in the morning.'

The heat that Dunphy generates inevitably gives him an unusual intimacy with libel laws, like a recidivist who gains an almost reassuring familiarity with police authority. Naturally, locating the mean between strident opinion and libellous comment is hardly a science, and Dunphy sometimes has got it wrong. A perfect example of this pattern arose from the long-running feud that he shared with his arch journalistic nemesis, Cathal Dervan. The two football correspondents have a colourful history. Together, they orchestrated a public, and frequently childish, tit-for-tat blizzard of barbs and counter-barbs that culminated in their public disagreement over Saipan in 2002. They loved to hate each other, with Dervan's support for Mick McCarthy's management of Ireland and his criticisms of Roy Keane being a constant sticking point in their rivalry. They even went toe-to-toe on the current affairs show *Prime Time* on two occasions to represent their respective corners, and they lined up against each other in print with Dervan ghosting McCarthy's account of the 2002 World Cup, while Dunphy worked on *Keane: The Autobiography*.

Another source of acrimony was Dunphy's support for former Premier League club Wimbledon FC's proposed move to Dublin in 1996, an idea that Dervan opposed on the grounds that it would damage the already fragile public interest in the League of Ireland. Dunphy begged to differ, believing that having clubs such as Liverpool and Manchester United visiting Dublin regularly could only benefit the domestic game. Wimbledon, at the time, was without its own stadium, and gave serious consideration to the move on the basis that the club could develop a healthy fan base in a city such as Dublin, where there was both a large population and an intense interest in the Premier League.

On the Wimbledon issue, Dervan was right. The frequent presence of Premier League clubs playing in Dublin would surely have dealt a hammer blow to the already ailing fortunes of the League of Ireland, a competition that typically leaks fans to its more glamorous equivalent in England. As for Dunphy, it was another instance of his unfair disregard for his country's domestic league. Although he freely admits that he has not set foot in a League of Ireland ground since his retirement from the game with Shamrock Rovers in 1978, and so cannot be in a position to make an informed judgment on its status, he has deigned to repeatedly write off the League as the preserve of small-mindedness and opportunistic backwoodsmen. This irrational attitude to a League that needs all the support it can get from people with a profile such as Dunphy's seems not to be based on any stable football argument, but to simply be the undigested, bitter aftertaste of his unhappy experiences at Shamrock Rovers three decades ago and more.

Dervan and Dunphy had insulted each other before. Dervan, however, took particular umbrage with a piece Dunphy wrote for the *Sunday Independent* on 10 March 1996. The context of the piece was the resignation of the FAI president Louis Kilcoyne because of public dissatisfaction with the manner in which international match tickets had been sold. Dunphy, a staunch supporter of Kilcoyne, rounded on those in the media whom he believed had orchestrated a reprehensible witch-hunt to bring Kilcoyne down and Dervan, in this regard, came in for special treatment. In what could hardly be described as a subtle reference, Dunphy wrote: 'One particularly scurvy little pup, a media non-entity, can boast of felling Mr President. RTÉ, *Morning Ireland* and *Prime Time*, in particular, offered this journalistic low-life a platform.'

Dervan was reportedly 'staggered' to read the words, certain that the Irish public would easily pick him out as the target of Dunphy's abuse. He brought legal proceedings against Independent Newspapers, its editor Aengus Fanning, and Dunphy himself, alleging that the writer's words had defamed him and in a two-day High Court action held in May 1999, the matter came to a head. Dunphy's counsel sought to argue that his client's views constituted fair comment on a matter of public interest and were consequently justified. Although a settlement was reached, the cross-examination of Dervan proved to be highly amusing and revealed the kind of intense feelings that Dunphy's opinions generate in other analysts. Dervan, it transpired, had himself dished out quite a lot of bile in Dunphy's direction. He was presented with his own words and invited to comment. In various pieces, written in the late 1990s, he had indirectly described Dunphy as a 'failed footballer', a 'pitiful radio host', a 'TV puppet' and even more bizarrely, in a strange kind of shorthand, he began referring to Dunphy simply as 'Eamon Dead'. In one article, which appeared in the *Sunday World* in 1996, attacking the idea of Wimbledon FC moving to Dublin, Dervan called Dunphy the 'Dead Man', with the feature also including a skull in place of Dunphy's head. Dervan explained to the court that what he had meant was that the campaign Dunphy had supported to bring the English Premier League club to Dublin, was dead; hence 'Eamon Dead'.

Matters took a surreal turn when Dunphy's counsel asked Dervan to explain what he had meant by 'Wimbledon Weasels', a phrase the writer had used in another piece to deride those behind the move, including Dunphy. Stephen Dodd, reporting on the case for the *Sunday Independent* in May 1999, paraphrased the absurd courtroom exchange, with Dervan scrambling desperately for a way to dodge the glaringly obvious interpretation:

'I felt they were weaselling their way into Ireland,' Mr Dervan said. 'I was suggesting they were trying to get in through the backdoor.' Mr Feeney gave the two usual dictionary definitions of the word 'weasel'. It referred either to an animal, or it described something that was sly and deceitful. Which of these definitions did Mr Dervan have in mind when he wrote the piece? Mr Feeney pressed him. 'You used the word weasel', he said. 'In the animal context', Mr Dervan replied. 'Oh, Mr Dervan,' said the Lawyer. 'Are you seriously suggesting that?' 'Yes,' said Cathal Dervan. 'Weasels go underground. They dig and ...' He left the sentence unfinished.

Perhaps wisely, Dervan did leave it at that, realising that it is not only weasels that are adept at digging holes for themselves.

Closely allied with the charge that Dunphy's views are compromised by his determination to always be more outrageous than the next aspiring controversialist is the idea that he is perhaps even more undermined by his frequent habit of blatantly contradicting himself. Any analysis of Dunphy's output has to address the issue, because Dunphy does not even try to conceal it. On the contrary, he flaunts it, adopting strikingly opposite opinions as and when he feels like it and, generally, without believing himself to be under any compulsion to inform the rest of us about the dramatic change of heart. Obviously this leaves Dunphy open to claims that he flip-flops with abandon and is, consequently, not to be taken seriously when he launches into yet another of his famous outbursts. The examples abound. Many times he has proclaimed the greatness of Liam Brady as a player while working alongside him as a panellist on RTÉ, yet in 1983, after Ireland had lost a two-goal lead against Holland, Brady was 'nothing of the kind. His performance on Wednesday was a disgrace, a monument to conceit adorned with vanity and self-indulgence, rendered all the more objectionable by the swagger of his gait'. In another example, from March 2007, Steven Gerrard was said, as previously noted, to be a 'nothing player', yet in 2010, while Dunphy was commenting on that year's World Cup Gerrard was, suddenly, 'world-class'.

There is no comfortable way around this for Dunphy. By changing position so drastically and with such alarming ease, Dunphy seems to confound common sense. It is one thing to alter your view over time as circumstances change – such shifts of opinion can be rationalised fairly straightforwardly on the basis that, as events change, one's views might naturally evolve also – but it is quite another simply to announce a diametrically opposite view and expect your audience to swallow it whole without offering any proviso or explanation. Yet this is precisely what Dunphy does. He delights in launching supremely provocative barbs from his seemingly endless supply of outrage, contradicting himself along the way in almost glorious fashion. Though perplexing, this weakness is actually an essential part of Dunphy's appeal. His habit of ritually reinventing himself gives him an enticing air of unpredictability. Viewers and readers just do not know what he is going to say next and so they invariably wait on his every word in the hope that he will drop another bombshell. His habit of contradicting himself only adds spice to an already colourful brew because he can tear up the rulebook at any time and perform an about-turn on dearly held opinions. This lends his views a marked 'churn' factor that sets him apart from ordinary commentators. He enjoys a level of looseness with accuracy that would not be allowed to any other football analyst. This leaves the meagre consolation that Dunphy has at least, as Michael Ross puts it writing in *The Irish Times* in May 2010, 'been constant in his inconstancy'.

Could there, however, perhaps be a defence for Dunphy's unique style or is it simply empty controversialism and unaccountable flip-flopping? According to Dunphy, there *is* rhyme and reason to the madness. He has argued repeatedly that consistency is an overrated virtue and is akin to the last refuge of the pedant. He has sought to turn commonplace attitudes on their head, arguing that the devil is not, in fact, in the detail. Quoting Ralph Waldo Emerson, the nineteenth-century American writer, Dunphy has claimed that 'a foolish consistency is the hobgoblin of little minds' and so is not something to which one should aspire. There is, he seems to suggest, a greatness of mind in not being lashed to the minute detail of your past utterances, a freedom that allows one to soar free of mediocrity, wiping the slate clean each time, in readiness for your next tantalising flare-up. Dunphy might equally have quoted Oscar Wilde when he wrote: 'The well-bred contradict other people. The wise contradict themselves.'

In Dunphy's defence, though he is sometimes guilty of sacrificing accuracy and moderation in his determination to be controversial, his analysis works on the grand level. At heart he is a polemicist who is obviously more at home with the drama of the sweeping statement rather than with impartial, cautiously constructed opinions, but this is very much part of his brilliance. Dunphy *is* partial, and in a world of inane football analysis, he is loved all the more for it. He is more than willing to put his neck on the line, shooting fast and loose with a penetrating directness and a fearlessness that other commentators cannot emulate. Revelling in what might be called the polemicist's poetic licence, complete factual accuracy is certainly a troublesome casualty of Dunphy's approach, but it is often compensated for by his ability to deliver thought-provoking and invigorating opinions that have set the agenda for many major football debates in Irish soccer.

At his best, he hits the mark spectacularly, uncovering the bigger issue in a way that other commentators cannot match. Dunphy himself, perhaps aware of his habit of sometimes getting the facts wrong, has extolled the virtues of this expansive style. 'By saying what I think, I can at least encourage a viewer to have another look. So you're challenging the prevailing orthodoxy. I don't think there's anything wrong with that; you don't even have to be right all the time, though you have to be right often enough to be credible.'

The fact that his critics also fail to mention is that, behind his sensational one-liners, Dunphy invariably offers detailed football reasoning to make his case. This is evidenced, for example, in the cogent tactical arguments that he has made against the negative football styles of Irish national managers, Jack Charlton and Giovanni Trapattoni. In Dunphy's case the bite is often as bad as the bark. If his only talent was for marching into the RTÉ studio, pulling up a seat alongside John Giles and Liam Brady for two hours or so, and directing tasty X-rated jabs at the nearest respected sports person, he would surely have received a gift of his P45 many years ago. But there is substance behind the neat turn of phrase. Beneath the biting put-downs and his obvious enjoyment of the conversational flourish is a highly perceptive football mind and an impressively wide-ranging intellect, the last trait helping to explain why he has enjoyed such durable success.

Michael McMullan's suggestion that Dunphy commands mass appeal simply because he has mastered the ignoble art of the soundbite misses the point. He enjoys such unrivalled popularity because of a rare capacity to speak to different audiences. He alone, in Irish journalism, with his heady mixture of intellect and attitude, has managed to straddle the divide between broadsheet and tabloid readerships. From lowbrow to highbrow, knee-jerk to nuance, Dunphy has arguably catered for a wider spectrum of audience than any other football writer or analyst working in Ireland or Britain during the last thirty years. Like a pantomime laced with double entendres, his sulphurous comments satisfy our appetite for controversy but at the same time manage to excite our intellects. It is sugar-coated gravitas; steel wrapped in silk. He is the likeable autodidact, the original pub philosopher who can identify with Everyman, enjoying immunity from the perception of being a haughty and out-of-touch intellectual. This also explains the diversity of newspapers for which he has written, from respected broadsheets such as *The Irish Times* to popular tabloids like the *Irish Daily Star*.

Dunphy's depth of penetration into so many facets of the media, whether it be through radio, television, print journalism or the various books he has written and ghosted, easily places him in a league of one in comparison with competing Irish commentators. Some critics, however, are not persuaded that it is journalistic talent alone that explains Dunphy's rise to the top of his profession. They prefer to highlight his undoubted skill for self-promotion, believing that it is his mastery of the dark arts of marketing that allows him routinely to pump-prime his profile and unerringly win the headlines. In an article entitled 'Secrets of brand Dunphy', Joe O'Shea, writing in the *Irish Independent* in January 2010, has referred to the frustration he and other journalists feel when, time and again, they are forced to observe what they consider to be Dunphy's lucrative and shameless self-branding being swallowed by the Irish public. O'Shea calls the phenomenon 'brand Dunphy' and quotes one sports broadcaster who has worked with Dunphy and who was firmly of the opinion that the popular analyst was well aware of the need to develop and maintain his hold on the public's often fickle attentions. 'I think he realises he is a brand; he works at it and he does know what will get him the headlines.' O'Shea, although with some humour, notes the hypocrisy of Dunphy's posturing: 'He has become an established figure by attacking the establishment, held two fingers up to convention and consensus and has had an unapologetically good time along the way. It's enough to make you sick.'

Taking a similar line, Terry Prone also writing in the *Irish Independent* in January 2010, considered Dunphy to be the 'greatest self-publicist of them all', highlighting how, in publicity terms, the controversial commentator can do no wrong, even when, well, doing wrong. Prone points to the fact that Dunphy's many well-publicised misdemeanours have not only been forgiven very easily, but have in fact managed even to add to the allure of his bad boy image. This gives Dunphy a Teflon quality. No matter what besets him, nothing seems to stick. He rides the storm, dusts himself off, puffs out his chest and emerges with his stock higher than ever. Prone points to the infamous incident in 2002 when Dunphy arrived for work at RTÉ visibly affected by heavy drinking from the night before and was sent home before receiving a short suspension from the station. For any other analyst or journalist this would surely have spelled career suicide, but in the ambiguous world of celebrity that Dunphy enjoys, nothing is this straightforward. As Prone points out:

> Thirty years ago, if a commentator had arrived in RTÉ wobbly and incoherent with drink, he would never have been employed by the station again.

But in today's ratings-driven context, all that happened when Eamon turned up to do a TV gig having, according to his own account, had a few drinks, no sleep and in no condition to fulfil his contract, was a temporary suspension. Someone who provides great excitement around a football match isn't just easy to forgive – they're arguably more interesting because of the possibility that they may turn up again the worse for alcoholic wear.

Prone makes a good point, but how does Dunphy manage to turn these setbacks into yet more career-boosting injections? Mainly, it has to be because of the considerable affection in which Dunphy is held with large numbers of the public. No matter how deviant he has been, his underlying likeability factor has seen him through the adversity. Dunphy has built up a large store of goodwill because he is a genuine case of a self-made man. Out of his modest working-class background and his unspectacular playing days, he has fashioned a most unlikely career as an incredibly successful and multi-talented journalist and broadcaster. Dunphy, in his rise from obscurity, is a phenomenon and people recognise and respect this fact. Enveloped in this image of lovable rogue and people's champion, Dunphy is to a great extent untouchable.

And this is borne out by the facts: he has no less than eight road traffic convictions to his name, three of which are for drink-driving offences. In February 1982, he was twice fined for driving without insurance. He was convicted of the same offence in June 1982, July 1984 and September 1992, receiving a two-year ban on the final occasion. His first drink-driving conviction was in July 1993 when he was punished with a further three-year ban.

His penultimate offence was in May 1997, when he had to accept a heftier seven-year ban for once more failing to have insurance on his vehicle. His final indiscretion was punished in December 2001 when his licence was revoked for ten years for a repetition of the offence of driving while drunk. Furthermore, Dunphy is a confessed former cocaine user (famously quipping: 'You can't get good coke in this town [Dublin]'), yet this busy rap sheet has not nearly been sufficient to knock him from his perch as Ireland's most important and most discussed football journalist and pundit. Although Dunphy has expressed complete regret for these incidents and it is hardly the work of this book to pass moral judgment on his personal life, the lack of a concerted backlash from these events exhibits more than anything else the enduring hold this man has over the Irish public's affections. He has even been able to turn his public image as a rabble-rousing party animal into an effective marketing tool. When he first began working for Newstalk in September 2004, with his own morning radio show, the promotional campaign, with some humour, traded on the presenter's infamous taste for the city's nightlife. Dublin was festooned with billboards cheekily inquiring: 'Will he turn up?'

A curious aspect of Dunphy's football analysis is his self-deprecating habit of frequently reminding the world of his less than memorable football career. When discussing football matters on the RTÉ panel, he will often refer to his avowedly lamentable playing career as the barometer for how poor a professional footballer can be, generally informing his colleagues in words such as: 'I know what a bad player is. I was one myself for nearly fifteen years.' Nothing seems to please him more than humbly prostrating himself before the greatness that his television colleagues, John Giles and Liam Brady, enjoyed as players. Better still, during World Cups, when RTÉ fill out the studio with former international players who join as guest panellists for the tournament's duration, Dunphy positively purrs with the possibilities inherent in such a line-up. As Mary Hannigan, writing in *The Irish Times* in June 2010, realised, the arrival of World Cup winner Ossie Ardiles to the RTÉ panel during the World Cup of that summer introduced Dunphy to previously unrealised opportunities for debasement. Here was a man who held the World Cup trophy aloft in Argentina's glorious triumph of 1978, compared to Dunphy, who finished his career kicking mud with Reading in the English Fourth Division: simply mouth-watering potential.

Although there is almost something a touch compulsive about this tendency of Dunphy, he has often seen the funny side of his lowly playing days. During one debate on RTÉ, John Giles noted, 'Football fans have short memories', whereupon Dunphy interrupted, 'I found at Millwall that fans had long memories, John. They never forgot how bad I was.' Similarly, when Dunphy was football correspondent for the *Sunday Tribune* in the early 1980s one irate reader, who had evidently tired of the analyst's outspoken style, simply wrote a one-sentence letter to the publication: 'A failed Third Division footballer.' Dunphy's response showed he laboured under no illusions about the precise low benchmark that his career had reached: 'I'll have you know that I am not a failed Third Division footballer. I am a failed Second Division footballer.' Again, in an interview with *The Guardian* in November 2004, when asked about the highlight of his playing career, he laughed at the idea that there were any highlights to recount and suggested that at least its many downs inured him to failure. 'It taught me the value of grafting hard and not being disappointed when things don't go your way. Yes, you could say my playing career was one long character-building exercise [laughs].'

A highly distinctive aspect of Dunphy's attitude to football, already alluded to in this book, is the way in which he sees the game in a much larger context than most other players or analysts. Speaking during an interview with the *Irish Examiner* in April 2010, Dunphy was effusive on the salutary role that football and, sport in general, can play in our lives. Describing his childhood, he said: 'Sport gave you something to dream about. People say the church down through history has been the succour of Irish people when they were impoverished, but sport was also a great enrichment of people's lives – wonderful and innocent. And the heroes of those sports were beloved.' In the same piece, he disclosed that in the early 1980s, when he was a member of the Fine Gael political party, he had lobbied then Taoiseach Garret FitzGerald to introduce a lottery to fund sports. FitzGerald, he relates, had no interest in the topic but Dunphy wrote a persuasive paper on the social importance of sport and the idea was subsequently put in place by the Fine Gael-Labour coalition, with proceeds from the national draw being channelled into local sports throughout Ireland.

If Dunphy has managed to emphasise the positive social aspects of football, it is in grasping the political dimensions of the game that he has stood out from other commentators. For instance, commenting on RTÉ about the decline of Italian and Spanish football at Euro '2004, he blamed the rise of economic prosperity in those countries for their lack of first-class new players. Although, with an admittedly tongue-in-cheek delivery, he argued persuasively that most footballers seem to emanate from

relatively poorer backgrounds, noting: 'You need dicta-
torships and poverty to produce great footballers.'

Even in his playing days with Millwall, Dunphy was
earning the dubious rubric of troublemaker for his agi-
tation on behalf of players' rights. For instance, he
campaigned for the right of professional footballers to
form and join trade unions, a move that he claims so
upset the establishment that it ruled him out of being
considered for managerial posts on his retirement. The
reputation that followed him marked him out as more
of an insubordinate working-class hero than what he has
termed 'the officer material' that clubs usually look for
in their manager. Moreover, hardly assisting Dunphy in
ingratiating himself with the powers that be was his brief
association with the British Communist Party during his
playing days, a rapprochement that publicly announced
his 'dangerous' leftist leanings. He was, for a time, a card-
carrying member of the British Communist Party before
eloping to join the more moderate British Labour Party.
Dunphy even found ways to bring his tendentious political beliefs onto the football pitch.

In February 1972, soon after the events of Bloody
Sunday in Derry when the actions of the British Armed
Forces led to the death of 14 civilians, Dunphy, in a
gesture that proved highly unpopular but required considerable courage, wore a black armband playing for Millwall
in an English League match to make his opinion clearly
known on the matter. On the same point of principle, he
also led a failed attempt to persuade his international colleagues to wear the armband in their next appearance for
the Republic of Ireland. His early attempts to promote
players' rights did, however, have one notable success. In
1971 he was a prominent party to a threatened players'
strike by the Republic of Ireland squad that objected to

the selection system the FAI used. The players wanted the removal of the Big Five, the cabal of FAI officials who wielded control over team selection. Ever since this protest, the Irish team has been chosen by the manager alone.

In this early political activism, Dunphy was displaying the beginnings of his lifelong anti-establishment ways, a pattern that would repeat again and again throughout his career as a football analyst. It is the same ideological strain that encourages him to back the player in any dispute with the football hierarchy, a habit this book has already had cause to note on more than one occasion. Also, the manner in which he has consistently shown himself to be fundamentally opposed to the power that the Football Association of Ireland holds, demonstrates this same innate mistrust of official authority. When Roger Greene asked him in 2006 to explain what motivates him as a journalist, without hesitation he said: 'I'm anti-establishment. I don't like the ruling class ... I don't like the powerful and the smug. I don't like those people. I identify more with the people on the street who are suffering generally ... I don't like the guys who run this show [Irish society] and I don't like the guys who run any show.'

Dunphy's involvement in a politically sensitive international match in Chile in 1974 demonstrated that he could also insist on the de-politicisation of football when he felt it was appropriate to isolate the sport from surrounding events. Dunphy, already known for his committed political views, was accused of 'swallowing his principles' by joining the Irish squad on a tour of Brazil but which also took in a game at Chile's National Stadium. The opprobrium was because Ireland would set the dubious precedent of becoming the first side to play in Chile since General Augusto Pinochet's military coup had overthrown the socialist government of Salvador Allende in

September 1973. The arrangement proved highly contentious in some quarters. The Irish Committee for Chile even wrote to then Minister for Foreign Affairs, Garret FitzGerald, urging him to denounce an event that they suggested 'can only enhance the prestige of the regime'.

What made matters worse was the macabre history of the game's venue, a stadium that only months earlier had been used as a mass detention centre where dissidents of the ruling regime could be held and tortured. In a *Sunday World* article from 23 June 1974, Dunphy told journalist Sam Smyth about the disturbing impression that the match had left on the Irish players. 'When we went out to inspect the pitch, armed guards ordered us back to the dressing rooms. It was a sobering experience ... The stadium was freshly painted for our visit so all traces of blood and torture were destroyed.' However, Dunphy insisted that he was not in any way endorsing Pinochet's rule by participating in the match, arguing that 'by going to Chile I certainly wasn't supporting the regime. I was playing football.' Though Dunphy sought to portray the game as a politically neutral sporting event, it is clear from the release of Irish government files in 2005 that the government of the day regarded the situation as very sensitive. As Maeve Sheehan has shown, writing in the *Sunday Independent* in January 2005, documents found in the National Archives reveal that the Department of Foreign Affairs at this time maintained a file on Dunphy.

If the situation in Chile did not stimulate Dunphy's political side, the injustice of the system of apartheid in South Africa seemed to have a much stronger effect on him. He, like many Irish people, had protested against the British and Irish Lions' rugby tour of South Africa in 1974 on the grounds that it lent some legitimacy to a regime that held sway over institutionalised racial discrimination.

Dunphy, again in the previously mentioned *Sunday World* article of 1974, offered a weak defence for his actions, claiming that 'the Chilean issue is vastly different from South Africa' and so, he claimed, there was no inconsistency in his choices. It is difficult to square these divergent responses: if apartheid had exercised his sense of injustice so much, how could the political situation in Chile have not provoked similar sentiments.

Although Dunphy has many detractors, much to their chagrin he has displayed the pugilistic tenacity and bulletproof hide to ride roughshod over their criticisms and maintain his enviable status as the most talked-about football journalist in Ireland. His proverbial nine lives must be the envy of every comparable football commentator. His ability to keep audiences and readers on tenterhooks, eagerly awaiting his comments on football matters of the day, puts him in a class of his own. Although age has mellowed him somewhat and tempered his fierceness, he remains unfailingly passionate and interesting in his opinions; he is still the volatile powder keg waiting to blow at any moment, and that, imperfections and all, is why we are still listening.

Although Dunphy, as a footballer, certainly did not disprove the adage 'nobody ever makes it after leaving Old Trafford', he has in his subsequent career surely laid that ghost to rest. He *has* made it, just not in the way anyone would have expected.

Appendix

Statistics

Football League Division Two 1973/74: Final Table

Pos	Team	Pld	Home							Away							Overall						
			W	D	L	F	A	Av	Pts	W	D	L	F	A	Av	Pts	W	D	L	F	A	Av	Pts
1	Middlesbro	42	16	4	1	40	8	5.000	36	11	7	3	37	22	1.682	29	27	11	4	77	30	2.567	65
2	Luton	42	12	5	4	42	25	1.680	29	7	7	7	22	26	0.846	21	19	12	11	64	51	1.255	50
3	Carlisle	42	13	5	3	40	17	2.353	31	7	4	10	21	31	0.677	18	20	9	13	61	48	1.271	49
4	Leyton Orient	42	9	8	4	28	17	1.647	26	6	10	5	27	25	1.080	22	15	18	9	55	42	1.340	48
5	Blackpool	42	11	5	5	35	17	2.059	27	6	8	7	22	23	0.957	20	17	13	12	57	40	1.425	47
6	Sunderland	42	11	6	4	32	15	2.133	28	8	3	10	26	29	0.897	19	19	9	14	58	44	1.318	47
7	Nottm Forest	42	12	6	3	40	19	2.105	30	3	9	9	17	24	0.708	15	15	15	12	57	43	1.326	45
8	West Brom	42	8	9	4	28	24	1.167	25	6	7	8	20	21	0.952	19	14	16	12	48	45	1.067	44
9	Hull	42	9	9	3	25	15	1.667	27	4	8	9	21	32	0.656	16	13	17	12	46	47	0.979	43
10	Notts Co	42	8	6	7	30	35	0.857	22	7	7	7	25	25	1.000	21	15	13	14	55	60	0.917	43
11	Bolton	42	12	5	4	30	17	1.765	29	3	7	11	14	23	0.609	13	15	12	15	44	40	1.100	42
12	Millwall	42	10	6	5	28	16	1.750	26	4	8	9	23	35	0.657	16	14	14	14	51	51	1.000	42
13	Fulham	42	11	4	6	26	20	1.300	26	5	6	10	13	23	0.565	16	16	10	16	39	43	0.907	42
14	Aston Villa	42	8	9	4	33	21	1.571	25	5	6	10	15	24	0.625	16	13	15	14	48	45	1.067	41
15	Portsmouth	42	9	8	4	26	16	1.625	26	5	4	12	19	46	0.413	14	14	12	16	45	62	0.726	40
16	Bristol C	42	9	5	7	25	20	1.250	23	5	5	11	22	34	0.647	15	14	10	18	47	54	0.870	38
17	Cardiff	42	8	7	6	27	20	1.350	23	2	9	10	22	42	0.524	13	10	16	16	49	62	0.790	36
18	Oxford	42	8	6	5	27	21	1.286	24	2	8	11	8	26	0.320	12	10	16	16	35	46	0.761	36
19	Sheff Wed	42	9	6	6	33	24	1.375	24	3	5	13	18	39	0.462	11	12	11	19	51	63	0.810	35
20	C Palace	42	6	7	8	24	24	1.000	19	5	5	11	19	32	0.594	15	11	12	19	43	56	0.768	34
21	Preston	42	7	8	6	24	23	1.043	22	2	6	13	16	39	0.410	10	9	14	19	40	62	0.645	32
22	Swindon	42	6	7	8	22	27	0.815	19	1	4	16	14	45	0.311	6	7	11	24	36	72	0.500	25

Eamon Dunphy's Football League Career

Clubs	Appearances	Goals
Manchester United FC 1962-65	0	0
York City FC 1965-66	22	3
Millwall FC 1966-73	303	25
Charlton Athletic FC 1973-75	44	3
Reading FC 1975-77	77	3
TOTAL	**446**	**34**

Eamon Dunphy's International Career

Country	Appearances	Goals
Republic of Ireland 1965-72	23	0

Republic of Ireland Managers

John Giles: 1973-80

Country	Games	Won	Drawn	Lost
Republic of Ireland	37	14	9	14

Eoin Hand: 1980-85

Country	Games	Won	Drawn	Lost
Republic of Ireland	40	11	9	20

Jack Charlton: 1986-1995

	Games	Won	Drawn	Lost
World Cup	29	13	11	5
European Championship	28	12	10	6
Friendly	36	21	9	6
Total	**93**	**46**	**30**	**17**

Mick McCarthy: 1996-2002

Country	Games	Won	Drawn	Lost
Republic of Ireland	68	29	19	20

Don Givens (Caretaker Manager) : November 2002-January 2003

Country	Games	Won	Drawn	Lost
Republic of Ireland	1	0	1	0

Brian Kerr: 2003-05

Country	Games	Won	Drawn	Lost
Republic of Ireland	32	17	11	4

Stephen Staunton: 2006-07

Country	Games	Won	Drawn	Lost
Republic of Ireland	17	6	5	6

Don Givens (Caretaker Manager) : October 2007-February 2008

Country	Games	Won	Drawn	Lost
Republic of Ireland	2	0	1	1

Giovanni Trapattoni: 2008-Present (Matches played up to 1 May 2012)

Country	Games	Won	Drawn	Lost
Republic of Ireland	43	19	16	8

Bibliography

Bolchover, David & Brady, Chris, *The 90-Minute Manager: Lessons from the Sharp End of Management*, Prentice Education Limited, 2002

Charlton, Jack with Peter Byrne, *Jack Charlton's World Cup Diary*, Gill & Macmillan Ltd, 1990

Jack Charlton's American World Cup Diary, Gill & Macmillan Ltd, 1994

Jack Charlton: The Autobiography, Partridge Press, 1996

Dunphy, Eamon, *Only a Game?*, Penguin Books, 1976

Dunphy, Eamon, *A Strange Kind of Glory: Sir Matt Busby & Manchester United*, Aurum Press, 1991

Dunphy, Eamon, *Eamon Dunphy's World Cup Diary: More than a Game*, William Heinemann Ltd, 1994.

Giles, John, *A Football Man: The Autobiography*, Hachette Books Ireland, 2010

Giulianotti, Richard, *Football: A Sociology of the Global Game*, Polity Press, 1999

Greene, Roger, *Under the Spotlight: Conversations with 18 Leading Irish Journalists*, The Liffey Press, 2005

Hartley, L.P., *The Go-Between*, New York Review of Books, 2002, originally published 1953

Honigstein, Raphael, *Englischer Fussball: A German View of Our Beautiful Game*, Yellow Jersey, 2008

Howard, Paul, *The Gaffers*, The O'Brien Press, 2002

Humphries, Tom, *Laptop Dancing and the Nanny Goat Mambo: A Sportswriter's Year*, Pocket/Townhouse, 2003

The Legend of Jack Charlton, Weidenfeld & Nicolson, 1994

Inglis, Simon, *The Football Grounds of Great Britain*, Willow Books, 1983

Keane, Roy with Eamon Dunphy, *Keane: The Autobiography*, Penguin Books, 2002

Keane, Trevor, *Gaffers: 50 Years of Irish Football Managers*, The Mercier Press Ltd, 2010

Kuper, Simon, 'Sporting Fictions', www.britishcouncil.org

Kuper, Simon & Stefan Szymanski, *Why England Lose & Other Curious Phenomena Explained*, Harper Sport, 2010

Lynch, Declan, *Days of Heaven: Italia '90 and the Charlton Years*, Gill & Macmillan Ltd, 2010

McCarthy, Mick, *Captain Fantastic: My Football Career and World Cup Experience*, The O'Brien Press, 1990

McCarthy, Mick with Cathal Dervan, *Mick McCarthy's World Cup Diary 2002*, Simon & Schuster/Townhouse, 2002

O'Callaghan, Conor, *Red Mist: Roy Keane & the Football Civil War*, Bloomsbury, 2004

O'Leary, David with Harry Miller, *David O'Leary: My Story*, (Mainstream Publishing, 1988)

Ronay, Barney, *The Manager: The Absurd Ascent of the Most Important Man in Football*, Sphere, 2009

Stapleton, Frank, *Frankly Speaking*, Blackwater Press, 1991

Storey, David, *This Sporting Life*, Penguin Books, 1968

Theiner, Egon & Elisabeth Schlammerl, *Trapattoni: A Life in Football*, Liberties Press, 2008

Titford, Roger with Eamon Dunphy, *More than a Job?: The Players' and Fans' Perspectives*, Further Thought Publishing, 1992

Vialli, Gianluca & Gabriele Marcotti, *The Italian Job: A Journey to the Heart of Two Footballing Cultures*, Bantam Press, 2006

Whelan, Daire, *Who Stole Our Game? The Fall and Fall of Irish Soccer*, Gill & Macmillan Ltd, 2006

Wilson, Jonathan, *Inverting the Pyramid: The History of Football Tactics*, Orion, 2008

Index